ELIOT HIGGINS is the founder and chief executive of Bellingcat, an independent international collective of researchers, investigators and citizen journalists using open-source and social media investigation to probe some of the world's most pressing stories. Higgins is a research fellow at UC Berkeley School of Law's Human Rights Centre, and is a member of the International Criminal Court's Technology Advisory Board.

@EliotHiggins | bellingcat.com

WE ARE BELLINGCAT

An Intelligence Agency for the People

ELIOT HIGGINS

BLOOMSBURY PUBLISHING
LONDON · OXFORD · NEW YORK · NEW DELHI · SYDNEY

BLOOMSBURY PUBLISHING
Bloomsbury Publishing Plc
50 Bedford Square, London, WC1B 3DP, UK
29 Earlsfort Terrace, Dublin 2, Ireland

BLOOMSBURY, BLOOMSBURY PUBLISHING and the Diana logo are
trademarks of Bloomsbury Publishing Plc

First published in Great Britain 2021
This edition published 2022

A catalogue record for this book is available from the British Library

ISBN: HB: 978-1-5266-1575-6; TPB: 978-1-5266-1573-2; PB: 978-1-5266-1571-8;
EBOOK: 978-1-5266-1572-5; EPDF: 978-1-5266-4506-7;

6 8 10 9 7 5

Typeset by Newgen KnowledgeWorks Pvt. Ltd., Chennai, India
Printed and bound in Great Britain by CPI Group (UK) Ltd, Croydon CR0 4YY

To find out more about our authors and books visit www.bloomsbury.com
and sign up for our newsletters

Contents

Introduction   1
1   Revolution on a Laptop   9
2   Becoming Bellingcat   63
3   Firewall of Facts   111
4   Mice Catch Cat   155
5   Next Steps   193

Afterword   223
Notes   243
Acknowledgements   267
Index   269

Introduction

Government ministers hurried into an underground conference room in central London for the COBRA crisis-response meeting. A chemical weapons attack had taken place on British soil; it looked like an assassination attempt. The Skripals remained on ventilators in a hospital, pumped full of atropine, under sedation and under armed guard. Britain needed to respond. Suspicions turned to the Kremlin – one victim had been a former colonel in Russian military intelligence who had worked as a double agent for the British. On 4 March 2018, he and his daughter were found slumped on a bench in the peaceful English city of Salisbury, both on the verge of death. Moscow denied responsibility.

'Our colleagues say with pathos, with serious faces that, if this was done by Russia, then the response will be such that Russia will remember it forever,' said Foreign Minister Sergey Lavrov. 'This is dishonest. This is pure propaganda, pure fanning of hysterics and hysteria.'[1]

Yet the Kremlin had been implicated in revenge poisonings before, notably in the case of Alexander Litvinenko, another former Russian intelligence officer who had defected to Britain and become a scathing critic of President Vladimir Putin. On 1 November 2006, Litvinenko met two former KGB agents at the Millennium Hotel in London. Later that night, he fell ill. Within weeks, he was dead of exposure to polonium-210.

By coincidence, the British defence lab that studies such poisons, Porton Down, happens to be a few miles outside Salisbury. Chemical-weapons experts there were urgently studying blood samples from the sixty-six-year-old Sergei Skripal and his thirty-three-year-old daughter, Yulia, trying to figure out what afflicted them. The results came back: Novichok A234, a nerve agent that the Soviet Union had developed in the 1970s and 1980s, back when Vladimir Putin was just an officer in the KGB. A smear on the skin could cause loss of vision, constricted breathing, incessant vomiting, convulsions, death. Intelligence analysts discovered that Russia had been intercepting communications between Skripal and his daughter before she flew from Moscow for a two-week holiday. Tracking Yulia, Russian operatives would have found her father.[2]

'Either this was a direct act by the Russian state against our country,' Prime Minister Theresa May told the House of Commons, 'or the Russian government lost control of this potentially catastrophically damaging nerve agent and allowed it to get into the hands of others.' Moscow had forty-eight hours to explain itself. 'Should there be no credible response, we will conclude that this action amounts to an unlawful use of force by the Russian state against the United Kingdom. And I will come back to this House and set out the full range of measures that we will take in response.'[3]

Russian state-funded news outlets spread conspiracy theories, alleging that Britain held the Skripals against their will. Also, if the nerve agent had been military-grade, why weren't the victims dead? This was a contention with a double effect, spreading doubt and menace at once, as if to say Kremlin violence would not have failed. The British expelled twenty-three Russian diplomats, identified as undeclared intelligence officers. Allied countries showed solidarity, throwing out their Russian 'diplomats', too. The United States sent home sixty, while imposing sanctions on banks and exports. Moscow retaliated with expulsions of its own.[4]

At Bellingcat, we watched, awaiting a point of entry. Scattered around the globe, we are an online collective, investigating war crimes and picking apart disinformation, basing our findings on clues that are openly available on the internet – in social-media postings, in leaked databases, in free satellite maps. Paradoxically, in this age of online disinformation, facts are easier to come by than ever. A core team of eighteen staffers works with scores of volunteers, producing reports seen by hundreds of thousands, including government officials, influential media figures, and policymakers. We have no agenda but we do have a credo: evidence exists and falsehoods exist, and people still care about the difference.

During the months after the attack, Sergei and Yulia Skripal recovered, but Scotland Yard struggled to solve the case. No surveillance cameras covered Sergei Skripal's front door, which was the probable contamination site. Detectives gathered and watched 11,000 hours of local CCTV footage, pored over credit-card payments and studied mobile-phone usage in the area.[5] As they sought answers, further poisonings occurred. A man from the Salisbury area whose addictions led him to scavenge in rubbish found what he thought was a bottle of Nina Ricci Premier Jour perfume and presented it to his girlfriend. She sprayed it on her wrists and became gravely ill. On 8 July, the hospital turned off her life support. The Organisation for the Prohibition of Chemical Weapons analysed samples from this fake perfume bottle and confirmed that it contained Novichok. 'The nerve agent is one of the rarest chemical warfare agents in the world and its discovery, twice, in such close proximity is beyond a coincidence,' British counter-terrorism police said.[6] The assassins seemed to have dumped the container, which was full of enough nerve agent to kill thousands of people.[7]

Six months after the Skripal attack, the police at last provided what we needed. Images showed two Russian men arriving at Gatwick Airport a couple of days before the poisoning, travelling together by train from London to Salisbury on consecutive days and lurking near the defector's home.[8] The authorities needed help identifying these two, so published images of the suspects, who had travelled under the names 'Alexander Petrov' and 'Ruslan Boshirov'. Scotland Yard hoped someone might recognise them. The Kremlin certainly did.

'We know who they are, we have found them,' Putin said. 'I hope they will turn up themselves and tell everything. This would be best for everyone. There is nothing special there, nothing criminal, I assure you. We'll see in the near future.'[9]

The future comes fast when the president demands it: the following day, 13 September 2018, the two suspects materialised in an interview on the Kremlin's international news channel, RT. On the Bellingcat internal chat forum we fired messages back and forth, transfixed by this broadcast. The two men proclaimed themselves innocent, merely two friends who had taken a last-minute holiday to Britain to admire a provincial cathedral. 'Petrov' glared as if furious about appearing in public. 'Boshirov' winced, a sheen of sweat on his face. They were not assassins, they protested, just entrepreneurs in the fitness industry.

RT interviewer: What were you doing there?
Petrov: Our friends have been suggesting for quite a long time that we visit this wonderful city.
Interviewer: Salisbury? A wonderful city?

Petrov: Yes.

Interviewer: What makes it so wonderful?

Boshirov: It's a tourist city. They have a famous cathedral there, Salisbury Cathedral. It's famous throughout Europe and, in fact, throughout the world, I think. It's famous for its 123-metre spire. It's famous for its clock. It's the oldest working clock in the world.

One day before the poisoning, the two burly Russians made their initial visit to Salisbury by train, a three-hour round trip from London, yet spent only thirty minutes there because, they said, the snow had put them off. The next day, they took the London–Salisbury trip again. They claimed not to have a clue where Skripal's house was. The interviewer inquired about the perfume bottle.

Boshirov: Don't you think that it's kind of stupid for two straight men to be carrying perfume for ladies? When you go through customs, they check all your belongings. So, if we had anything suspicious, they would definitely have questions. Why would a man have women's perfume in his bag? …

Interviewer: Do you work for the GRU [military intelligence]?

Petrov (to interviewer): And you, do you?

Interviewer: Me? No, I don't, and you?

Petrov: I don't.

Boshirov: Me neither.[10]

Back on our internal message board, we were unanimous. These two were lying. 'Famous for its 123-metre spire'? Who spoke like that, as if reciting a Wikipedia entry? If the British authorities could not determine who these men were, we would try. But there was little to go on. Photos of their faces. Their supposed names.

Within days, we had cracked the case.

Our Skripal investigations drew headlines around the world, and questions, too. How had a collective of self-taught internet sleuths identified a Russian 'hit team'? Was that even plausible? Where had we come from? And what was 'Bellingcat'?

The answers begin a decade ago, in that period when smartphones were beginning to spread globally and social media became the platform for personal relationships, opinions, images. Without intending to, humanity presented for public viewing the most revealing account of itself that the world had ever known. The innocents did not realise how much they were giving away. Nor did the guilty.

At the time I was just another computer enthusiast, an office worker in my early thirties with an unsatisfying job and an interest in the news. Then I had an epiphany. If you searched online, you could find facts that neither the press nor the experts knew yet. A smattering of other people had a similar realisation, and an online community drew together, converging around news events that had left clues on YouTube, Facebook, Twitter and beyond. As our efforts progressed, we gained sophistication, teaching each other the latest investigative hacks, cobbling together what cohered into a new field, one that connects journalism and rights advocacy and crime investigation.

We proved that the Syrian dictator Bashar al-Assad fired chemical weapons at his own people. We showed who was behind the downing of Flight MH17. We located ISIS supporters in Europe. We identified neo-Nazis rampaging through Charlottesville, Virginia. We helped quash the floods of disinformation spreading alongside Covid-19. And we exposed a Kremlin 'kill team'.

This discipline is so new that it lacks a single name. Most common is 'OSINT', for open-source intelligence. But that shorthand derives from government intelligence, whose secretive practices diverge from the open and public mission of Bellingcat. A more accurate description is 'online open-source investigation'. What we do is far more than just internet research, though. We battle the counterfactual forces warping society. We insist on evidence. And we show ordinary citizens how to expose wrongdoing and demand accountability from the powerful.

The private investigator Michael Bazzell – a guru of open-source techniques – used to pursue criminals in his work for the FBI, trawling databases so expensive that they excluded amateurs. 'But today with OSINT, I'd say 98-plus percent of everything I need to find out about someone, I don't need to pay for anymore. That's where I really jumped into the OSINT side,' he says. 'It dawned on me that anyone can have this.'[11]

When General Michael Flynn ran the Defense Intelligence Agency (before disgracing himself in the Trump administration), he remarked that secret sources used to contribute 90 per cent of valuable intelligence. After the arrival of social media, it was the opposite: 90 per cent of worthy intelligence came from open sources, available to all.[12]

Spy agencies have always gathered open-source intelligence, poring over newspapers and listening to radio broadcasts. But they tended to disdain such material, preferring clandestine sources, which justified their immense budgets and influence. For the rest of us, there was a problem with secret intel: we had to trust those who controlled it. Public trust has been brittle since the Iraq War, when the US-led coalition justified invasion with claims about Saddam Hussein's weapons of mass destruction that proved unfounded.

Social mistrust today has become a broader problem than just the masses doubting the elites. Citizens view other citizens with deep suspicion, each political tribe inside its own information bubble. There is the temptation to consider oneself – readers of books like this, opponents of disinformation – as a different grade of human from those who fall for deception and conspiracy theories. Yet much of what each of us believes is just what someone else once told us. That makes experts vital. But they are not sufficient anymore. Allowing truth to become a matter of group loyalty has been a disaster. Today, claims must be laid out for all to see. The Bellingcat method is that: click the links and check our conclusions for yourself.

Years ago, the internet was advertised as a cyberutopia around the corner. Lately, public opinion has swung in the opposite direction. The digital era is viewed as a wrecking ball, smashing journalism, civility and politics. At Bellingcat, we do not accept this cyber-miserabilism. The marvels of the internet can still have an impact for the better. However, guarding society and upholding truth are not the exclusive domain of institutions anymore. It is for all of us.

This is not about Top Secret clearance, or restricting information to the initiated. Bellingcat is something that has never been before: an intelligence agency for the people.

1

Revolution on a Laptop

The discovery of online investigation

Following afternoon prayers on 2 February 2011, buses pulled up at Tahrir Square. For days, thousands of protesters had engulfed this traffic circle in the centre of Cairo, demanding the ousting of President Hosni Mubarak, dictator of Egypt for thirty years. The men on the buses disembarked, holding machetes, clubs and straight razors. They had not arrived to join the protesters, but to assault them.

At first they circled, issuing threats. Elsewhere, men on horseback rode in. A few had saddled up camels, and charged the crowd, brandishing swords. The boldest demonstrators sought to form a perimeter. But attacks came from above, too, supporters of the regime flinging bricks from rooftops and pouring boiling water on fleeing protesters. Facing clouds of tear gas, demonstrators clutched wet rags to their mouths. Soldiers merely looked on as journalists were targeted, too. Protesters dug up the roads, grabbing rocks to defend themselves. A tank commander, confounded by the order to do nothing to protect the innocent, thrust a gun in his mouth, threatening to kill himself rather than stand by. Other soldiers just abandoned their posts. By night, pitched battles still flared, but many reporters had left to file their stories. With the battle lines surging and receding, those who roamed outside faced injury.

One journalist, Andy Carvin of National Public Radio, held his position that entire day, piecing together a running narrative of the Battle of the Camel. He never needed to take cover or press a vinegar-soaked rag to his mouth against the tear gas. He sat at a computer in Washington DC, chronicling the Arab Spring through social media. 'With each incoming tweet, the better I could visualize the situation on the ground,' he later wrote. 'The people tweeting from Tahrir had their own extraordinary perspective – but it was limited to each's immediate field of view. There was no way for them to report on what was going on everywhere.

'I imagined myself flying over Tahrir in a helicopter, looking down at the field of battle,' he explained. 'It was coming together in my mind – a situational awareness I probably couldn't have achieved on the ground.'[1]

For months, Carvin tweeted up to eighteen hours a day, seven days a week, recounting the uprisings in Tunisia, Egypt, Bahrain, Libya, Yemen, Syria. Often, he exceeded 1,000 tweets in a day – so many that Twitter once blocked his account, mistaking him for a spammer.[2] Foreign correspondents, who pride themselves on rushing towards danger, tended to view this work as not true reporting. But for a news industry struggling with financial cuts, outsourcing research to social media was an attractive option. The problem was that many of those who tweeted were activists with agendas. How could journalists – reading tweets from afar, without knowing the local language, let alone the cultural context – get it right?

The Arab Spring raised what was to become the most serious news question of the digital age: verification. How to say if this stuff was true? How to know *what* you were looking at?

I was asking myself this same question at my admin job in Leicester, where I spent downtime at my desk viewing live-streaming video, filmed from a hotel window over Tahrir Square. The police pushed back protesters, then the police were themselves repelled, creating an odd theatre: crowds rolling out, crowds rolling in, tear gas fogging the scene, rocks soaring through the air, water cannons spraying.

Long before, I had considered becoming a journalist, perhaps even covering stories like this from the ground. But I had not thrived at college and dropped out, taking a series of office jobs that left me unsatisfied. From afar, I watched politicians and celebrities and journalists as if they were another breed. I found no place in the larger world, and had no prospect of ever having an impact. Instead, I took refuge in online video games, which I played with obsessive devotion, organising large groups of players spread across various countries. But when 9/11 happened, my interests shifted. News was happening so fast, and papers were so slow. I wanted to know more, and discovered an online message board, Something Awful, that was full of argument and insight on almost any topic imaginable. I gained a new obsession: current affairs. By 2011, the most compelling part of my day came each morning, when I arrived far too early at the office. Alone at my computer, I scoured the internet for the latest updates on the Arab Spring.

Among the best sources was Middle East Live, a breaking-news blog on the *Guardian* website. What captivated me were threads on the Libyan civil war, which had broken out after the country's long-time dictator, Muammar Gaddafi, violently suppressed protests in the eastern city of Benghazi. The result was armed rebellion, involving men without formal military training but with AK-47s, leaping on pick-up trucks and driving to the front line. Gaddafi warned them: 'I'm going to march with the masses, to purify Libya inch by inch, house by house, room by room, street by street, one by one, until the country is cleansed of filth.' In March 2011, the UN Security Council authorised attacks to protect civilians, and NATO launched airstrikes against the government.[3] The war turned in the rebels' favour. They pushed towards the capital, Tripoli, and Gaddafi's hometown of Sirte from rebel strongholds in Misrata, Benghazi and the Nafusa Mountains.

I studied every English-language article I could find, scrolled through Something Awful message boards, and scanned the Twitter feeds of Carvin and others. The internet was cut off across Libya, so limited information emerged. A few vociferous Twitter accounts made claims – but they tended to have a strong bias, either pro-revolution or pro-Gaddafi. To evaluate their assertions, I also studied the tweets of foreign correspondents travelling through the war zone. These reporters, I noticed, gathered more material than they could fit into their published articles. Twitter was where they emptied their notebooks, including facts I had not read anywhere else.

In mid-August 2011, a group of journalists happened to drive past the town of Tawergha, not far from a rebel stronghold, Misrata. They observed buildings burning. However, bigger news was happening in a key government-held city, Sirte, where fighting was underway. Only later did the world learn of what had happened in Tawergha. The town had been a pro-Gaddafi stronghold, and when rebels took control they exacted revenge, ordering 10,000 residents to flee. Afterwards, they burned and vandalised Tawergha, turning it into a ghost town.[4] Those tweets – habitations on fire, glimpsed from car windows – were the first clues to an act of ethnic cleansing.

Anytime I found an intriguing detail that news articles had no space for, I posted it on Something Awful and in the comments section of the *Guardian* live blog. I became competitive, trying to post overlooked items before anyone else. Each morning at work I trawled through material that had popped up overnight about Libya, compiling a summary of links. Over the months, I broadened my sources, throwing in reports from human rights groups, YouTube footage, statements on Facebook, photos from Tumblr. My niche, as it developed in thousands of posts, was the detail. I never attempted to tell a complete story, as a news reporter strives to do. I unearthed nuggets that others might use.

This simple ambition proved more important than I realised. An alternative-media ecosystem was expanding in those days, with plenty of dubious websites misrepresenting videos and images to win political arguments. By contrast, I had no personal connection to the Arab Spring, and no partisan views. I was just fascinated, and I hungered for extra titbits. Plenty circulated but plenty were false. My focus became *valid* information. I cited all sources, making it clear where information derived from, always acknowledging the limits of my knowledge. This approach developed into what would become a guiding principle at Bellingcat: the response to information chaos is transparency.

In the early morning of Friday 12 August 2011, I impatiently loaded up the computer at my office, wondering what the Arab Spring had in store. Hundreds of thousands of people had been demonstrating in Yemen, demanding the ousting of President Ali Abdullah Saleh, who was recuperating after an assassination attempt. In Syria, security forces had opened fire on pro-democracy protesters in several cities – President Bashar al-Assad was refusing to cede power.[5] And in Libya, fighting had intensified for key towns such as Brega, a settlement of a few thousand people on the northern shores of Africa at the southernmost point of the Mediterranean.

A charmless outpost, Brega had become a battlefield because it contained an oil refinery, an airstrip and a strategic port. After six months of fighting, Gaddafi's army occupied it but were set on by rebels, marking a possible turning point in the civil war.[6] Combat raged in the east of the town, with artillery shells blasting down in both directions. The evening before, rebels had claimed to control part of Brega. But today, 12 August, the Libyan government said that *it* controlled Brega.[7]

A rebel video appeared on YouTube. This was part of a new genre, the soldier selfie, where combatants brag of their conquests to the camera. In shaky footage, a shaven-headed, bearded gunman walked confidently around what he claimed was newly captured Brega. The buildings were shuttered, and the streets empty but for a handful of fellow rebels in desert camouflage. This could have been evidence of victory. Then again, the rebels might have been lying.[8]

While traditional journalists guard exclusives from competitors, the online ethos was to post anything of interest and make sense of it together, pooling insights. The collaborative spirit marked online investigation from the start and infuses Bellingcat to this day. But the assertion of facts online also led to furious disputes, with anonymous supporters of one side or another railing against findings that challenged their preferred narrative. When I posted in the comments of the *Guardian* live blog, linking to that footage of the rebel claiming his forces controlled Brega, another commenter slapped me down. *How is that proof of anything? Do you KNOW this is Brega? Could've been filmed ANYWHERE.*

The person had a point. How could I, who had never visited the town, say this was Brega at all? I watched the video again, looking for something to identify. A clue like a shop sign would not have helped me since I could not read Arabic. The soldier's face filled most of the frame as he spoke. In the background were single-storey, white-walled concrete buildings and lampposts, all jumping in his shaky camerawork.

I clicked pause and took a lap around the empty office to clear my thoughts. Stopping at the printer, I helped myself to a piece of paper, picked up a pen and reran the YouTube video at my desk. Again, the soldier was talking, striding through the two-lane streets, turning this way and that. I kept pausing, sketching the roadways around him, creating a little street map. He started up a sharply curving road, turned left at the T-junction, passed an armed rebel seated on the corner, reached another T-junction, turned left again.[9] I went to Google Maps, typed in 'Brega' and switched to a mode that superimposes satellite imagery over the road map. The town had three residential areas. One contained multi-storey buildings. Nope, not there – my video showed low-rise concrete houses. The western and eastern residential areas looked more plausible. I studied each, checking the layout against my scrawled fragment of a map. On the sketch, I didn't even know which way was north. I kept rotating it and checking it against the satellite image.

I noticed something: only the eastern residential area had curving roads. That was a start. Still, I was looking at a labyrinth of roadways on Google Maps. I kept rotating my drawn shape until, suddenly, it fitted the street layout, exactly as on the Google map. To double-check, I replayed the video, homing in on every background detail. If I was right, everything needed to match up. That open area visible behind the cameraman, for example – was that in the satellite image? Yes.[10] Everything fitted. I had it. And I had a mini scoop. What my finding meant was that the rebels had taken part of Brega, specifically the eastern residential quarter called New Brega. That explained how Gaddafi loyalists could also claim that they held Brega – they may have been in the western quarter.

Seated in my office in Middle England, I had clarified the front line of a war zone thousands of miles away. All I had needed was a YouTube clip and Google Maps, aided by a sketch on printer paper. I fast-typed my findings into the *Guardian* live-blog comments, and tweeted a copy of my drawing, aligned on a map. In the years to come, Twitter would become my main outlet to disseminate findings; by now, I have tweeted a quarter of a million times. But this was only my seventh tweet. I was just setting out. But already, I had found evidence nobody else had, not even the journalists on the ground. I watched as my discovery filtered through the message boards. Even news professionals took note.

This was a rush, and it contained a revelation. With a bit of a brain shift, you could construe video images from a top-down perspective, flattening the distraction of three dimensions, transforming wobbly footage into something as precise as a map. From there, it became a matching game. I had stumbled across 'geolocation', as we came to call it – the first technique of the digital detective.

At every opportunity I sought to regain the thrill of that discovery. On my next workday, Monday 15 August 2011, Libyan rebels were claiming to have captured the small town of Tiji and they posted a video online as proof. The five-minute clip showed gunfire in a nearly featureless desert setting. Towards the end, the cameraman filmed a tank driving down a road, passing a mosque. Tiji is a small town, so there could not have been many mosques. The road itself had clues to narrow the search. It contained a small median strip dividing the lanes. Pausing the clip, I estimated that the lane closest to the camera was about two tanks wide. Across from the mosque were single-storey buildings.

I found Tiji on Google Maps and switched to the satellite-image view. A simple search turned up a listing of mosques in Tiji, which allowed me to check the roads where each was located, seeing if any layout matched that in the video. Promptly, I had a suitable road, including a mosque whose minaret was on the south side. In this video, the minaret was on the side closest to the road, with the dome to the right of the minaret – this matched the satellite imagery. Also present in both video and satellite images were trees visible behind the tank as it drove by; a wall outside the mosque; and the northward curve of the road. The more details I compared, the more matches I made. Everything was lining up. The day after, I pinned down the location of a video of a burning Gaddafi billboard, geolocating it via Google Maps to the south-western oasis of Sabha. And on I went, posting all to the *Guardian* live blog. Previously, I had been a passive consumer of news, scavenging from others' findings. Now, I had findings of my own. The incoming flow of social-media information only seemed unfathomable. If you sorted it shrewdly, you might detect something.

On 20 October 2011, rebels converged around a drainage pipe on the outskirts of Sirte. From the garbage-strewn hole, they dragged a sixty-nine-year-old with the most recognisable face in the country. Gaddafi was dazed, bloodied and finally deposed. He looked around, bewildered, asking the rebels, 'What did I do to you?' A mob dragged Gaddafi across the sand while others held up camera phones. They tore his shirt and beat him. Soon, Gaddafi lay dead, and the footage was online.[11]

But history was no longer written by the victors alone. The defeated, the passer-by, the neighbour – they had smartphones, too.

THE PRESS IS DYING, LONG LIVE THE NEWS

When I posted findings to the *Guardian* comments section or on Something Awful message boards, they appeared briefly, only to vanish under pages of subsequent entries. I wanted to keep an archive of discoveries, so began a blog under my long-time online handle, Brown Moses, taken from the name of a Frank Zappa song.

The Brown Moses blog, I decided, would deal with more than Libya; it should accommodate any subject. And those subjects kept increasing. After the death of Gaddafi, the news junkies who followed the Arab Spring shifted their attention elsewhere in the region, especially to the worsening conflict in Syria. The Assad regime kept arresting and killing protesters, the opposition took up arms and the conflict degenerated. Social media was full of claims and counterclaims, which made much to dig into. But first, I found myself delving into a news story about news itself.

The phone-hacking scandal tore apart elements of the British newspaper industry in 2011, exposing a pattern of illegal and immoral behaviour. With the rise of cell phones in the 1990s, tabloid reporters had discovered that they could call newsmakers' mobile numbers, reach voicemail, input the default code that few bothered to change and listen to private messages. Unscrupulous journalists used this trick, among other underhanded practices such as bribing police officers, to report articles as if they had obtained information from legitimate sources. I wondered if I could find further clues to these misdeeds online. There was irony in this. I was about to apply a new form of investigative journalism, entirely based on open sources, to expose the old ways of investigative journalism, which thrived on closed sources.

At the heart of the scandal was a prized part of Rupert Murdoch's media empire, the *News of the World*, the best-selling newspaper in Britain with 3.5 million copies every Sunday, more than triple the circulation of the daily *New York Times*.[12] 'To begin with, when libelled, or when my privacy was egregiously invaded, I did take legal action,' the actor Hugh Grant, who became a vocal opponent of tabloid malfeasance, explained in 2011. 'What I didn't do was openly criticize the worst practices of some papers. This would have been, and still is, to invite brutal editorial revenge.'[13] Politicians were equally fearful of the Murdoch press, which included the best-selling daily the *Sun* and establishment organ *The Times*. If the Murdoch empire disliked members of parliament, it meant surveillance of their private lives and attempts to destroy them through public humiliation.[14] But it was the case of Milly Dowler, a thirteen-year-old girl murdered by a serial killer in 2002, that led to the unspooling of this system. When she went missing and her fate was unknown, tabloid journalists illicitly listened to her voicemails. Her family noticed that the schoolgirl's voicemails had been deleted, and gained false hope that Milly was still alive. Once all this came to light in 2011, the public[15] recognised that predatory techniques harmed more than celebrities and politicians.[16]

After the scandal broke, there were so many cases and so many details that much never made it into print. But they did appear online. This included a massive leak of emails that I hoped might prove ties between corrupt policemen and the Murdoch press. The leak consisted of 14,400 messages from the laptop of a former top police officer, Ray Adams, who had quit the force and joined the Murdoch empire. *The Australian Financial Review* acquired the emails as unsorted raw text files and asked the public for help digging through them.[17] A number of us discussing the case most obsessively on Som

Awful leapt to the task, and I posted their best findings on my blog, from what I thought showed links between hackers and a News Corporation subsidiary,[18] to references to an apparent slush fund. Ray Adams, for his part, denied any wrongdoing.

What took shape were the early flickers of the online investigative community. We were a small group, and I had no vision of what we would achieve in a few years; I was simply pleased to see my blog hit 10,000 page views in its first full month, April 2012. I promoted my blogging through Twitter, where I still had only a few hundred followers. The currency of our community was verified information – who found the fact did not matter greatly, except to flag that person as someone worth following on Twitter. The same principle remains at Bellingcat. Open-source investigation is not about formal qualifications. Your reputation is your results.

This was epitomised by my first close collaborator, a gifted online detective without the slightest background in journalism. She was a retired history teacher who ran a guesthouse in the West Country, and had followed the phone-hacking scandal closely, appalled by what she read. We noticed each other's contributions on the Something Awful message boards, and I asked if she would consider writing a post for Brown Moses. She preferred anonymity, so became 'The Regular Contributor'.

The Regular Contributor trawled through hundreds of hours of testimony in the phone-hacking inquiry, unearthing links to previous cases, searching online company records for financial ties among suspects, scouring digitised court records. She brought the meticulousness of a historian in dusty archives to the wilds of the internet. The Regular Contributor helped earn my blog an avid audience of people unsatisfied by phone-hacking coverage in the news media, including journalists themselves, even a few politicians. Many speculated that my contributor might be a senior member of parliament or a mole in the media. The truth was more telling. Newspapers based their sales on the notion that they alone accessed the corridors of power as the average citizen could not. They cultivated confidential sources and wielded influence to extract what they wanted. By contrast, the Regular Contributor wanted no glory and had no sway. 'If someone heard a tip from an insider, I wasn't going to use it,' she recalled. 'There were other people who had contacts and leads and moles, and that's not me.'

In hindsight, the phone-hacking scandal had a lasting impact, deepening an existing stereotype of journalists as a sleazy elite, both corrupt and corrupting. This reputation, which fails to distinguish between the ruthless reporters and the responsible, has been exploited by politicians (most notoriously President Donald Trump), with convenient dismissals of facts as 'fake news'. As for Brown Moses, the phone-hacking scandal stood as a vital first stop, one that helped shape the Bellingcat method. I knew with absolute clarity that our work must stand in opposition to the worst traditional journalism. Our sourcing would remain as open to public scrutiny as possible. Political agendas should have nothing to do with our work. And evidence-based citations had to underpin all findings. Lastly, we would never become a closed trade whose selling point was proximity to power. We were an open community of amateurs on a collaborative hunt for evidence.

The media critic Jay Rosen anticipated the rise of citizen journalism, predicting years ago that it would gain influence as the institutions clutching the levers of information lost control. 'The people formerly known as the audience wish to inform media people of our existence, and of a shift in power,' Rosen wrote in 2006. 'A highly centralized media system had connected people "up" to big social agencies and centers of power but not "across" to each other. Now the horizontal flow, citizen-to-citizen, is as real and consequential as the vertical one.'[19]

SYRIA: THE WAR THAT JOURNALISTS COULD NOT COVER

If tabloid manipulation represented the ugliest side of reporting, Marie Colvin of the *Sunday Times* stood for its nobler motives. In early 2012, she was among the few foreign journalists to risk a trip to Homs, a Syrian city under bombardment from the Assad regime. An experienced war correspondent of fifty-six, she was renowned for courage and her distinctive eye patch, worn because of a wound in another war zone.[20] 'It's a complete and utter lie that they're only going after terrorists,' she told CNN via satellite linkup. 'The Syrian Army is simply shelling a city of cold, starving civilians.'[21] The following day, Assad forces attacked a makeshift media centre, killing Colvin herself. Some believe that the live TV linkups hours before allowed them to obtain GPS coordinates of her location.

After Colvin's death, even fewer Western journalists dared to enter Syria. In their absence, the war grew crueller. Its evils would have been hidden from international view, were it not for the internet. More than any conflict in history, this war included social media as a component of the fighting, with combatants and victims alike chronicling bombardment and weaponry on hundreds of YouTube channels and blogs, desperate for outsiders to take their side. Back in 1982, the Syrian regime had crushed an uprising in the city of Hama, killing thousands of people; the exact number is unknown because the authorities concealed the crime. 'But today we have the internet,' a Syrian rebel remarked in 2012. 'We photograph and film and have Al Jazeera, so people know. They can see what is happening.'[22] The government tried to halt that, cutting electricity and landlines, while disabling mobile phones and the internet in opposition-held cities.[23] So activists created 'media centres' – often just a residence with a satellite-phone linkup.

In parallel, newsrooms around the world were in catastrophic decline, with circulations plummeting and ad revenues decimated, leading to mass layoffs. More information was available than ever before, yet the industry designated to evaluate and disseminate facts was overwhelmed. Who had time to go through all the footage from the Syrian conflict flooding the internet?

As it happened, I did.

Although I spoke no Arabic and had never visited Syria, I became intimately involved in studying its war, observing civilians' despair worsening every day via YouTube. From a distance of thousands of miles, I saw the regime indiscriminately bombing defiant towns like Daraa and Homs, and hundreds of competing rebel groups threatening revenge. In the early weeks of the Brown Moses blog, I persisted with my practice from message boards of compiling lists of notable videos that I found:

- 'Tank firing directly at the cameraman, unknown location'[24]
- 'Assad security forces beating and abusing a detained student in Aleppo University'
- 'Assad military helicopter firing missiles or rockets over Taftanaz'[25]

Each subject I dug into – Libya, the phone-hacking scandal, now Syria – brought me new Twitter followers, and linked me to others who were equally obsessed with parsing the deluge of information online. Twitter is often criticised as being an echo chamber, with people following only those with whom they already agree. But in niche pursuits like ours, where findings matter far more than opinions, creative networks can form, each member feeding into the progress of the group.

Among these who joined this informal Twitter hub were freelance foreign correspondents on whom major news organisations increasingly relied, since they were cheap and took the risks upon themselves. Such reporters were often young and highly engaged with social media. A pattern of cooperation ensued between on-the-ground reporters and computer-bound investigators: they provided up-close details; we shared revelations from social media. Together, we triangulated the truth.

However, their side of the collaboration grew unsustainable in Syria. Violence came not just from the Assad regime but from rebels and criminals who saw Western reporters as a target. Among those I tweeted with was Austin Tice, who freelanced for the *Washington Post*. In August 2012, he disappeared. At the time of writing, he was still missing, perhaps still in captivity. Kevin Dawes, a troubled Californian who had fought in Libya and whom I interviewed for my blog, tried to freelance in Syria, too. He was arrested in October 2012, confined in Assad's horrific prisons, and only released in 2016. The American freelancer James Foley tweeted a Brown Moses article hours before his abduction in late 2012. Two years later, he appeared in an online video, beheaded by ISIS.

The only viable option was to comprehensively monitor what Syrians were posting on social media. This new branch of war reporting, it turned out, is especially suited to the most savage conflicts, those that can be reached only at a high risk of injury. Obviously, online investigation is far safer – yet it is not without risk of harm to the mind of the researcher. Each time I thought I had seen every way a human body could be harmed on YouTube, I witnessed another. My approach was to resist a personal connection with what I saw. This was practical as well as protective: if my attention fixated on upsetting details, I might miss the most relevant ones.

What happened on 25 May 2012 challenged my detachment. News spread via Twitter of a massacre in Houla, a village near Homs. 'The number of dead varies greatly depending on reports,' I wrote on Brown Moses, 'but from videos posted on YouTube it seems apparent many have been killed, including a very large number of children.'[26] Activists said that regime forces had slit the throats of civilians. But this had to be checked carefully – the opposition pumped out propaganda, too. What was beyond doubt was what I saw: dozens of corpses, including women and children. More footage appeared, including horrifying audio of locals keening over slaughtered relatives. I paused the videos, trying to count corpses. The outpouring of information was so abundant that I decided to replicate the *Guardian*'s approach, producing my own live blog.[27] I posted activists' tweets, Facebook entries, links to live video from the mobile-streaming platform Bambuser, which broadcast protests breaking out around Syria in solidarity with the Houla victims. Gradually, I pieced together what seemed to have happened. After Friday midday prayers, a protest broke out in the area, which was a hotbed of hostility towards Assad yet surrounded by villages supportive of the regime. According to activists, the Syrian military shelled the rebellious town, prompting armed groups to retaliate. Then the *shabiha* moved in. These were pro-government militiamen who carried themselves like mobsters, often musclebound thugs in track suits and trainers, some with tattoos of Assad on their biceps. Their unofficial status permitted the regime to deny responsibility[28] – *shabiha* derives from the Arabic for 'ghosts'.

According to the opposition, *shabiha* had stormed into civilians' homes, looting and executing[29] residents. In the final count, 108 people were killed: 49 children, 34 women, 25 men. Artillery and tank shells killed some of these, but most had been executed.[30] The government blamed 'terrorists'.[31] In response, the United States, Britain and other nations expelled Syrian diplomats.[32] A later UN investigation confirmed that the Syrian government and *shabiha* had committed crimes against humanity, including murder, torture, indiscriminate attacks against civilians and sexual violence. These atrocities pointed 'to the involvement at the highest levels of the armed and security forces and the government',[33] the UN inquiry said. But at the time facts were bitterly disputed online – a pattern that followed every outrage in the Syrian civil war. Newspapers were not the first draft of history anymore; social media was. And everyone there was shouting.

In parallel to my community of fact-finding obsessives were partisans who denounced any contradiction of their worldview, an approach that I had first encountered when dealing with the Libyan uprising. Several such characters found platforms in the propaganda arms of the pro-Gaddafi press. I watched the same process repeat itself with Syria, where counterfactual zealots linked up with the pro-Assad media. Later still, another iteration of such alliances came into effect, when fringe conspiracists found themselves elevated by Kremlin news-manipulation outfits, invited on air by Russia Today or to write for Sputnik.

During the Houla massacre, online disputes sowed confusion, making verification imperative. I kept updating the live blog until after 1 a.m. and slept only a few hours before returning to it early on Saturday morning. To my surprise, NPR had mentioned my work – the first major media source to acknowledge Brown Moses. The American public broadcaster's website said: 'Note that we did not publish any of the images we described. If you're so inclined, the videos from where those images were taken, were collected by Brown Moses on his blog. Be warned – they are gruesome.'[34] On the internet, people want to see for themselves. NPR's caution prompted thousands to click.

Previously, the Brown Moses blog was receiving about 100 to 200 site visitors a day. This soared to around 3,000. Many who discovered the live blog kept returning. Brown Moses monthly total page views, which had hit 10,000 back in April 2012, more than tripled to 32,000 two months later. Those are not vast figures online but were gratifying to me, given that I was still doing this in my free time while working a day job. Among those who now followed me on Twitter were top academics, members of think tanks, foreign policy officials – influential types who sought titbits beyond what the news outlets provided. They did not want just another rant about Syria. They wanted granular facts, day by day, video by video, claim by claim. That is what I offered.

To start, my approach had been reactive, reposting videos and tweets of note. But covering the Houla massacre nudged me towards a more proactive method. Many YouTube channels, I noticed, were reposting videos from other sources, sometimes omitting key information or mislabelling footage. Original footage on this massacre derived from four YouTube channels. That was it: just four.[35] Multitudes of Syrians were filming the surrounding nightmare, but the regime was not letting anyone just upload content from their mobiles. Residents who wanted to disseminate footage had to do so via a media centre, those ramshackle rooms where a rare satellite connection could be had. Also, armed groups had satellite phones. Another option was smuggling a memory stick to activists in Turkey. These three sources accounted for almost every new video. I reasoned that, if I could figure out which media centres, which armed groups, and which expat activists covered each opposition-controlled area, I could pin down all sources of fresh footage. Rather than wait for someone to post intriguing material on Twitter, I developed a systematised way to survey Syria in full, dividing up the country geographically, creating a patchwork social-media map of the war.

This started with around fifteen channels, which I posted as a public directory on the Brown Moses blog. In the end, I had compiled more than 500 sources,[36] from original YouTube channels to profiles on Bambuser linked with specific areas to Facebook pages for towns or regions. Each day, I surveyed this massive list, checking for fresh material, cutting and pasting Arabic titles of clips into Google Translate to learn what each video purported to show. It was impossible to watch hundreds of hours of footage daily, so I ran my mouse pointer along the timeline under each YouTube clip, scanning the thumbnail preview, which alerted me to relevant material.

Assad supporters condemned my efforts because most footage came from the opposition, but this was unavoidable. The Syrian government knew that the outside world would condemn its strategy of violent suppression, while the opposition calculated that it would earn sympathy by exposing the security state at work. Still, I always reminded myself that the supposedly 'raw footage' had been selected to support one side in the war. For this, I sought to keep my approach dry and forensic. Other Syria observers – either partial from the start, or horrified by what they saw – picked a side. I myself had no personal stake. I just kept unearthing material and worried that, if I did not write about it, perhaps nobody would.

Midway through 2012, I noticed an intriguing development during my exhaustive daily video monitoring: the Free Syrian

Army rebels had become well armed. They no longer relied on AK-47s and rocket-propelled grenades; they had heavy weapons. My attention to arms dated back to Libya, when questions kept arising there about what the revolutionaries had. This became even more vital to understanding the prospects of the Syria uprising.

In one Syrian video, a young man in military fatigues declared the formation of Al-Hamza Brigade. Perhaps a hundred others stood behind him, some in camouflage and sneakers, others in street clothing. Nearly all held Kalashnikovs, pointing the barrels upwards for their induction into this Free Syrian Army faction in Rastan, between Homs and Hama. '*Allahu akbar!*' the men cried in unison, pumping their weapons in the air.[37] In the background, a man in blue trousers stood out. He held a shoulder-fired missile system with a high-explosive warhead, the Strela-2,[38] which was first produced in 1968 in the Soviet Union, commonly used in Cold War-era conflicts and by guerrilla movements ever since.[39] If those details make me sound like an arms expert, I was no such thing at the time. However, I had seen many such videos because the formation of new opposition fighting units was rampant by mid-2012. The routine was a few minutes of bellicose announcements (fast-forward), then soldiers holding up arms (pause). The rare weapons were what I focused on.[40]

My real-life experience with armaments was nil, so I searched online for articles about the revolutionaries' arsenal. One magazine spoke of AK-47s coming with defectors who had quit the army[41] and taken their guns. A news site cited a rebel who claimed that 50 per cent of Free Syrian Army weaponry was captured in battle, 40 per cent gained by ransoming soldiers and buying arms from corrupt military officers,[42] while 10 per cent had been donated or smuggled from outside the country.

One newspaper spoke of rebel emissaries meeting with top US officials and pleading for heavier weaponry, bringing an iPad loaded with Google Earth to show rebel positions and regime targets.[43] With the proper firepower, they pledged to knock out regime tanks and aircraft. The international community hesitated, unsure which of the hundreds of fighting outfits to deal with.

Despite this smattering of clues, I failed to find a clear account of what the rebels actually had. So I decided to compile one based on social-media videos, collating images of rocket-propelled grenades (RPGs), along with captured Soviet-era amphibious infantry fighting vehicles, even a captured tank driven around Homs. I added footage of a battalion firing 120mm mortars and a recoilless rifle. Others shot anti-aircraft cannons powerful enough to take down regime helicopters, or Soviet-made DShK heavy machine guns mounted on trucks. How did I identify all of this? Simple: I matched the images in paused footage to Wikipedia entries, or via internet message boards that discussed munitions, or through websites that specialised in unexploded ordnance. It was time-consuming, and I had to get this right or I would lose credibility.

Another rebel trend I documented was improvisation. In YouTube videos, I found driverless cars rigged with bombs and directed by remote control, along with bizarre-looking trucks converted into mobile forts with slabs of protective metal, armoured wheels and firing posts. I found a heavy machine gun mounted on a trolley; fuse-lit explosive bottles fired with an oversized slingshot; a homemade missile that looked like a hybrid of a firework and a space rocket.[44]

Paradoxically, my lack of Arabic could be an asset in pattern recognition. Videos showed furious young men shouting at wobbly cameras, or victims crying about lost loved ones. Such emotional declarations would affect anyone who understood them. But I could not, so ignored the foreground and scrutinised what I could judge: objects. This directed me to a key precept of digital sleuthing. What people mean to show is not all they are revealing.

A pivotal example came in July 2012, when a clip exposed the brutal descent of Assad's military strategy. I was about to go to bed after a long day's work and blogging, when a video popped up on my Twitter feed from a Syrian activist, Sami al-Hamwi, who went by the handle @HamaEcho. 'Anyone know what this weird bombs is?'[45] he asked.

By this time, a few dozen Syria obsessives were communicating this way via Twitter – strangers with the common aim of studying the internet to understand the war. The group included academics, reporters, Syrian activists, plus outsiders like me. Some gave witness accounts; others monitored Arabic media and provided translations; I could geolocate and identify weapons. This was long before the multiperson staff of Bellingcat came together, yet my efforts were never solitary.

The video that @HamaEcho flagged was forty-five seconds long, filmed in the dark of night in the Hama countryside, showing a man picking through sandy earth, pointing out about fifteen turquoise canisters, each the size of an aerosol spray but with tail fins,[46] and describing these objects as shrapnel. I had been viewing Syrian munitions every day for months and knew this was not shrapnel.

Weeks earlier, UN monitors had confirmed a longstanding claim of the opposition, that Assad forces were firing machine guns and smaller arms from helicopters.[47] I myself had video evidence of the Syrian Air Force tossing out unguided bombs in the area where this clip had purportedly been filmed: the opposition stronghold of Jabal Shashabo, a mountainous area north-west of the city of Hama. Rebels took shelter in caves there, and the Syrian military had been bombarding them for the preceding two weeks with artillery, the occasional warplane and helicopters.[48]

In this latest video, the cameraman picked up one of the canisters and turned it to face his lens, displaying black markings on the side: 'A-IX-2'. I had my lead. All I had to do was type the markings into Google Search. Nearly all industrial munitions are catalogued on specialist military sites and the webpages of arms dealers; even Wikipedia is remarkably reliable.[49] These particular markings did not denote rockets, I learned. They were for Russian-made explosive fill for packing inside military shells. They must have failed to detonate. The man on the video, I realised, was picking through live explosives while speaking offscreen to what sounded like a small boy.

I wondered if the objects that @HamaEcho called 'this weird bombs' might be cluster munitions, a widely denounced form of weaponry, outlawed in many countries. The way they work is that a main shell breaks apart, releasing explosive bomblets, sometimes as many as hundreds, that can spread over an area as large as several football fields. Cluster bomblets often fail to explode, and sit like landmines, waiting for someone – often a child – to pick them up.[50] During the Libyan conflict, the *New York Times* war correspondent C. J. Chivers, a former US marine and weapons expert, wrote about Gaddafi loyalists dropping cluster munitions when attacking rebel-held Misrata. If Syrian government forces had used them in an area where civilians lived, I was looking at a major escalation.[51]

A giveaway trait of cluster munitions is that they leave behind a bomb casing, and @HamaEcho had a second video from the same location, showing a large shell split in two, seemingly the delivery device.[52] @HamaEcho had also tweeted these two short clips to Bjørn Jespersen (@bjoernen_dk) of the.processing blog, another amateur identifying Syrian weaponry with open-source information. Jespersen drew a sketch of the split shell, so we had something to match online. We scoured images of bombs that could be used to drop cluster munitions, and found that each had a distinct shape and tailfin configuration, while only delivering certain types of bomblets. From there, it was a process of elimination. Only one delivery munition of this configuration matched with the A-IX-2 explosive fill of the bomblets: the Russian-made RBK-250-275 cluster bomb, which we cross-referenced on various sites, from the defence-industry publisher Jane's, to the webpages of the unexploded ordnance site Uxoinfo.[53] Cluster bombs *were* being deployed in Syria, and we had evidence.[54]

By this point, the original video itself had only been watched about two hundred times on YouTube, and would have likely escaped the world's notice. My Twitter followers numbered around 1,500 people – far higher than months before, but still too few for my tweets to reverberate widely. Somehow, I needed to attract high-level attention, so tweeted a link to my blog article to any account that I thought might be interested, from Chivers of the *New York Times* to Amnesty International, to Human Rights Watch, to a reporter at the *Guardian*, to Andy Carvin of NPR, even members of the UK parliament whom I had come across for their role in confronting the phone-hacking scandal. For good measure, I sent a link to the top diplomat in Britain, Foreign Secretary William Hague.

Chivers cited my findings on his own blog, rightly cautioning that my analysis was preliminary. However, he confirmed that the videos did suggest a RBK canister shell containing bomblets, writing, 'Brown Moses gets points for an alert set of eyes and a careful mind.'[55] Human Rights Watch seemed to have read my post, too, publishing its own report, with arms experts confirming my findings, while independently determining that the video uploader had indeed filmed this in Jabal Shashabo.[56]

On his blog, Chivers answered a common question about why cluster bombs matter more than the other horrific tools of war. It is the indiscriminate harm, but also what this munition represents. 'Arab governments do not need anyone to tell them how resonant the use of cluster bombs against Muslims and Arabs has been, whether it was Israel's use in 2006 in Lebanon or Libya's use against its own citizens last year,' he wrote. If Damascus was confirmed to have taken this step, 'it would signal a regime crossing another psychological threshold, and a willingness to escalate another notch'.[57]

In passing, Chivers chided Human Rights Watch for failing to cite the Brown Moses blog – an omission that I had scarcely registered. Yet it spoke to a common assumption back in 2012: that one could dip into the internet and take whatever one found, not needing to acknowledge it. What existed online was deemed less worthy, and yet the internet was increasingly likely to be the basis of public knowledge. This gap is what led many institutions to underestimate what was happening online.

After Chivers' comment, Human Rights Watch invited me to join a private Facebook group called Mystery Munitions, consisting of arms experts from various organisations, all studying unidentified weaponry. In an earlier era, professionals of this calibre would have consorted only at universities, military facilities, academic conferences, or within the walls of a think tank. An outsider like me – still just an admin worker – could never have tapped such expertise; nor would they have heard mine. As it turned out, I had insights that eluded them, especially regarding stranger forms of weaponry in Syria, such as those homemade artillery launchers that rebels improvised because of their limited arsenal. On conventional weapons, their feedback sharpened my judgement immeasurably.

A further lesson I took from the Mystery Munitions group was that, if not in the same field, experts rarely talk to each other. Partly, this is intentional. Arms experts, for instance, hesitate to share findings with reporters or activists, concerned that the information could end up as splashy headlines or lobbying. But nobody was threatened by me. My aim was finding facts, nothing more, and nobody was paying me to produce or to promote one side or another. As such, I gained access to a range of online nodes – journalists, Syrian activists, rights advocates, arms experts – finding myself at the centre of a broadening knowledge network. Besides gaining access to their expertise, the position allowed me to connect others when they needed help.

For months to come, I was studying crashed bombs in paused YouTube images, comparing the tiniest details of a shell's configuration against photos online – high-resolution amateur snapshots posted from air shows, for example, where model bombs were on display, all varieties lined up in a row. Online hobbyists proved invaluable, too. They set up chat groups and exchanged lists and photos online that you found nowhere else. In future Bellingcat investigations, we were to make breakthroughs via plane-spotter webpages, websites of licence plates and countless other obscure niches online. But in the Brown Moses days I focused on the military hardware of the Syrian Air Force, still a mere amateur yet proficient enough from online experience – recognising the tell-tale placement of lug holes, grooves along the fins, distinctive tail rings – to make authoritative identifications from a mere bomb fragment.

INFORMATION WARS AND BARREL BOMBS

By late July 2012, the Assad regime had lost control of districts in Aleppo, Syria's largest city and economic hub. Anybody observing the civil war had the same question: how were the rebels doing it? For my part, I sought to identify each unexploded munition caught on video. Every weapon bigger than a machine gun, I wanted to name. Besides the endless AK-47s, rebels were brandishing anti-aircraft cannons and rocket-propelled grenade launchers, mostly taken from the army. They also built improvised explosive devices, IEDs, alongside homemade contraptions to hurl explosives at Assad forces.

Amid this, a major publication asked me to contribute an article, my first such invitation. *Foreign Policy*, esteemed magazine of diplomats, academics and policy analysts, sought a piece on the revolutionaries' armoury. Rather than worrying about how to appeal to this elevated audience, I just wrote what interested me, pulling together recent findings from Brown Moses posts. Free Syrian Army rebels had adapted regular trucks into fighting machines, mounting them with heavy weaponry like the captured Soviet-era DShK heavy machine gun, nicknamed 'Dushka', or 'sweetie' in English. These could challenge Syrian Air Force helicopters, which flew at around the height of a skyscraper, firing machine guns down or throwing unguided bombs such as the OFAB 250-270, a metal shell as heavy as a Harley-Davidson plummeting wherever the wind took it.[58] The guerrillas' use of IEDs, as with attacks on the US military in neighbouring Iraq, proved highly effective. Their homemade weaponry was even more extraordinary. One group produced an impromptu flamethrower by commandeering a fuel truck, uncoiling its hose and spraying gasoline at a target building, then setting the flow alight. They also had workshops producing ammo, taking used grenade rockets and filling them with homemade explosives.[59] These methods stirred debate over international military intervention – Western powers kept denouncing Assad yet were not rushing to send weaponry to defeat the Syrian dictator. In the meantime, Russia and Iran were solidly backing him, so taking the opposing side risked a wider war. Also, the rebels remained divided, and the international community worried about which groups to support.

My own objective – to unearth evidence about the Syrian civil war – itself made enemies. Ever since the Houla massacre, when international condemnation flared against Assad, many supporters of the Syrian president denounced any allegation against his forces as a devious conspiracy to engineer regime change. By this twisted logic, to document war crimes was to want war.

I myself was not advocating foreign intervention or inaction; I was not advocating at all. But anger about the leadup to the Iraq War remained so intense that some, especially on the far left, could not see criticism of an Arab dictator as anything but a neo-conservative plot to remake the Middle East and steal its oil.[60] Meanwhile, those on the far right also supported Assad, but for his willingness to torture and murder, ostensibly to crush Muslim extremists, even though those were only a small fraction of his victims. When it came to Assad, the far left and the far right united in sympathy. This meant that I found myself deemed 'imperialist scum' online while also receiving racist abuse from people who assumed that as 'Brown Moses', I must be Jewish and/or non-white.

Paid propagandists entered the fray, too, seeking to muddy facts from Syria. At the end of April 2012, the Syrian channel Addounia TV, following two months of devastating bombardment in Homs, broadcast video purportedly by an

Algerian traveller filming from his hotel window, showing that the city was fine and that journalists were lying. The clip showed a peaceful metropolis, cars driving freely around.[61] But when the camera panned past billboards with phone numbers, they included the area code of the capital, Damascus. I, along with fellow online detectives, drew a street layout using this video, then checked it against the Google Maps satellite images of Damascus. We had a match: that same tall apartment block in the background with a distinct pattern of windows; two structures with canopies on top; every tree lining up.[62] They had broadcast a shameless fabrication.

The Kremlin's news network in English (initially Russia Today, later rebranded RT to downplay its origins) also slipped lies into its Syria coverage, smearing the opposition to Assad. In a typical case, RT ran a piece under the headline: 'Nothing safe, nothing sacred: Syrian rebels desecrate Christian churches?' The article based its assertions on the website Prison Planet of far-right conspiracy theorist Alex Jones, which contained photos supposedly showing a vandalised church and 'a man who is said to be a member of the Free Syrian Army' posing 'in a stolen priest's robe while brandishing a looted cross in one hand and a machine gun in the other'. RT said the images had been taken by a Christian woman in Homs who had spoken to Prison Planet.[63] In fact, the photograph had been lifted from Lens Young Homsi, a group of young photographers based in Homs whose watermark had been conveniently cropped, hiding its true origin. In my monitoring of activists' YouTube channels, I had seen footage of this same church. During a two-minute sequence, a Syrian man pointed to rubble on the floor, to overturned pew seats, and damage to a picture of Jesus – after which the camera angled upward to the ceiling, zooming towards a hole in the roof. The rubble was not from anti-Christian looting, but from artillery fire.[64]

I did not realise it then, but what I saw were early indications of a coming contest: the Information Wars. Repressive states, which had long faced bad press abroad, could now bypass independent journalists, injecting propaganda directly into foreign countries. Disinformation became a key lever of foreign policy.

RT, established in 2005, has been among the most energetic purveyors. In its early incarnation, the Kremlin-funded channel broadcast dull stories about the Russian motherland, only to realise that few overseas cared. In 2009, in parallel with the RT rebrand, the broadcaster shifted its focus to the decay of the Western world. Even if few watched its TV broadcasts, RT could still reach millions online, with segments spreading on YouTube, Facebook and Twitter.

RT's editor-in-chief, Margarita Simonyan (who conducted the infamous interview with the two Skripal poisoning suspects), said in 2012 that she did not believe in journalistic objectivity, and characterised her operation as an arm of Russian information warfare. 'It's impossible to start making a weapon only when the war has already started!' she told the Russian newspaper *Kommersant*. 'The Defense Ministry isn't fighting anyone at the moment, but it's ready for defense. So are we.'[65]

Baseless claims proved the perfect fodder for conspiracy theorists looking to pad their online operations with fresh content. Alex Jones's InfoWars published a Syrian piece on 4 July 2012 that said: 'Whereas the establishment media, particularly the likes of CNN and the *Guardian*, have prostrated themselves as 24-hour rolling propaganda platforms for anonymous "activists" with Twitter accounts, showcasing unverified YouTube clips of alleged atrocities, equally disturbing footage of rebels committing acts of savagery have been buried.' Below this, the website published a series of disturbing videos, all purportedly documenting rebel crimes. I fact-checked this and found a litany of falsehoods. The list started poorly, featuring an RT video that falsely claimed to show a family of Syrians blaming rebels for an atrocity. Another clip showed a grieving woman talking to Syrian state TV, captioned: 'This woman's son, Sari Saoud, was shot in Homs. While Al-Jazeera claimed it was the army that killed him, the woman insisted it was the insurgents.' But in my YouTube channel monitoring, I had seen an earlier video in which this woman was grieving over the body of her son, during which she shouted, 'Fuck you, Bashar!' in Arabic.

InfoWars captioned another video: 'This disturbing clip shows rebels insulting an Alawite Syrian civilian before decapitating him.'[66] With minimal research, I found that the video was not from Syria but Tunisia. InfoWars also linked to the dubious article claiming Syrian rebels had ransacked a church.[67] In another posted video, InfoWars showed the United Nations transporting a rebel by truck, claiming that the supposedly neutral observers actually favoured the opposition. However, I knew this clip from my monitoring. It showed UN observers telling an activist, Hadi al-Abdallah, that they would *not* protect him.[68] Paul Joseph Watson on InfoWars also pointed out that men in the clip exclaimed '*Allahu akbar!*' and described this as 'a phrase widely associated with fundamentalist Muslims who are engaged in jihad'.[69] This proved only the site's ignorance. '*Allahu akbar!*' is a common expression among Muslims,[70] akin to saying, 'Thank God!'[71] Fakery ramped up online, but it was not always sophisticated: exposing all those InfoWars falsehoods took me just an hour.

My article for *Foreign Policy* from July 2012 – 'Syria's DIY Revolt' – allowed me to access a new set of readers, delivering open-source investigation to the upper echelon of the Syria debate. Traffic to Brown Moses climbed yet again, and, less than six months into the blog, monthly page views had more than quadrupled, up to 46,000 in August 2012. Then came my most significant discovery yet, which exposed just how desperate the Syrian government had become.

In a YouTube video, townspeople gathered around a rusty barrel flattened on the ground. It looked like a burned-out dustbin, kicked over and squashed. Locals said the object had fallen from a helicopter.[72] Only the regime had helicopters, but it seemed strange that a professional military should use a crude device like a barrel bomb – explosives stuffed into a metal drum – and push it from an aircraft. I kept studying clips of that scene, uploaded by opposition supporters in Batbo, a town west of Aleppo. 'This time,' I wrote on Brown Moses, 'I've come across something that's really got me stumped.'

I solicited input from others online[73] and theories soon proliferated. Maybe it was a rebel IED that the military had disarmed, then thrown back onto territory held by the Free Syrian Army. Perhaps besieged regime airbases had run out of supplies and resorted to DIY bombs themselves. Some wondered if the videos could have been fakes created by the opposition.

When it came to accusations of barrel-bomb use, the Saudi-owned news channel Al Arabiya said the Syrian Air Force had dropped them filled with 200 kilos of TNT onto residential buildings in Homs, to demolish possible hiding places for the rebels.[74] But the evidence was limited. A journalist for the *Daily Telegraph* in Aleppo cited activists saying barrel bombs had been dropped on a public park.[75] Again, a strong claim without strong evidence. My search for barrel-bomb clips turned up many questionable leads. Often, footage marked as 'barrel bomb' displayed Syrian L-39 warplanes dropping Soviet-era munitions, the OFABs. Predictably, RT had something to say on the subject. In an article headlined 'Barrel Bomb Baloney', the analyst Colonel Evgeny Khrushchev ridiculed assertions that Assad's forces would resort to such methods. 'Welcome to the latest spin of the Al-Qaeda psychological operation against the Syrian government, backed by their Western advisers,' he wrote, deeming it 'malarkey', 'black propaganda' and American trickery to justify a NATO intervention.[76]

Finally, damning evidence appeared: five videos filmed inside a Syrian helicopter gunship, either leaked or taken from a captured airman, and showing rows of barrel bombs lined up in an airborne chopper, the back door wide open. Men in military fatigues posed for each other's phone cameras, taking vertiginous looks at the town below. In the fifth video, an airman smoked a cigarette, blowing the lit end to make it glow, then touched this to a barrel bomb's wick fuse, which sparked alight. He pushed the bomb out of the open back door.

Before, those of us studying Syrian weaponry had not known that barrel bombs operated on wick fuses, but this explained a great deal. If the fuse was too long, a barrel bomb would hit the earth before detonating, and the impact could knock out that fuse, which explained the discovery of unexploded barrel bombs. I had also seen videos of purported barrel bombs falling from helicopters and exploding in mid-air – the fuse must have been too short.

After the airman pushed out that barrel bomb, the cameraman filmed the explosive somersaulting towards a town below – vivid evidence of an indiscriminate attack on a civilian area. The cameraman kept filming, offering a top-down view of roadways and habitations. Sceptics online said the footage could have been filmed anywhere, perhaps not even in Syria. But a top-down shot was ideal for comparing with maps. Josh Lyons of

Human Rights Watch, an early user of open-source investigative techniques, spent hours scouring satellite imagery of Syria and found that exact road layout. I checked his claim, adjusting a map on Google Earth, comparing this to the paused image on YouTube. The street layout was identical: Al Dabaa, a town in central Syria, outside Homs.[77]

In the years ahead, barrel bombs became an emblematic weapon of Assad's forces, which rained down thousands more as a devastating and cheap alternative to conventional munitions. By the end of 2017, regime barrel bombs had killed nearly 11,000 civilians, according to the Syrian Network for Human Rights.[78] Assad denied that his forces had dropped even one. 'I haven't heard of army using barrels, or maybe cooking pots,' he joked in a 2015 interview with the BBC. 'There's no indiscriminate weapons. When you shoot, you aim. And when you aim, you aim at terrorists in order to protect civilians. Again, if you're talking about casualty, that's war. You cannot have war without casualty.'[79]

By September 2012, my blog had surpassed 200,000 page views – a notable milestone but nowhere near enough to support myself through ad revenue. Also, my previous job had ended, which ratcheted up the pressure to decide whether I could afford to keep putting every free moment into Brown Moses. While this question preoccupied me, NPR's *Weekend Edition* reached out, asking me to appear on air to discuss my findings, in what was my first major broadcast interview. I prepared exhaustively, bringing pages of notes to the Leicester studio of the BBC, which patched me through to host Scott Simon in Washington.

SIMON: Where do rebels get rocket launchers?
HIGGINS: As far as I can see, most of this is actually
    coming from military bases, arms depots and the like.

SIMON: So, they're taking the government's weapons and using them against the government?
(I was tense, but had answers.)

HIGGINS: That's correct. I've not seen any evidence that they're coming from abroad. Although it's always quite difficult to tell. I mean, we don't really get to see the packing slips that come along with them.

SIMON: You've written a good deal about what you've called DIY – do-it-yourself – weapons systems.

HIGGINS: That's correct.

SIMON: Give us an example of what you've noticed in the Syrian conflict.

HIGGINS: One of the most popular weapons I've seen is simple pipe bombs. They're made from a variety of explosive, some of which is actually harvested from unexploded bombs that have been dropped onto Syrian rebels. They break them open, take out the explosives, and put them into their own pipe bombs. They also use oversized slingshots to actually launch these and clear the distances over walls and into military compounds and fortified areas.

SIMON: Did you say *oversized slingshots*?

I had. And I hadn't needed those copious notes: the challenge was not answering his questions, but simplifying my replies. In the coming weeks, an Austrian newspaper interviewed me about my findings.[80] CNN cited my work.[81] So did the *Christian Science Monitor*[82] and the *Financial Times*.[83]

At the end of the interview, Scott Simon of NPR sought to assure his listeners. 'Mr Higgins, you often are cited as a source on the arms that are used in the conflict. We have to ask: you're sitting there in some kind of studio in the United

Kingdom. How do you know this stuff?'[84] I mentioned my network of contacts, plus all the uploaded videos that provided daily insights. But I never dubbed myself 'an expert'. Those who opposed my findings used this language – 'so-called expert Eliot Higgins' – to discredit me, noting my lack of formal training, and sneering that I was only a blogger. I never hid that; rather, it was the point.

Still, my expertise was growing, and this delivered a troubling realisation: many policymakers, top officials and politicians taking decisions about going to war knew far less about the Syrian conflict than I had learned merely by looking at open sources. I had stumbled onto a gap in the information system – one that I have spent every day since working to fill.

FRONT PAGE OF THE *NEW YORK TIMES*

By early 2013, the Syrian government seemed incapable of regaining control of the country. But each time the opposition advanced, the regime pulled out a worse weapon. The latest were incendiary munitions. The opposition gained extreme elements, too, including foreigners with guerrilla experience across the border in Iraq. I started finding videos of rebel jihadi attacks against civilians. The war looked like a stalemate, and the future of Syria would depend on foreign nations. A country I never expected to find on the battlefield was the former Yugoslavia.

In clips from the Hauran region in south-western Syria, near the border with Jordan, an unusual rocket launcher appeared in rebels' hands. In one video, a guerrilla knelt in wait by an intersection, propping an M79 Osa portable anti-tank rocket launcher on his shoulder, the weighty metal tube as long as the man himself. A tank came into view and the rebel fired. In my nine months of scrutiny, I had never come across this weapon.

Later, Syrian state television broadcast footage from the same region near Jordan of weapons seized from rebels that matched what I had seen in the tank-attack video.

Normally, rebels acquired arms from the Syrian Army through defectors, or by looting when they overcame a military outpost. However, the military did not have the M79 Osa rocket launcher. It originated in republics of the former Yugoslavia: Serbia, Macedonia, or Croatia.[85] Another state TV segment showed more captured rebel armaments, including rows of rocket launchers and RPGs and recoilless rifles. I identified them, again finding that they were models developed in Yugoslavia and not known to be used by the Syrian armed forces.

I went to my list of YouTube channels and tracked back through the media feeds of rebel groups based near where the weapons had been seized, finding that such arms showed up near the beginning of 2013. Insurgents in the south-west, it seemed, had received a major shipment, perhaps across the border with Jordan. My hypothesis was that a foreign supporter had delivered a huge cache to one of the larger armed groups around Daraa, and this group distributed weapons to other factions in the region. Notably, all the rebel groups that brandished these fresh weapons were aligned to the more moderate end of the opposition spectrum, suggesting that weapons may have been supplied specifically to groups that would oppose the growing influence of the Al-Qaeda affiliate Jabhat al-Nusra.

If I had uncovered evidence of international arms smuggling, this would be extraordinary – not only as a news event, but in demonstrating what open-source investigation could achieve. All I had done was monitor social-media channels, particularly on YouTube, spotted anomalous weapons and recorded this on a spreadsheet. This was rudimentary given the complexity of

Bellingcat investigations a couple of years later. Yet it was proof of concept, even more powerfully so because of its simplicity.

In coming days and weeks, I spotted other ex-Yugoslav weapons, sometimes distant from the border area. This arms-smuggling operation was serious,[86] and perhaps marked a turning point in the war. I posted my work on Brown Moses but soon found a larger platform. A *New York Times* blog called At War published contributions from those with knowledge of conflicts, and approached me in February 2013 to ask if I had anything to interest their readers. I rushed them a summary of my recent findings – then waited. Finally, they replied: they were interested but wanted to report it further themselves. C. J. Chivers, along with the Washington reporter Eric Schmitt, took my evidence to officials. Their response was this: it's true, and it's the Saudis, with the knowledge of the US government, purchasing arms from the Croatian government, flying them to Jordan and moving them across the border to the Free Syrian Army. It was the first time a major arms route to the Syrian opposition had been exposed.

On the front page of the *New York Times* of 26 February 2013, the lead story bore the headline 'IN SHIFT, SAUDIS ARE SAID TO ARM REBELS IN SYRIA':[87]

Saudi Arabia has financed a large purchase of infantry weapons from Croatia and quietly funneled them to antigovernment fighters in Syria in a drive to break the bloody stalemate that has allowed President Bashar al-Assad to cling to power, according to American and Western officials familiar with the purchases …

Many of the weapons – which include a particular type of Yugoslav-made recoilless gun, as well as assault rifles, grenade launchers, machine guns, mortars and shoulder-fired rockets for use against tanks and other armored vehicles – have been extensively documented by one blogger, Eliot Higgins, who writes under the name Brown Moses and has mapped the new weapons' spread through the conflict.

Officials cited in the article said the weapons derived from a surplus held by Croatia after the Balkan wars of the 1990s. The previous summer, a senior Croatian official reportedly mentioned this surplus to the Americans, in case anyone might be interested in supplying them to the Syrian rebels.[88]

I wrote a companion piece for At War, discussing my methods. Meanwhile, in Britain, the reports came up in parliament, raised by Tom Watson, an MP who had become part of my online network through his interest in the Brown Moses work on phone hacking.[89] My monthly page views skyrocketed, up to 72,000 in March 2013, then 137,000 by May. In my first year of blogging, I had gone from total obscurity to more than half a million views.

Curious about this blogger from nowhere, the *Guardian* decided to profile me. I had granted a smattering of interviews before, but always just about my findings – nothing that focused on me personally. 'Journalists assume I've worked in the arms trade,' I told the reporter. 'But before the Arab Spring, I knew no more about weapons that the average Xbox owner. I had no knowledge beyond what I'd learned from Arnold Schwarzenegger and Rambo.'[90] My detractors still cite this quote, saying that it proves I am unqualified. They miss the point. I *was* unqualified, but even an outsider like me could add to the debate.

After the *Guardian* profile, TV interview requests poured in: CNN, Channel 4 News in Britain, ARD from Germany. The CNN segment featured shots of me on a laptop in my kitchen, my daughter's highchair and toys in the background. At the time, I was between jobs, and this became part of the narrative: jobless house husband looks after toddler while discovering scoops about the Syrian civil war.

A different TV crew visited our house nearly every day that week, which produced a strange dissonance for me. After years of admin work, I had found something that I valued, seemed to excel at and wanted to pursue every waking hour. Yet I was not earning a living. Indeed, I was barely coping, and had a young family to support. The only option seemed to be to end Brown Moses. 'I'd like to blog forever, but I'd also like to pay my mortgage,' I wrote on Twitter. A flurry of tweets came back. I could at least try crowdfunding, they said.

Contributions trickled in – mostly small, but a steady stream. Within a few weeks, I had surpassed my modest goal[91] of £6,000. I had breathing room for a few months. In that time, I was to produce my biggest investigation yet.

A CHEMICAL-WEAPONS BREAKTHROUGH

When I woke on the morning of 21 August 2013,[92] videos were coming in fast and they were appalling. Overnight in the suburbs of Damascus, rockets had landed, hitting with a thud but no explosion. Vapours spread across the neighbourhood and civilians fell in the streets, froth coming from their noses, pupils constricted, their chests heaving. Clinics filled fast, and the victims all had the same glassy-eyed glare, whether alive or dead. Syrians had previously accused regime forces of attacking opposition areas with chemical weapons, but those strikes had been small and hard to confirm. Here, perhaps a thousand people were dead, with thousands more suffering neurotoxic symptoms. They were civilians, guilty of nothing but residing in Ghouta, a rebel-held suburb of the Syrian capital. Furious debate raged online between partisans of both sides, disputing who had been behind the attack.

A year earlier, President Obama had urged Assad to step down but said the United States was not prepared to intervene militarily – with one caveat. 'A red line for us is we start seeing a whole bunch of chemical weapons moving around or being utilized,' he warned.[93]

I had been trying to assess chemical-warfare allegations in Syria for months. Everyone knew the Syrian government had a chemical arsenal; it had admitted[94] that much. But establishing that the Assad regime was actually murdering its own citizens with poison was another matter. To confirm the chemical agents used in an attack, one needed chemical-weapons experts on the ground, gathering samples. Presumably, an online observer could contribute almost nothing.

The wider public had largely lost interest in the horrors of the Syria civil war, but a chemical attack of this magnitude drew renewed attention. As with future chemical weapon attacks in Syria, the Assad regime denied responsibility for the attack. Prime Minister David Cameron asked British legislative bodies to authorise airstrikes against Assad. During the parliamentary debate, a number of MPs spoke, most revealing a worrying ignorance about the topic, simply reciting what ill-informed newspaper columnists had written. Ultimately, parliament voted against military action,[95] which left Obama without this key ally. The White House released an intelligence summary on the Ghouta attacks, accusing the Assad government.[96] I read the four-page document and was once again dismayed. It was so flimsy and overlooked the wealth of online videos, which already numbered more than two hundred.

I was piecing together everything I could from social-media footage and still images on the day of the attacks. Residents of

Ghouta had found long, thin, grey, tubular rockets, each around ten feet long, which had crashed into the ground. The rockets had tailfins on the butt end and an oversized warhead on the front. I had come across these unusual rockets in online videos before, first in January 2013, but they had always been loaded with explosives, not chemical weapons.

For answers, I appealed to my knowledge network, querying arms and chemical-weapons experts from the Mystery Munitions group on Facebook. Nobody recognised the tubular rockets, so I called them the UMLACA, for Unidentified Munitions Linked to Alleged Chemical Attacks. The presence of several intact rockets suggested they had not been intended to cause explosive damage, but to distribute a payload. The base of the warhead had two ports, one of which was a screw cap. That meant it could not have been filled with a gas, and the port was too small to readily fill with a solid. The most likely content would have been liquid. This reduced the possible chemical agents.[97]

In one especially useful image, an UMLACA protruded from the soil in an open field, the metal buckled from impact. We needed to geolocate this rocket, so I alerted the investigative community on Twitter. One user proposed a possible site, dropping a pin on Google Maps for me to check out. A key to geolocation is to avoid losing yourself in an abundance of details. You pick a standout element: a distinctive minaret, say, or an unusually landscaped park. This allows you to bypass the confusion of visual information. Once you match the first element, you seek a second notable detail, and so on.

In this case, I used five separate images of the rocket site, each showing a background view of a different part of the area, allowing me to patch together the surroundings. Bit by bit, I matched everything with satellite imagery from Google

Maps. We had the location. And using shadows in the photo, I determined the angle of the rocket, thereby estimating the direction from which it had come. With that, I went to Wikimapia, which allows users to annotate maps by inserting names and types of structures. I traced back the likely trajectory of the rocket to determine who held the area where it had come from. I found a Syrian military installation,[98] largely encircled by rebel-held territory.

In addition to the first attacks around 2:30 a.m. in the eastern suburbs of Damascus, a second chemical-weapons strike took place at about 5 a.m. in the south-western suburbs. While the first attack came from the pipe-shaped UMLACA rockets, the second involved a different munition. During all this, a UN team of investigators was working in Syria, with the mandate to determine if chemical weapons had been used – but not *who* had used them. One inspector was filmed studying munitions, measuring an artillery shell reported to have emitted poison gas or vapour. I paused the frame while the inspector's measuring tape was extended. I copied the image, cut and pasted the ruler and then used it to gauge the width of the munition: 140mm. With this measurement plus images of the shell, me and my investigative companions online consulted reference material, identifying it as a Soviet 140mm M14 artillery rocket. As with the UMLACA rockets that had hit the eastern suburbs, only the warhead had been damaged, suggesting this had not been packed with high explosives. According to reference material, one potential warhead of the M14 was a chemical payload: 2.2 kilograms of the nerve agent sarin.[99]

While Obama pondered military retaliation, conspiracy theories spread online, several claiming that rebels had been behind the attacks. According to one theory, the Saudis had supplied rebels with chemical weapons, which had leaked by accident. The origin of this claim was an article on MintPress News,[100] a small website based in Minnesota that followed a pro-Assad line. But the article had problems: not only was it wild speculation without evidence, but one of its supposed authors denied having written it at all.[101, 102]

While I could not tell which chemicals had been used by looking at images, I could determine what munitions had been used, which would point strongly to the guilty party. For eighteen months I had been checking almost every new video from Syria. Never had I seen the opposition with either of the two munitions used in these attacks. Nor did they have the systems to launch them. If rebels possessed advanced rockets, they would not have bothered with slipshod homemade artillery.

As for government forces, they definitely had M14 artillery rockets, while the mysterious tubular UMLACAs had appeared in previous confirmed regime attacks. I had also spotted the rockets in alleged chemical attacks that had been poorly documented, including in the southern town of Adra two weeks earlier, where footage showed a dog convulsing in the street, its hindlegs and head twitching[103] as if affected by a nerve agent. The sight of this wounded dog is what most viewers fixated on, but I was not watching to stir my sense of outrage. I watched for hard evidence, and the munition is what interested me. When the Ghouta attacks took place, I saw UMLACAs again. I made the connection.

If UN experts determined that the munitions had contained chemical weapons, one had to conclude that the government was responsible.[104] In the end, Obama chose not to launch military strikes, accepting a Russian proposal under which Syria was to declare its stockpile of chemical weapons for destruction.[105] The UN inspectors' report came out soon after, confirming the use of sarin.[106] Two munitions had been deployed, they added: the

M14 artillery rocket and the 330mm rocket of unknown origin, the UMLACA.

Another key piece of evidence appeared, thanks to the Russian-language ANNA news agency, which had embedded journalists with Assad forces in the weeks before the chemical attacks, chronicling a major offensive in Damascus with GoPro cameras mounted on tanks. Using photos of an impacted UMLACA, I had already estimated the incoming trajectory of one rocket, tracing it back via Wikimapia to an area where a Syrian military installation was encircled by rebel-held land. This setting now came into play. By geolocating the ANNA videos, I was able to reconstruct the gradual Syrian military conquest of a strip of land that connected the isolated military base to government-controlled territory. I could map out precisely where government forces had been, and when.[107] In one ANNA video, the Syrian military explained its plan: to gain this strategic strip of territory, then launch attacks on surrounding rebel-held parts of Ghouta. That phase of the campaign was to begin on 21 August 2013 – the very day of the sarin attacks. The UN report included measurements indicating the point of origin of the chemical munitions. When I plotted this, it confirmed the hypothesised launch sites, exactly within the territory that regime forces had just retaken.[108] 'The report makes for chilling reading,' the UN secretary-general, Ban Ki-moon, said. 'The findings are beyond doubt and beyond the pale. This is a war crime.'[109]

Assad forces alone had such weapons. Assad forces held the launch sites. Assad forces stood to gain by the attacks. Assad forces were on record planning an aggressive campaign on the day the sarin attacks took place in the location where the attacks occurred. Nevertheless, his supporters maintained their denials. The Iranian news channel Press TV published an article headlined '5 lies invented to spin UN report on Syria' and blamed me – 'a UK-based armchair observer' – for the first supposed lie. I had established that the two types of munitions used in the Ghouta attacks were in the hands of government forces, the article noted, but I had bypassed the fact that the rebels had 'rockets similar in construction and operation, but smaller'.[110] This was a bizarre defence, as if casting suspicion on a person who never touched the murder weapon but *had* touched a weapon that was different. But disinformation need not be rational. It is enough for the propagandist to accuse, then watch doubt seep into the discussion. In another peculiar incident, I received a strange email, advising me to study three videos that would supposedly prove that rebels had carried out the Ghouta attacks. What I found were amateur theatrics of supposed guerrillas, ostentatiously showing off logos of an Islamist faction while declaring that they were shooting UMLACAs, all while wearing gas masks to prove how deadly their warheads must have been. However, the cameraman could be heard talking clearly throughout – with no gas mask. They also fired a D-30 howitzer, which was never linked to the attack.[111, 112]

Russian officials uttered a range of lies, too, trying to spread so much confusion that the public would give up attempting to figure out who was responsible. At first, they insisted that rebels had fired the rockets. Next, that rebels had faked it all, pointing out that videos of the aftermath bore a timestamp of 20 August, a day before the attacks. However, the YouTube videos in question were marked with the time where the servers were located, in California, which is ten hours behind Syria. Next, Russia began citing a nun called Mother Agnes who had previously allied herself with the Assad regime by blaming the opposition for the Houla massacre.[113]

When I heard that the legendary reporter Seymour Hersh had published a major article on the Ghouta attacks in the

London Review of Books[114] in December 2013, I read it eagerly. I had first come across the Pulitzer Prize-winning journalist's work as a teenager, when in awe of the investigative journalists who exposed American foreign-policy misdeeds. Over the years, Hersh produced a stream of scoops, specialising in US government deception. Here, he claimed to have another, and threw doubt on whether the Assad regime had carried out this war crime, positing that jihadi rebels had mastered the manufacture of sarin, and that the Obama administration 'cherry-picked intelligence to justify a strike against Assad'. The Hersh story posed many questions; the problem was, I had answered most of them long before. Ultimately, his piece was an embarrassing muddle.

Today, when journalists cover hard-to-access conflict zones, they are negligent if they overlook the mountains of online evidence. Traditional reporting is still irreplaceable, but it is incomplete. No longer can journalists simply rummage through the Rolodex and phone for the opinions of a retired CIA analyst. Nor do they need to transform into OSINT specialists. Hersh needed only to read my blog.

HOW FAR CAN WE TAKE THIS?

My work on the Ghouta attacks attracted more attention than anything I had published at the time. The *New Yorker* profiled me under the headline 'Rocket Man'.[115] The Google Ideas summit in New York invited me to lecture, seated onstage in the prop of a brown-leather club chair, making the point that I was 'the armchair detective'.[116] Christiane Amanpour of CNN interviewed me. Months before, I had been on the verge of quitting. Now, Brown Moses page views soared again, reaching 245,000 in September 2013, up from the 10,000 that had delighted me a year and a half earlier. I had to make the most of this momentum; this needed to become more than a blog.

That same year I found myself in the wooded hills of northern Italy for a retreat of the Tactical Technology Collective, a Berlin non-profit that brought together rights campaigners and hackers to a complex overlooking Lake Orta. They had designated me one of five teachers of the investigation group,[117] alongside an award-winning journalist who had reported on human trafficking;[118] a technologist who fought for government transparency;[119] a campaigner previously involved in UN meetings on fighting corruption;[120] and a Tunisian activist whose blog had leaked US diplomatic cables that helped spark the Arab Spring.[121]

When it was my turn to deliver a lecture, I did so with trepidation: my audience included those who risked their lives at the front lines of wars, whereas my work took place before a laptop at home. Still, they had invited me, so I proceeded, explaining step-by-step how I had geolocated battle zones in Libya, identified weapons around Syria and recently uncovered a clandestine international arms-smuggling operation. I looked at the audience. They were listening with rapt attention.

Afterward, many of them had versions of the same question: how do *we* put this to use? One group wanted to study arms used by riot police. When I directed them to promising open sources, they were soon in a headlong rush through untapped information. Three Syrian men approached me, too, among them Hadi Al Khatib, whose speciality was teaching rights workers and journalists how to secure digital data from those who would spy on or sabotage them. Hadi – later a key Bellingcat contributor – had worked with international NGOs in his homeland but left Syria in 2011, shortly before the uprising. From Germany, he followed the Syrian war on social media.

What he had not realised was that videos from his homeland contained more than a nightmare; they contained evidence.

The public was beginning to hear of online sleuthing around this time, but what they learned was not always great. Shortly before my trip to Italy, the Boston Bombings took place, when two terrorists detonated explosives near the marathon finishing line on 15 April 2013, killing three people and wounding hundreds. Users of Reddit sought to solve the case and botched it, mistakenly circulating false claims that various dark-skinned men with backpacks were guilty. This was termed 'digilantism', a reckless version of open-source investigation where scaremongering masqueraded as[122] detective work.

Others wondered if open-source investigation was what WikiLeaks did. Absolutely not. WikiLeaks was about leaking classified information, while open-source investigators analyse what sits in public. The secrecy of WikiLeaks placed vast power into its hands, which became problematic when Julian Assange exhibited strong political preferences, timing drops to harm those he despised, notably Hillary Clinton during the 2016 presidential campaign.[123] Another problem with WikiLeaks is that it is hard to verify huge data dumps of shadowy origin. Are the floods of diplomatic cables legitimate? Perhaps, but how can you tell? At best, I consider WikiLeaks a potential source among many that I would need to cross-reference.

By the Tactical Tech retreat in the summer of 2013, the open-source investigative community amounted to a loose grouping that had formed organically, most of us amateurs plus a few pioneering professionals such as Andy Carvin, who had harnessed social media during the Arab Spring; Josh Lyons of Human Rights Watch, a master of satellite-imagery analysis; Christoph Koettl of Amnesty International, who pored over aerial photos of North Korean prison camps; and former computer programmer Malachy Browne of Storyful, a company that was among the first to monitor social-media feeds for facts that had yet to make it into the news. Although few of us had met, a spirit of cooperation ruled, even friendship.

In those early days, we scarcely had terms for our work. When I stumbled across my first geolocation from Libyan footage, I did not even know what to call it. After the Tactical Tech retreat, I kept thinking about those experienced activists who had expressed such enthusiasm for our budding techniques. This was becoming a discipline with teachable skills, I realised. So many topics were fertile for open-source scrutiny, yet most remained untouched. If a small number of us were already producing results while working on the fringes, what would happen if hundreds, even thousands of people, joined the search for online evidence? I had stumbled across something here, and I kept getting much of the attention, profiled in magazines and newspaper articles and on television. But other digital detectives were doing spectacular work, and more would join. They deserved a platform.

When I first ventured into seeking facts online, my aims had been modest: gather nuggets of evidence and offer them to the real experts. As findings mounted, people started calling *me* an expert. Throughout, I kept expecting a major organisation to take over the field and professionalise it. It never happened. Was it up to me? This seemed beyond my capabilities. Yet, in retrospect, I see that I had advantages. Major institutions did not want to be the first to get this wrong; they needed an example before jumping in. Moreover, Brown Moses had already become something of a hub, linking me with established experts and amateur investigators who trusted my motives and approach.

I reached out to prospective contributors for a new hub, which would be about proof, gathered openly on the internet, and for anyone to inspect. A dozen people in my network – freelance journalists, a chemical-weapons expert, an arms-control specialist, independent researchers, analysts, tech-security pros – offered reports on Iraq, Turkey, Kurdistan, Nigeria, police corruption, jihadis, and more. I set up a Kickstarter crowdfunding appeal, pledging ambitious open-source investigations, a place to share cutting-edge techniques, with how-to guides – a collective that would invite everyone to join in the detective work while setting standards for our new field.

I never worried that a bad actor could infiltrate this project. If someone materialised with startling claims of new evidence, I would not blindly publish the work. First, I would evaluate the research on its merits, while checking the personal data trail that the individual had left online, to ensure that nothing was awry. The question of who can join touches on a key principle: we care only what you can find, what you can substantiate, what you can lay out for all to see.

The motto of this new platform would be 'Identify, Verify, Amplify':

- **Identify** issues both overlooked and discoverable online.
- **Verify** all evidence, and never indulge in speculation.
- **Amplify** what we learn, while amplifying the field as a whole.

In this burgeoning investigative community, I recognised a common personality type. We tended to be detail-oriented obsessives, many of whom had spent our formative years at computers, enthralled by the power of the internet. We were not missionaries out to fix the world, but we had enough of a moral compass to repudiate the other routes to an outsized impact online, such as trolling and hacking. Most of us grew up assuming we would remain peripheral to the issues of the day, that the powers that be could just ignore small people like us. Suddenly, this was not so. It was intoxicating.

We needed a name for this project. I sat at my kitchen table, laptop open, cursor blinking. I phoned Peter Jukes, a citizen journalist who had written successfully for stage and screen before reporting on the phone-hacking scandal, which is how I had connected with him. If anyone could invent a clever name, he could.

'You know that old fable, where the cat is terrorising the mice?' he said.

'Never heard of it.'

'Okay, so these mice are holding a meeting,' Peter went on. 'They need a way to protect themselves. This one mouse pipes up. "We're all faster than the cat, right? Problem being, we can't tell *when* he's coming. So here's what we do," the mouse says. "We hang a bell around the cat's neck, and he'll never catch us again." The other mice burst into applause. They have a plan; they'll be saved. Only one problem. Who'll put a bell on the cat?'

That was it: our name and our mission. Belling the cats.

2

Becoming Bellingcat

A team of detectives takes shape

On 17 July 2014, Malaysian Airlines Flight MH17 took off from Amsterdam with 298 people aboard, many of them families setting out for Kuala Lumpur on summer holidays. After nearly three hours, the Boeing 777-200ER had traversed the width of Germany and Poland. The flight map showed eastern Ukraine six miles straight down.

An arm's length from the cockpit window came an explosion.

At first, the news reports were fragmentary, with mentions on Twitter of a plane crash in south-eastern Ukraine. An armed conflict had broken out there a few months earlier, following the ousting of President Viktor Yanukovych, a close ally of the Kremlin. Once he was deposed, pro-Russian militants in this region, the Donbass, rebelled against rule from the capital, Kiev. A social-media post regarding the downing of a plane appeared on a well-connected fan page of Igor Strelkov, a Russian former colonel in the FSB (the agency which succeeded the KGB), also known as Igor Girkin. Donbass insurgents had declared two breakaway 'people's republics', Luhansk and Donetsk, and Strelkov led rebel forces in the latter. On VKontakte, the Russian equivalent of Facebook, the Strelkov fan page reported that insurgents had downed a Ukrainian Air Force transport plane near Torez. 'We have issued warnings not to fly in our airspace,' the post said. 'The bird fell on a waste heap. Residential areas were not hit. Civilians were not injured.' Previously, separatist militias had indeed shot down Ukrainian Air Force planes, including an Antonov An-30 surveillance aircraft, an Ilyushin Il-76 transport plane and Sukhoi Su-25 fighter jets.[1] But the only downed plane in Donbass on 17 July 2014 was a civilian passenger jet. Abruptly, the post[2] was removed.

Online, competing narratives circulated. Some claimed that Ukrainian military jets had suspiciously been escorting the Malaysian Airlines plane before it exploded, or that Ukraine had sought to shoot down Putin's plane but accidentally hit MH17. The separatists insisted that they lacked the weaponry to hit a plane at that altitude. Amid the information blizzard, someone posted footage on YouTube, claiming to show 'the murder weapon'. This brief clip filmed from a distance, apparently with a phone, showed a Buk missile launcher driven down a road in a wooded residential area, purportedly Snizhne, a town within insurgent-held territory.[3] The Buk missile system was designed during the Soviet era, entering service in 1980. After the fall of the Soviet Union, Buks remained in the arsenals of various former communist states, including both Russia and Ukraine. To an untrained eye, a Buk resembles a tank – army-green on rolling treads. But instead of a gun barrel and turret on top is a battery of four missiles, while internally the vehicle contains radar equipment to target military aircraft. The selling point was mobility: this surface-to-air missile could fire, then drive from the scene.

If someone verified that such an advanced weapon had been moving through territory held by pro-Russian insurgents on the day of the attack, it indicated that their forces *did* have something capable of hitting a passenger plane at cruising altitude. Instantly, I downloaded the thirty-five-second video of the supposed 'murder weapon' to my computer – I knew from Syria investigations how often crucial evidence popped up on social media, only to vanish. I was proved right: minutes later, the original Buk video was deleted. But the question remained whether this footage really showed Snizhne. To geolocate it, I sought landmarks in the clip. The road had two lanes and a median divider with trees. In satellite images of Snizhne, this configuration of road and greenery seemed unusual. But the town was large and full of twisting roads. I sought to involve other sleuths, sharing the clip with my Twitter followers: 'Gold star sticker to the first person who geolocates this video,' I wrote.

Seven minutes later, I received the first hypothesis. Several people were pointing to an area south of the centre of Snizhne. A two-lane road there shared the layout of trees in the middle and a slight turn, as in the video. To nail the location, we needed to figure out where the camera had been. With that, you can confirm that other sights at the same perspective all line up. The footage had been shot at a downward angle, suggesting higher ground. I loaded one of the most useful apps in our toolbox, Google Earth, which patches together satellite images and aerial photos into a model of the globe, allowing the user to zoom into any area, tilting whole cities up and down, left and right. You can also measure distances and compare satellite images from different times with a slider that shifts between then and now – vital when tracking conflicts, as I had found when studying neighbourhoods of Damascus a few months apart, seeing a once-bustling area wiped out. Another key feature of Google Earth is its 3D view, which allows you to tilt an aerial image to the perspective of someone on the ground, viewing the landscape head-on. From this, you can match hills or mountains or other background landmarks that appear within social-media images.

In this case of the Buk video, I sought to replicate on Google Earth the perspective in the clip, and this meant finding that same high vantage point. The only hills were in the distance, but I noticed something else: apartment buildings. Testing this as the camera's location, I picked out landmarks from the video: three specific trees; junctions in the road; the red roof of a house. I had a match. The Buk missile launcher had been heading south from here, leaving the town of Snizhne.

But I, along with my improvised team of online collaborators, had proved little. We did not yet know whether a Buk had shot down the passenger plane, let alone this particular Buk. Nor did we know for certain who had been in possession of the Buk, where it had come from, or who had supplied it. Still, we had a first piece of evidence, gathered in mere minutes from online sources available to anyone. It was a start.

A GATHERING OF STRANGERS

By chance, I had founded Bellingcat three days before the downing of MH17. My goal was a hub where citizen investigators could study cases of precisely this kind, where an atrocity had occurred and nobody took responsibility. In the coming months and years, this case proved to be the making of Bellingcat, drawing together a core team of investigators, raising the sophistication of our methods and establishing the global platform I had envisaged.

But first I needed to figure out the basics. I spent weeks developing a website, splitting it according to Bellingcat's dual missions: conducting investigations and teaching others how to carry out their own. I rented a tiny office space in Leicester and installed a microphone to produce a podcast, which was to consist of interviews with my network of contacts established during Brown Moses days. From this same pool, I solicited articles and how-to guides. Among my earliest volunteer collaborators were the chemical-weapons expert Dan Kaszeta, who wrote an early explanation about nerve agents; Peter Jukes on the notorious Daniel Morgan murder, which touched on corruption in the British police; a prolific tweeter, Chris Brace, who delved into redacted documents on the phone-hacking scandal. I posted a beginner's guide to geolocating videos along with case studies on video verification and the Ghouta attacks. We were working this out as we went along, from the writing style, to the best visual presentation, to simple technical issues like how to upload a podcast to iTunes. While balancing all that, I kept close watch on the news, awaiting major cases where we might employ our tools.

At first, making sense of the MH17 tragedy might have looked impossible for online investigators. The destruction of the plane occurred so high up that the explosion scattered debris over a vast area by the time it fell to earth. Hunks of fuselage and electrical cables littered farmland, along with passports, teddy bears and luggage. Channel Four News producer Federico Escher recalled arriving on the scene about a day and a half after the tragedy. He had covered disasters and conflicts around the world, but this situation unnerved him. Nobody seemed to be in control, just separatist militiamen wandering around, poorly trained, recklessly pointing AK-47s into a journalist's car. In a field, Escher came across part of a plane wing; nobody seemed to know it was there. At another location, he was able to walk up to the cockpit, still with human remains inside but not a single investigator to be seen.

The Russian Defence Ministry was now contending that a Buk missile system had shot down the plane – but that it came from Ukrainian-controlled territory.[4] A bizarre new statement came from Strelkov, the Russian operative, suggesting that the downing of MH17 had been a false-flag operation, that the airliner had taken off with dead bodies inside, and was shot down to frame the insurgents.[5]

A correspondent for RT, Sara Firth, resigned in protest at the broadcaster's falsehoods, saying, 'Every single day we're lying and finding sexier ways to do it.' An RT spokeswoman responded: 'Sara has declared that she chooses the truth; apparently we have different definitions of truth.'[6]

Far away in a North Carolina office building, twenty-five-year-old Aric Toler was monitoring online reports of the tragedy. At his desk job with Bank of America, Aric watched for major news that might affect company employees. For example, if a bomb exploded at an Istanbul railway station, it was Aric who checked whether bank staff were in the vicinity. No employees had been aboard MH17, which ended his duties but not his curiosity. Aric had been a student of the region ever since studying Russian at college. When he was off work the following day, the plane crash lingered in his mind and he spent 18 July 2014 searching for more details. Three hours before the plane went down, it turned out, a photographer and cameraman from the Associated Press happened to be in Snizhne. A rebel convoy drove past, consisting of two civilian cars and a Buk missile launcher. Plenty of military hardware had passed through the town before, including tanks. But a Buk was different. In that part of the world, where so many men had done military service, civilians knew what a powerful anti-aircraft missile system represented – a significant escalation that the separatists were not hiding. They moved the new weapon around in broad daylight, as if boasting of what they had. Before the AP journalists could raise their cameras, a soldier with a Russian accent cautioned them not to film[7] anything. The Buk missile launcher drove out of Snizhne,[8] where it was captured in the geolocated YouTube video.

Mine was among the Twitter accounts that Aric followed for work. What he noticed the day after the downing of MH17 were tweets pinging back and forth about a newly discovered photo of a Buk. Ukrainians had a habit of taking pictures and recording videos of separatists' military hardware and posting them on social media. In some cases, this was to alert Ukrainian intelligence monitors to what their enemy had and where it was heading. This new photo provided little to go on: a parking area in the foreground, perhaps a petrol station; the yellow sign of a shop, its name obscured by a tree; and a Buk launcher on a flatbed truck towards the rear. Again, the location was purportedly Snizhne.

Aric had never attempted a geolocation, but he was able to read the letters on the store's obscured yellow sign, which he typed into simple web searches, discovering that a hardware chain contained the same characters: Строй Дом. He searched for a branch of Строй Дом in Snizhne, but none came up, so he looked through Google results for outlets of the hardware store in the surrounding area. On a Russian-language wiki site, he found reference to a branch in the small city of Torez. The wiki site did not contain a full address, just a street name: 50 Years of the USSR. Aric searched Google for results that incorporated the store name, the city name and the street name: 'строй дом' and 'торез' and '50 лет ссср'. A court document appeared. A fight had broken out at the shop, and witness testimony included the address. He typed this into the maps app of the leading Russian search engine, Yandex. From this, he turned up a promising satellite map, showing what looked like a petrol station, plus trees, as in the photograph. Then he found something even better.

Among the most peculiar hobbies in Eastern Europe is the practice of mounting a camera on your car dashboard, and just driving around, filming the journey, then uploading the footage to YouTube with a soundtrack. Someone in Torez had done this for 50 Years of the USSR Street. Aric scanned through the video, and there it was: the store in high-resolution video, seen in passing through the windscreen, every distinctive landmark matching up. On the satellite map, Aric stuck a pin exactly where the camera must have been positioned in the forecourt of a garage south of the store, and pointed out his finding via Twitter. Such a discovery is normally swallowed up by other amateur sleuths, all rushing towards the next step in an investigation. But I wanted to highlight Aric's impressive finding – his first geolocation, achieved with no specialised knowledge besides language skills. This illustrated exactly what Bellingcat sought to popularise. I asked him to forward me the details of his efforts and wrote them up into an article.[9]

Today, Bellingcat staff and our core collaborators exchange our initial findings via an internal Slack messaging board, where we jointly decide how best to proceed before publishing our discoveries. This allows for long-term investigations rather than putting out each small fact as we uncover it. But early Bellingcat took a more organic path, led by the hive mind of amateur sleuths on Twitter, all converging around the next big question, whether geolocating a fresh photo or parsing the validity of a social-media video. That early investigative network on Twitter had various circles of involvement, starting with an outer ring of several thousand users who followed the MH17 case but rarely sought to answer questions themselves. The next circle inward contained a few hundred people who occasionally joined in

Twitter threads. Then came us, an innermost circle of a few dozen people, restlessly scanning for verifiable facts.

After geolocating the garage image, our next step was to estimate the time of the image, which we did using an app designed for photographers, SunCalc, which measures shadows in pictures. I had not been familiar with the app, so experimented in my garden, taking snapshots at different moments of the day, testing whether SunCalc correctly extrapolated the time. It worked. The photo Aric geolocated had been taken around 12:30 p.m. local time, which was before the AP journalists had seen a missile launcher in Snizhne.

Andrew Haggard, a blogger who took a close interest in military hardware and wrote as KoreanDefense.com, came across another tweeted photo of a Buk, also taken on 17 July 2014. The image showed a Buk moving on its own tank tracks, not on a flatbed truck, as in the Torez picture. In this new image, the missile launcher was partly hidden behind what looked like an apartment block. In the foreground was a dusty clearing, shaded by a lone tree. The tweet included a line of Cyrillic script: '#Снежное О русских зенитчиках и "Буке" в Снежном "это дом 50 лет октября, в нем пирка, недалеко уголек и фуршет".'[10] Andrew pasted this into Google Translate, which detected it as Russian and spat out a perplexing translation: '# About snowy Russian anti-aircraft gunners and "Bouquet" in the Snow "is the home of 50 years in October, it Piercy, near coal and buffet".' Luckily, Andrew had language skills of his own, as well as experience in fiddling with quirky Google translations. From the original tweet, he plucked out '50 лет октября' or '50 Years of October'. This sounded like a street name, another Soviet-era commemoration of the October Revolution of 1917. Andrew considered the hashtagged word at the start of the message, '#Снежное', which Google

Translate rendered as 'About snowy'. However, 'Снежное' was not 'snowy' – it was the Cyrillic spelling of Snizhne.

Another part of the Google translation that drew Andrew's attention was 'near coal and buffet', which he surmised to be a garbled location. From the original text, he plucked out the word for 'coal' and did a Google search for this alongside the Cyrillic spelling of Snizhne. On Wikimapia, he found a 'уголек' ('Coal') in Snizhne; it was a restaurant. This was not 'coal and buffet', as Google Translate said, but the Coal buffet restaurant, which happened to be at the end of 50 Years of October Street. On a satellite map, next to the restaurant and before a tall apartment block, was that barren plot of land,[11] shaded by a lone tree, just as in the tweeted photo. Shadows allowed us to estimate the time of the photo at 2 p.m. to 2:30 p.m.

Now we had four Buk locations: on a flatbed truck before a hardware store in Torez around midday (the photo geolocated by Aric); personally witnessed in Snizhne (the Associated Press journalists); near a restaurant in Snizhne around 2 p.m. (the photo geolocated by Andrew); and rolling out of Snizhne on its own caterpillar tracks (that first YouTube video). At 4:19 p.m., the airliner had its last communication with air-traffic controllers.

The Ukrainian government provided a further clue, releasing a shaky clip of deep-green trees with a patch of empty grey tarmac in the centre and a car dealership billboard in the background – then a flatbed truck carrying a Buk launcher driving briefly across the frame. Supposedly, this had been filmed after the downing of MH17, with the Buk heading in the direction of the Russian border.[12] The flatbed truck was the same as before, with an identical blue stripe on its white cabin and the same loading ramps. Yet the Buk launcher itself had a notable difference: one missile was gone.[13]

DECEIT VS EVIDENCE

Russian generals sat at a table with giant screens behind them showing illustrated mockups of the flight path of MH17. Four days had passed since the tragedy, and more evidence kept appearing on social media, all pointing towards Russian-backed insurgents. Moscow set up this event, broadcast live on RT with consecutive translation into English. The generals were ready to lay out their evidence.[14] The online investigative community, dispersed around the world, watched as they presented four claims:

1) that the Ukrainians had deliberately changed the flight path of MH17 to pass right above the war zone, thereby setting up the plane for attack;
2) that Russian radar data showed a Ukrainian aircraft near MH17, suggesting that Kiev's military had shot down the airliner;
3) that a Buk missile system belonging to Ukraine left a military base shortly before MH17 went down, and that two Buks were in a field near Zaroshchenske, a Ukrainian-government-held area, where a missile was fired;
4) that a video the Ukrainian government had released – the one showing a Buk on that flatbed truck driving past a car-dealership billboard – had not been filmed in separatist territory on the way back to Russia but in Ukrainian-held Krasnoarmeysk.[15]

What stood out to those of us in the investigative community on Twitter was that the four claims did not connect. The Russians were not piecing together a case, but scattering doubts. How could Ukraine have simultaneously set up the plane for mistaken attack, while the Ukrainian Air Force had blown up the plane and a Ukrainian surface-to-air Buk missile had downed the plane? The Russian generals also highlighted a feature in the video of the Buk with the car-dealership billboard in the background, zooming in on the bottom-right corner to show an address: 34 Dnepropetrovsk Street, Krasnoarmeysk. A *Ukrainian* area, not held by the pro-Russian insurgents. That proved it: the Buk hadn't been in the hands of separatists at all!

But a pro-Ukrainian account on Twitter rebutted this, saying that the video actually showed one of the insurgents' main outposts, the city of Luhansk. The Twitter user presented a street-view photo from Yandex maps, supposedly showing the location in that city. Andrew Haggard, the blogger who studied military hardware, found a website that broadcast traffic cameras from the area. The live cameras had been turned off, but preview images were still visible. One showed that same billboard. The Buk video matched up: a lamppost with white paint at its base and the layout of cables above the road. At the beginning of the shaky video, you saw a window frame or perhaps a curtain – the filmmaker had been inside, then zoomed the camera onto the road. With Wikimapia, we discovered an apartment building in Luhansk that matched the exact vantage point.[16]

A local in the city provided corroboration, going to the location and taking photos, then posting them on the popular Russian blogging site LiveJournal.[17] Everything lined up. Most damning were the local's close-ups of the car-dealership billboard. The Russian generals had said the corner of the sign contained an address in Ukrainian-held territory. On the actual billboard there was no address whatsoever. They had simply falsified it.[18]

In the past, citizens heard governments lying and had little recourse, knowing there was no way of doing anything about it.

Events on the news happened so far outside our control. That is not the case anymore, and nothing stirs the online investigative community like fabrications from the powerful. Moreover, contradictory narratives about an event are useful, providing something concrete to either verify or debunk.

As for the Kremlin, it had a long history with disinformation. Even the Russian word '*dezinformatsiya*' was meant to deceive, coined by Stalin to sound like a French term, implying that capitalist countries had created this underhanded tactic. Soviet governments deemed 'active measures' – including assassination, forgery and propaganda – an arm of foreign policy.[19, 20] Active measures diminished with the fall of communism, but those who had been raised in the system were not giving up so fast. Putin entered the KGB in 1975 and served at least sixteen years. In 1991, having reached the rank of lieutenant colonel, he became deputy mayor of St Petersburg, then director of the FSB. By 1999, he was the acting president[21] of Russia, and active measures became a central feature of government policy again. In the age of the internet, information meddling had never been easier. The West – still basking in post-Cold War primacy, preoccupied by terrorism and diverted by thrilling new technology – was unprepared.

The Kremlin employs what disinformation expert Ben Nimmo has dubbed the 4D Approach: Dismiss, Distort, Distract, Dismay. First, Russian officials aggressively dismiss uncomfortable facts, perhaps insulting the sources themselves, deeming them 'Russophobes' or shills for a rival nation. Next is distort, either exaggerating the truth into something unrecognisable, such as citing a minor rally and characterising a country as racked by protests, or simply inventing claims, as in an article by the Russian state news agency ITAR-TASS on the day of the MH17 downing, which cited eyewitnesses as saying that separatists had downed a Ukrainian An-26 – something we now know never happened. The third tactic, distract, involves conspiratorial theories and 'whataboutism', turning accusations back on the accuser, as in: 'You say that the separatists downed an aircraft in Ukraine, but what about the *thousands* of civilians killed during the Iraq War?' The outcome of whataboutism is a worldview of such moral bewilderment that nobody is believable, and anything could be true.[22] The fourth tactic is dismay, threatening grave consequences to those who persist in disputing the Kremlin's preferred narrative.

Western governments concerned about the downing of MH17 struggled to counter the Moscow information operation. A day after Russian generals broadcast their press spectacle, US officials merely tweeted a satellite image with the supposed launch site of the missile. This poor-quality graphic cited no source and earned ridicule online. As a news headline from the time said of Bellingcat's efforts, 'Group of Bloggers Unearthing MH17 Intel Quicker Than U.S. Spies'.[23] The American contribution reminded me of what had followed the Ghouta chemical attacks in Syria a year earlier, when the White House published a limp four-page intelligence dossier including an inaccurate map, while ignoring open-source information that made a far stronger case. Again, the United States – notwithstanding its varied intelligence agencies – contributed little to the public discussion. If anything, they had detracted from it, conveying the impression that no evidence existed.

General Michael Hayden, former director of both the CIA and the NSA, recalled a turning point for American intel back in the mid-1990s, when espionage officials faced a question: try to dominate cyberspace, or to dominate the information sphere generally, including diplomacy, public affairs, disinformation, and more? 'We had a sharp debate, and we finally decided that we're probably in the cyber-dominance business,' he recalled. 'Now the important punchline here is that the Russians went to door number two. The Russians went to not just cyber-dominance, but information-dominance.'[24]

Less than an hour after MH17 went down, the Internet Research Agency – a notorious 'troll factory' based in St Petersburg, where desk workers are paid to spew out vast amounts of disinformation online – went to work. During those first three days, its Twitter accounts posted 111,486 times, a pace that it has never matched before or since.[25] Most tweets were in Russian, starting with the claim that the downed plane had been a Ukrainian military aircraft, and was therefore a legitimate target. Soon, this shifted to saying that the culprits had been Ukrainian and had shot down a passenger plane to stir hatred against Russian-backed separatists. Additionally, the paid trolls posted disinformation on LiveJournal blogs, then shared this via Twitter, a classic recycling technique where one lie claims corroboration from another source that was itself planted.

Catherine A. Fitzpatrick, an analyst for The Interpreter, an online publication that studies Kremlin misdeeds, recalled watching one particular Russian lie about MH17 spreading through the internet. First came a gush of identical posts on Russian social media, in tweets and on Facebook, all insisting that the video of the Buk with a missile gone had been filmed in a Ukrainian-controlled town. Next, identical fake posts turned up on Western social media, then Russian state TV and separatist websites. Last stop in the disinformation chain was the Russian Defence Ministry briefing of 21 July 2014. 'This was a deliberate attempt to simulate "crowd-sourcing" of geolocation efforts,'[26] she said.

Unfortunately for the Kremlin, our efforts were not over. A fresh clip appeared on YouTube, seemingly filmed from within another building, this time overlooking a communal patch of dry grass and a roadway. A flatbed truck passed, transporting the Buk. The person who had posted this seemed aware of the need to verify online claims, so included geographical coordinates – 48°01′01.1″N, 38°18′06.6″E – and the time of day of the footage. To us, this counted only as a lead; anyone could say anything. First, we checked the claimed coordinates on Google Earth. Satellite imagery showed buildings, paths, a two-lane road. We moved backwards to the camera's vantage point and found an apartment building. Comparing the paused footage with the satellite pictures, we matched more and more precise details until everything lined up: dusty pathways in the communal lawn; features of the building across the way; a large blue box on the grassy area. This was the town of Zuhres, as claimed. Next, the purported time of day. Trees in the video cast shadows, so became our sundial with the help of the SunCalc app. As the YouTuber asserted, it had been filmed around 11:40 a.m., our earliest sighting of the Buk yet.

A second fresh clue emerged from the French magazine *Paris Match*, which published online an image of a flatbed truck transporting a Buk missile launcher, supposedly on the outskirts of Snizhne on the day of the attack. The image had been taken from inside a passing vehicle. We had never seen such a close and clear shot of the truck. What immediately leapt out was a yellow sign behind the cab, including a phone number in the rebel-held city of Donetsk. *Paris Match* journalists called it, and reached a construction company, where someone said the truck had been commandeered by separatists and that its current whereabouts were unknown.

However, *Paris Match* made a mistake. Supposedly, the image showed Snizhne, but the publication never verified this. What we knew from the other open-source images was that the Buk had later passed through Zuhres, Torez and Snizhne. To find where exactly this image had been taken, you could have driven the entire Donetsk-to-Snizhne route, scouring the roadside till you matched the background of the photo. However, making one's way to a war zone was not a practical solution. Instead, a sleuth 'drove' the route online, using a route planner to map the trip, and clicking down the road on Google Street View.[27] This person's work first appeared on the Ukraine@War blog, a fiercely pro-Kiev site that referred in the same article to 'Terrorussians' – hardly an impartial source. Moreover, the researcher was identified just as 'Chris Postal', without further details or credentials mentioned. That murkiness would frighten away a traditional journalist, but the Bellingcat method is independent verification. We did not need to know about Chris Postal, only whether we could replicate the research. To us, an online claim is nothing more than a hypothesis, one validated only with backing evidence that others should be able to corroborate themselves. It's akin to the scientific method applied to journalism.

We checked whether this supposed match lined up with the roadside in Google Street View. I even sketched limbs of the trees in that *Paris Match* image and in the Google image to check if the foliage and growth structure looked the same. Yes, we had it. But the location was not Snizhne, it was Donetsk. To determine what time of day, we sought further clues from the trees, using them as clocks by measuring the shadow length on SunCalc: early morning, around nine o'clock.[28] This was starting to fit together.

According to the Ukrainian counter-terrorism chief, Vitaly Nayda, communications intercepts showed that the Buk missile launcher had come from Russia, crossing the border on a transporter in the middle of the night before the downing of

MH17. By 9 a.m., the launcher had reached Donetsk, 125 miles from the border. At some point, the missile launcher was driven off the Russian transporter and loaded onto the flatbed truck that rebels had commandeered from the Donetsk construction company. The Ukraine@War blog also found tweets from Donetsk describing a missile launcher seen at an intersection around 9 a.m. We established a timeline for the day of the attack, all from open sources:

1) **Donetsk at 9 a.m.** The Buk is on the back of a flatbed truck, moving through the capital of the breakaway pro-Russian republic. (*Paris Match* photo)
2) **Zuhres at 11:40 a.m.** The Buk on the same flatbed truck, about twenty miles due east now. (YouTube video)
3) **Torez at 12:30 p.m.** The Buk on the flatbed truck, further east, passing a hardware store. (Photo geolocated by Aric Toler)
4) **Snizhne at 1:30 p.m.** The Buk is off the truck now – preparing for a launch? (Photo geolocated by Andrew Haggard)
5) **Snizhne, after 1:30 p.m.** The Buk rumbles out of town on its own caterpillar tracks. (The very first YouTube video that appeared after the downing)
6) **MH17 shot down, approximately 4:20 p.m.**
7) **Luhansk, July 18, around 4 a.m.** The Buk is back on the flatbed truck, a short drive from the Russian border, with one missile gone. (The Ukrainian government's video with the car-dealership billboard)

The critical gap was between points 5 and 7. The Buk rolled south out of the town of Snizhne. Where had it gone? What had it done?

Storyful – the innovative Dublin-based startup that combed social media to gather newsworthy content – found a clue in Google Earth satellite imagery from three days after the attack. At a location beyond the road out of Snizhne, you saw twin tracks like those of a Buk. The Ukraine@War blog also flagged a photo circulating online of a landscape with a blue sky and, supposedly, a smoke trail from the missile itself.[29]

Those details remained unverified but tantalising. More remarkable was how much had already been confirmed. The downing of MH17 was spurring a greater flurry of citizen sleuthing than any event yet. In ten days since the atrocity, the community of digital detectives had tracked a suspected murder weapon to within hours of the crime.

But we still had to prove that such a weapon had downed the plane. Critical evidence came from a new Bellingcat contributor. Veli-Pekka Kivimäki, a thirty-five-year-old Finn who worked for Microsoft, was at home, unable to stop looking at images on social media of the MH17 wreckage: fragments of wings, engines, the fuselage. Years before, VP (as he is known to all) had served in the Finnish military, conscripted into an anti-aircraft regiment that had Buk missile systems. The Finns had navigated a tense middle ground between West and East during the Cold War, an independent democracy but obliged to buy military equipment from the neighbouring Soviet Union. Buk missile systems were among the last pieces of hardware Finland bought before the USSR collapsed.

The plane had been flying at cruising altitude, VP knew. That high, only a couple of weapons systems could have hit it: a nearby warplane firing at the airliner; or a missile deployed from the ground. A surface-to-air warhead – fired from the ground to hit airborne targets – is designed to detonate just outside the enemy aircraft, and is filled with industrially formed metal fragments that blast through the target to kill the pilot and/or disable the engine and/or shred the airframe. Each model of missile contains different shapes of metal fragments, meaning that the shrapnel holes are like a fingerprint. Yet this was not a straightforward matter: MH17 had been torn apart six miles up, then fell all that way to the ground, suffering further damage on impact.

On a chat forum, the Professional Pilots Rumour Network, someone posted a schematic diagram of the front of a Boeing 777-200ER, which helped VP and others piece together images of the debris. The densest damage was to the left side, near the cockpit. This suggested an explosive charge, that a warhead had blasted in that location, with lesser fragmentation spray extending down the plane. A missile fired from a plane would have had a modest payload, creating a smaller shrapnel radius. There was nothing small about this damage.[30]

VP gathered all crash-site photos available on social media and posted them in an online album. He knew of Bellingcat from our geolocations of the Buk and messaged me a link to his own work. This was how we communicated with fellow amateur sleuths at first, via direct messaging on Twitter or emails; rarely did I speak with anyone. They approached me with a finding, and I tried to confirm it from open sources, ensuring that the work (and they themselves) checked out as legitimate. If their efforts deserved an article, I asked if they wanted to write it – in most cases, the investigator becomes the author at Bellingcat. I offered no training in news writing, not least because I'd had none myself. Rather, we figured this out as we went, seeking to achieve the sober authority of the best journalism while adjusting the tone to the informal mood of online writing. We took note of the success or failure of various forms of headlines, and soon learned how important images were to draw readers in. As our investigations grew more detailed, we had to account for this complexity, presenting each pertinent scrap of evidence while also keeping the articles accessible for those just happening across our work. The abiding principle has been simple: write articles we would want to read.

Involving the public was always central to the Bellingcat ethos, so when VP approached me with his online album I asked if he would lead a live blog, guiding others to collaboratively verify the images. I had discovered a new app, Checkdesk, that allowed anyone to add input while also tracking the discussions, so that research remained both transparent and available for later reference. VP accepted the invitation, bringing to Bellingcat a level of missile-system expertise I could not offer. Nor could I offer remuneration. The terms of participation in Bellingcat were long hours, no pay. Paradoxically, that had a beneficial effect. Volunteers embarking on an investigation did so from a dedication to getting the answers, obsessed by the possibility of discovering something nobody else had – in addition to the chance of nudging a tragic event ever so slightly in the direction of justice.

VP consulted other Finnish military experts, people who had operated the Buk system themselves, and they all agreed that the locus of worst damage indicated a missile, while the spray radius indicated a surface-to-air warhead. The shapes of the holes in the wreckage narrowed it down further: a Buk missile system. What remained a mystery was how insurgents battling in a poor corner of a poor country ended up with a surface-to-air missile, the kind that only national military forces kept. Ukraine had them. Russia, too. Also Belarus, North Korea, Finland. But the suspect Buk system – the one on that flatbed truck – where had that come from?

THE STUDENT WHO POINTED AT MOSCOW

A highly decorated elite operative in the Russian special forces, Ilya Gorelyh, arrived at the border with Ukraine days after the downing of MH17. According to the Kremlin narrative, Ukrainian nationalists were tormenting the Russian-speaking population of the Donbass region, compelling locals to take up arms in self-defence, and Moscow itself had not sent troops across the frontier. At least, that was the official line. This meant Gorelyh was entering Ukraine undercover. Yet at the border crossing, he took a photo and posted it on Instagram.

One of Gorelyh's social-media followers asked if the trip had been work or pleasure. 'Work, of course! It's to do with our profession,' he replied, adding gun emojis. Two days later, he posted another photo on his Instagram account: himself and a second man in a car, one holding a Makarov handgun, the other a special-forces knife. He added hashtags referring to 'the Little Green Men' – unmarked Russian soldiers who in February 2014 had covertly invaded Crimea – and Alpha Group, Russia's equivalent of the Navy SEALs. Later, he added, 'I went to bed early yesterday … Didn't sleep for two days, while we were riding around free Ukraine, and the training was very good we let them know about us.' Seemingly, the boasts about 'training' and 'we let them know about us' implied that he and his cohorts had engaged in combat with Ukrainian government forces. He posted a picture of himself in T-shirt, cargo shorts, flip-flops, brandishing an assault rifle, grinning. To eliminate any doubt, he had set his Instagram location to DNR, the Russian-language acronym for the breakaway Donetsk People's Republic. A follower encouraged him to tear the Ukrainians apart. 'We're already tearing them,' he replied.[31]

All this appeared on a public account; Gorelyh was just one of many social-media-happy Russian soldiers sharing their lives with their friends and other members of the public who happened across them. Among those who noticed was a twenty-five-year-old student, Iggy Ostanin. Born in Izhevsk, Russia, Iggy grew up in the 1990s, when his post-Soviet country faced hard times, with wholesale looting of state industries and the economy in freefall. Eventually, his father found academic work abroad, moving to Munich, then Strasbourg, then Glasgow, then Warwick in central England. Iggy found continuity through computers. When MH17 was shot down, he was living in the Netherlands with his girlfriend.

Dutch victims numbered 193. In the small and tight-knit nation, some called it Holland's 9/11. When people gathered on bridges, throwing flowers on the passing hearses, Iggy was moved. He wondered what people were saying about this on Russian social media, and spent hours clicking link after link – until he happened upon the Instagram profile of that *Spetsnaz* special-forces soldier, Gorelyh, bragging about crossing the border to fight in contradiction to what the Kremlin had told the world. Surely this was newsworthy. He found other titbits on social media and offered them to online news outlets, but struggled to interest anyone.

On the *Guardian* website he had come across my profile, which introduced him to the concept of open-source investigation. He sent me a note about what he had discovered. This was exactly what Bellingcat sought, so we published it. Iggy preferred anonymity, for he was about to expose a Russian special-forces operator and nobody could guess what fallout would follow. He had recently read a biography of Sergei Magnitsky, the Russian lawyer who had accused officials of massive fraud, only to be thrown in a Moscow prison, where he was kept in squalor, dying in 2009. Iggy chose to assume this pseudonym, and we published his contributions under the byline 'Magnitsky'.

Next, he turned to the *Paris Match* image of the Buk, taken from a passing car on a road in Donetsk, occupied south-eastern Ukraine. On the side of the missile launcher, Iggy distinguished faint markings but was unable to read them. When Russian forces deployed military equipment across the border into Ukraine they often painted over ID markings, but those soldiers assigned to do the cover-up did not always apply themselves. In this case, faint white markings remained. Iggy fiddled with the screen contrast. They were still unclear.

His hypothesis about MH17 was this: the Russian military had recklessly provided an advanced piece of military gear to the insurgents, and incompetent separatists fired the missile at an approaching passenger jet, believing they were targeting a Ukrainian Air Force plane. If the Russians had supplied the Buk, they would have transported it overland from a military base. This was a region where people loved dashcams, so someone might have filmed the Buk on its way through Russia. If Iggy could only find such footage, he would prove it was the Russian military that had supplied the murder weapon.

What he did next marked a pivot in digital detective work. Previously, Bellingcat analysed clips and photos that were generating buzz online. And in the case of my Brown Moses list of Syria video channels, I had established a methodical monitoring system. But those approaches were relatively passive. Iggy, without recognising his own innovation, dived into the haystack, searching for needles nobody else knew about. The challenge was figuring out what to look for. Simply typing 'Buk' would not work. Not everyone knew the specific name of a piece of military hardware if it rumbled past, even if they had experience enough to recognise that it was rare. Iggy logged onto

Instagram, which had served him well in the special-forces case, and searched for a more generic Russian-language acronym for 'anti-aircraft defence'.

He clicked plenty of duds, scrolling across thumbnail previews of videos, scanning hours of mind-numbing footage. He passed four days this way, hardly sleeping. Finally, something caught his attention. A photo on Instagram showed a Buk on the back of an army-green military truck on the evening of 23 June 2014, almost a month before the attack. This Buk, marked clearly with *232* on the side, looked fresher and newer than the missile launcher documented in Ukraine on the day of the downing. The Instagram post said it had been part of a large convoy of military vehicles, including several Buk missile launchers, that had passed through Stary Oskol, a Russian city ninety miles north of the Ukrainian border.

Iggy now had a focal point. He expanded his searches to VKontakte, where he found a clip from a day after the sighting in Stary Oskol. Someone had filmed an eleven-minute video outside a Magnit supermarket, showing a convoy of military vehicles driving through the town of Alexeyevka. Dozens of vehicles crossed the screen. But the convoy had encountered a problem. Some vehicles could not pass under an obstacle, so they turned around and headed back. As the convoy grumbled past the camera again, a number of Buks crossed the screen, most of them neat and tidy. But one Buk was scruffier than the rest; it stood out like the ugly duckling. The three-digit ID on the side lacked most of the middle number, appearing as *3 ' 2*.

Iggy pressed pause, and scrolled back a few frames, then ran it forward, and back again. Could he have hit the jackpot already? He scrambled for the *Paris Match* photo, studying the suspect Buk's markings again. That had been taken inside Ukraine, so the Russian three-digit ID would have been painted over. But he saw the ghostly remnants of *3 ' 2*.

From this new datapoint, the town of Alexeyevka, he used an online route planner to set the likely convoy route from Stary Oskol. Using the Pixifly app, he searched Instagram by location and time. Again, he scrolled through endless tedious footage. Eventually, he found a video of the convoy outside Stary Oskol. There it was, clearer than before: the ugly duckling Buk, with the marking *3 ' 2*.

Next, Iggy discovered a dashcam video, passing the convoy in the opposite lane as it headed into Alexeyevka. The resolution was crisp enough to copy down licence-plate numbers. Every vehicle whooshing past had the same number at the end of its plates: '50' – the region where it had been registered. On Wikipedia, Iggy found an entry listing Russian registration codes. The Moscow Military District was '50'. He went to a Russian military enthusiasts' forum. How many units within the Moscow Military District possessed Buk missile launchers? Only one, it turned out: the 53rd Brigade, based in the city of Kursk.

Iggy calmed himself, cleared his head. This is what he knew. A huge military column of the Russian 53rd Brigade had driven, possibly from its base in Kursk, to the south-east, reaching the city of Stary Oskol on the evening of 23 June. By the next day, the convoy had moved farther south-east, reaching Alexeyevka. The route took them ever closer to Ukrainian territory.

On VKontakte, Iggy found postings by a sergeant in the 53rd Brigade, showing a photo of a truck from the procession, even an image of the sergeant himself on the unit's parade ground, with a monumental display in the background of missiles pointing skywards. What he had found was huge, and nerve-racking. When published on Bellingcat, we would be levelling serious allegations against Russia, a major world power whose current leadership displayed both a propensity for information warfare and for violence. Our team was still in its first few months, and the Bellingcat project was on the line with every assertion we made. This was no longer just tweeting back and forth among investigative hobbyists; we were taking a major step into public view. Before publishing, I went over Iggy's work again and again, careful to ensure that everything checked out. Iggy concluded his article with a solemn declaration: 'The Russian government bears responsibility for the tragedy.'[32]

The report was a breakout moment for Bellingcat, with readership of the website soaring to more than 100,000 page views in the first twenty-four hours. For maximum impact, we had timed publication to the day before a report from the Dutch Safety Board, which had been assigned to determine the cause of the downing, although not to identify any culprits. This professional squad of experts confirmed findings that we had made weeks before, which was to become a theme of the MH17 case, our fledgling collective often far ahead of official inquiries whose resources dwarfed our own.

The BBC World Service and Sky News invited me on air to explain our work, while media from Russia and Ukraine began to pay close attention, too. RT cast aspersions on me personally, describing the rise of citizen reporters as a 'dangerous trend'. They were right: we *are* dangerous to those who falsify evidence. Our work also directly affected the reporting of traditional journalists, who sought to follow up what we had found. This had rarely happened in my coverage of Syria, where so few independent journalists remained on the ground after the death of Marie Colvin and the kidnappings of others. Now, we experienced a positive feedback loop between what we published and what reporters turned up. We might geolocate a photo, and journalists would rush to the site to consult locals on what we had discovered. In turn, we gained a better understanding of the events and timeline. Always, our ambition is to proceed as far as possible with open sources, but collaboration with other valid methods is fundamental, too. An investigation might be 95 per cent open source, augmented by 5 per cent traditional reporting. Other times, it could be 10 per cent open source, to substantiate a report that is 90 per cent old-fashioned methods.

Amid the strong response to our 53rd Brigade article, an email reached me from a stranger. Timmi Allen ran a business for users of the virtual world Second Life, creating 3D buildings, animals, even mountainscapes they could buy. Timmi emailed me because he had applied his graphical skills to images that Bellingcat had written about, creating a video clip in which the *Paris Match* photo morphed into the clearest image yet of the Buk in the convoy from Russia, to show how they compared. The fifty-two-year-old, who was to become a key staff member of Bellingcat, had been born in East Berlin during the Cold War, and formerly worked as an analyst for the communist regime's notorious secret service the Stasi. But by this time he was a single father, trying to raise a severely disabled daughter on his own. When Timmi watched news reports of MH17, he thought of all the children on board. He also became incensed at the Russian response – Moscow disinformation methods had not changed, he saw. So he worked up that morphing video, using advanced photo-editing software to flatten the *Paris Match* video, calculating image horizon, intersecting the vanishing point of the road and that of the Buk itself, correcting perspective distortion. When I watched the two images morphing into each other, the effect was striking. These were not two vehicles, but one and the same.

The expanding Bellingcat investigation of MH17 made me realise that we had the capacity for long-term projects. Most of my efforts on the Brown Moses blog had dealt with individual cases in the Syrian civil war. But I saw in us how a core group could push beyond an initial successful finding, drawing together the efforts of volunteers and journalists on the ground, to amass something far more comprehensive. We advanced from scattered evidence towards proof.

While I pondered this, I received a letter. Officers of the Leicestershire Police Force wished to inform me that international investigators looking into the downing of MH17 sought me as a witness. The Joint Investigation Team consisted of police and prosecutors from the Netherlands, Australia, Belgium, Malaysia and Ukraine. While the Dutch Safety Board aimed only to find out what had happened to the plane, the Joint Investigation Team had a deeper mandate: to discover who was responsible.

At Leicester's main police station an officer led me to a private room where two investigators from the Netherlands and one from Australia awaited. Also present were a few British officers, ensuring that all went according to protocol. 'Could you please start, Eliot, by explaining what you've found out,' the lead Dutch officer said. 'If you don't mind – very important – could you also say how?' The more I spoke and the more I saw and heard their reactions, the more I developed a dizzy sensation: *we* were the only ones doing this. The investigators realised that they had to take this open-source stuff seriously.

Bellingcat needed to take it more seriously, too. In the past I had shared Syrian open-source findings with Human Rights Watch or Amnesty International. At best, I hoped that the international criminal justice system might notice the contributions. Now, we had a direct line to senior police investigators – for the first time, we were contributing directly to a criminal investigation.

Once back home, I drafted an email while it was fresh in my mind – a proposal to Iggy, VP, Aric and Timmi, who had become my key partners through their devotion to Bellingcat's defining early investigation. I would set up an online workspace on the app Slack, where we could collaborate remotely on a private message board, uploading photos, videos, maps – working as if seated around a conference table, though I would be in England, Iggy in the Netherlands, VP in Finland, Aric in America, Timmi in Germany. Once again, I could not afford to pay anyone; all I offered were long hours. 'If this is something you'd be interested in being part of,' I wrote, 'let me know.'

They all responded immediately: yes.

'FINGERPRINTS' OF THE MURDER WEAPON

A member of the public tweeted an eagle-eyed observation, noting that two images – the *Paris Match* picture and Iggy's frame grab from Stary Oskol – had another element that matched. It was something so obscure that you would scarcely notice it: the side skirt, a horizontal mudflap above the tank tracks. When a Buk launcher came out of the factory, each side skirt would have looked identical. But, over time, the hard rubber of the skirt banged against obstacles, assuming a unique pattern of bumps, bends, tears. Most images of passing Buks captured a side view, showing military vehicles rolling past. Timmi realised that, if he froze the frame and zoomed in on a Buk's side skirt, he could trace its unique pattern. We collected all possible photos and videos of side skirts of different Buks and forwarded them to Timmi. Gradually, he compiled a database of side-skirt 'fingerprints', each unique to a specific launcher.

Against this, we could check all future images of any Buks, to see if they matched the suspected one, which stood out for a notable tear in its side skirt. Time and again, we checked the 'fingerprint' against images believed to show the suspect missile launcher. Time and again, it matched.

As we built up our evidence, the denialists were busy, too, with abundant disinformation from Kremlin sources. A state-funded TV channel, Russia-1, which enjoys a vast national audience, broadcast a special report on MH17. The presenter was Arkady Mamontov, whose previous work included suggesting that a meteorite explosion had been a holy warning against gay activism in Russia.[33] Now, he sought to bolster the claim that MH17 had been shot down by the Ukrainian Air Force. The show conducted a field test, getting a military plane to fire at parked aircraft, granting us a rare chance to see exactly what fresh cannon damage looked like on a fuselage, with entry holes of consistent shape and consistently large circumference. This, the broadcast stated, matched the damage to MH17. The reverse was true. As VP and others had shown with extensive photographic evidence of the wreckage, the entry holes in MH17 were not at all uniform, and many were far smaller than a cannon would have produced. The damage came in sizes and shapes consistent with a blast from a missile packed with metal fragments. Rather than prove their case, they had inadvertently debunked it[34] further.

In November, Russian state television took another crack at obfuscating the truth, even more absurdly this time, with what purported to be foreign satellite imagery of the last moments of Flight MH17, even showing a fighter jet firing at the plane. This image had first appeared on a Russian message board in mid-October 2014, supposedly from WikiLeaks. However, it was a crude fabrication, a composite of a Google

Earth satellite image from 2012 and another picture lifted from Yandex maps, with a passenger plane clumsily superimposed on top. Their image of the aeroplane even had the Malaysian Airlines logo in the wrong place.[35]

As their lies crumbled, our evidence accumulated. In early November 2014, we issued the first major Bellingcat report, a thirty-five-page dossier titled 'MH17: Source of the Separatists' Buk', summarising the mountain of evidence from open sources[36] and jointly written by the newly established Bellingcat Investigation Team: me, Aric, Iggy, VP, Timmi and now Andrew Haggard. Our inquiry had become so complex that we decided to present the report as a separate PDF document, rather than as just another article, allowing us to provide a summary of the investigation on the website while linking it to the much more complete PDF report..

This is what we had verified. In late June 2014, a Russian military convoy left the 53rd Anti-Aircraft Missile Brigade in Kursk, and travelled to the Ukrainian frontier, officially part of a 'training exercise' which lasted from 22 June until eight days after the downing of MH17. In this convoy, we had established the presence of a Buk marked on its left side with the identification number *3' 2*. The convoy moved southwards until 25 June, when it was recorded in Millerovo, twenty miles east of Ukrainian territory. After this, the Buk marked *3' 2* disappeared from public view for about three weeks. Stashed at a Russian base? We could not say. But the Russian military, we posited, had eventually provided the Buk to separatist forces in south-eastern Ukraine, who moved it with the flatbed truck on the day of the attack, 17 July 2014, taking it from the key insurgent outpost, Donetsk, to Snizhne – the trip we had mapped with video clips and photos from social media. In Snizhne, the Buk missile launcher was unloaded from the flatbed truck and driven under its own power out of the town, approximately three hours before the downing of MH17. Lastly, the suspect Buk had been filmed without one missile, on the same flatbed truck again, now proceeding through separatist-controlled Luhansk, back in the direction of Russia.

I publicised our report via Twitter, which I found was the best wedge into the news media. Publications around the world covered our release. Journalists were watching closely by now, aware that Bellingcat was ahead of the curve. Also, anyone could double-check every point of contention, all backed up with information one could view and judge oneself. With evidence such as this, you'd be kidding yourself if you now denied the culpability of the Donbass rebels and the Russian military.

However, one important piece of the puzzle was still missing: the launch site. Hours after the downing of MH17, a snapshot had appeared on Twitter. It looked unpromising, showing a bare landscape, a few houses and trees in the foreground, dry farmland beyond. Much of the image showed blue sky, but for a faint vertical white puff that did not look quite like a cloud. According to the anonymous photographer who had tweeted the image, this was the missile trail. If that was true, we could geolocate downwards, finding where the weapon had been fired.

Our lead investigator on this angle was a new volunteer, Daniel Romein, a Dutch IT specialist. Like many of our early contributors, he had been stirred into action by MH17 – not just the tragedy itself but the pitiless dishonesty of Russian officials afterwards. When it came to the 'smoke-trail' photo, questions and doubts circulated online, with some noting, for example, that the timestamp on the tweet was hours before the plane went down. This was explained by the default setting of Twitter, the time zone of its San Francisco headquarters. Meanwhile, we had a possible lead on the geolocation. The Ukraine@War blog – the pro-Kiev source that had nonetheless presented valid research before – said the photo had been taken north of Torez, and had persuaded a local to take a photograph at the location where the original image had purportedly been snapped, including identifiable landmarks, such as a long pole standing among houses in the foreground. We found a photo on Panoramio of the area from 2009, whose landmarks we matched with Google satellite imagery from 2010. Ukraine@War had a local replicate the view from the Panoramio snapshot, which afforded us a further clear match. The smoke-trail photo depicted an area in eastern Torez, taken in the direction of Snizhne.

On Panoramio, where users posted geotagged snapshots, we cross-referenced the location where the smoke-trail photographer had stood. Other images appeared apparently taken from the very same balcony. The photographer had identifying links that led back to him, so we reached out. He provided us with the original smoke-trail images in a raw format, whose metadata confirmed that none of them had been edited or manipulated. A Dutch news outlet, RTL Nieuws, also interviewed him, and obtained the memory card itself, which included other shots taken at the same location right after the plane went down. With the help of research organisations and the Technical University in Delft, the news outlet confirmed the authenticity of the photos.

We still had only half of the story, and the less significant half. We knew where the photos had been taken and that they were authentic, but we had not determined what they showed. Sceptics online said this was not missile smoke but an aeroplane's vapour contrail. However, the billowy puffs in the original photo followed a course that wavered back and forth, whereas jet contrails are straighter, even when dispersed by the wind.

We studied YouTube footage of other Buks firing missiles, and noted that they left grey smoke at the lowest stage of a launch. We enlarged the original tweeted photo, and checked – yes, there was a small grey smoke trail to the left of the main white upward shaft. When you enhanced the contrast and details of the photo, you saw that these two trails were connected. Why would the grey smoke waft horizontally? In the first video we had ever studied in the MH17 case, where a Buk was seen driving on its own caterpillar tracks out of Snizhne, you could see smoke from artillery fire on the horizon because fighting was taking place between the Ukrainian Army and the pro-Russian insurgents. The smoke was billowing to one side, owing to wind blowing in from the east. We cross-referenced this on a Ukrainian weather website. The wind in Snizhne near the time of launch had indeed been blowing in the direction shown in the smoke-trail photo.[37]

Daniel studied satellite imagery of the presumed launch area and found tracks in wheat fields, along with what appeared to be scorched earth south of Snizhne. To fire the Buk missile, they had first to unload this weapon system from the flatbed truck. That explained why it had been filmed driving out of town on its own tracks, headed in the direction of the fighting, probably to provide anti-aircraft support. Shortly after the downing, Roland Oliphant of the *Daily Telegraph* visited the area outside Snizhne, and found a field whose corner had been burned, and he took photos. Geolocations showed that this field was just south of where tracks showed up in the 20 July 2014 satellite imagery. The smoke-trail photo pointed directly to that same field. A further clue came in an audio clip, apparently a recording of locals near Snizhne on the day of the attack talking in Russian on the chat app Zello, which is popular in separatist areas. Citizen spies who support the Ukrainian government seek information that reveals the activities of the insurgents, often uploading findings to social media – probably how this audio clip ended up on YouTube.

'Roger, guys, a plane has crashed,' someone says.

'Well, probably, the guys have shot it down with a slingshot. Good job,' another local remarks.

'Have they caught the pilot and shoved something up his arse?'

'Our guys are awesome.'

They clearly believed that the downed plane was a military aircraft, perhaps a Ukrainian An-26 transport. When further facts reached them, indicating that it may have been a passenger plane, some dismissed this possibility. When mentioning the missile launch, they cited locations in this same area, which again helped us triangulate the launch site.[38]

Final corroboration came from that otherwise poor US release on 22 July 2014: a black and white satellite map showing the purported path of the Buk missile. It was so low-resolution and unclear that it had seemed valueless, but the image did contain large geographical features that we could cross-reference on higher-quality Google Earth satellite maps, allowing us to match where American intelligence believed the launch had taken place. Again, very close to that same field.

None of the four clues – the smoke-trail photo, burn damage in a field, the audio recordings, the US satellite image – was sufficient alone. But when clusters of evidence point to the same answer, a hypothesis looks ever more likely.[39]

The Kremlin and its online sympathisers continued to dissemble, often citing claims made by the Russian Defence Ministry in its briefing four days after the crash. But the generals' assertions were falling apart. In May 2015 we published a forty-five-page report debunking the satellite images they had used, which supposedly showed two Ukrainian Buk missile launchers south of the village of Zaroschinskoe, in shooting range of the plane. We checked those images, purportedly from 14 July 2014 and 17 July 2014 – three days before the downing of MH17 and on the day itself. However, both images were actually from June 2014. To prove this, we simply went to Google Earth and studied aerial imagery from May, early July and late July 2014. In the 30 May image, we saw an area of trees and shrubs. By 2 July, this greenery had been hacked away, leaving reddish earth, which was still visible in a 21 July satellite image. The Russian pictures showed those trees and shrubs miraculously still in place. The images could not possibly have been taken in mid-July, but weeks earlier. We also found that the Russians had manipulated their pictures, removing one Ukrainian missile launcher from an image to make it appear as if it could have been active elsewhere on the launch date.[40]

Although the Google Earth images displayed 2 July and 21 July, the app lacked pictures from the day of the attack. Moscow propagandists could have alleged that a Ukrainian Buk launcher had slipped away during the unmonitored period. Fortunately, a commercial producer of satellite imagery, Digital Globe, had a picture from the day itself, at 11:08 a.m. local time. The image was not available in open sources, so we crowdfunded its purchase, collecting £1,435 in donations[41] then posting it online for all to see. The image showed all the relevant vehicles at the base,[42] thus debunking the Russian fakes. By this point, we had disproved every claim made at the generals' briefing. But a major question remained: who had authorised the use of the Buk?

Once before, Iggy had exposed a Russian special-forces officer naïve enough to reveal operational secrets on Instagram. That man had been *Spetsnaz*, trained to kill and conceal, yet still disclosing details on the public internet. If someone like him had been so heedless, we suspected that even more evidence could be out there from enlisted Russian soldiers who had helped move the Buk, men who didn't want to be there in the first place and were missing home, longing to be among friends and family – and posting updates via social media.

We knew that the Buk from south-eastern Ukraine on the day of the downing of MH17 originated from the 53rd Anti-Aircraft Missile Brigade, and we reasoned that Russian forces would not hand over an expensive missile launcher to separatists without guidance or a Russian crew. Senior officers in the 53rd Brigade must have known something. To identify them, we clicked through countless Russian postings to learn about the brigade's organisational structure, its place in the Russian military and the senior officers most likely to be culpable for downing MH17. The project – pursued in parallel with a range of Bellingcat cases on different topics – took Daniel Romein and Andrew Haggard about a year of solid work, backed by the rest of the core Bellingcat Investigation Team.

To start digging into the 53rd Brigade we went to VKontakte, or VK. On this Russian version of Facebook, you could set search parameters to find only those who a) lived in the brigade's base city, Kursk; and b) served in the Russian military. You could even search by unit and years of service, which instantly popped up several dozen soldiers. As we had hoped, young conscripts posted on social media, showing off for friends back home and keeping their families informed. For men barely out of their teens, a 'training exercise' near the Ukrainian border probably felt like a road trip. They posted photos in army fatigues, their arms slung around each other, posing by the roadside with guns, snapping a buddy dozing in the bus. We could see ranks on their uniforms, thereby identifying members of the battalion, and identified the vehicles in the convoy, too, with soldiers posing in front of missile launchers, vans and trucks, whose licence plates we matched with those from dashcam videos of the convoy travelling towards the Ukrainian border in late June 2014.

A second revealing source was their mothers and girlfriends. In the Russian military, bullying is a terrible problem and service can be a nightmare for young men. Worried family members turn to internet forums to share warnings and gossip. On a message board for mothers and wives of those assigned to the 53rd Brigade, we found messages complaining in June 2014 of difficulty contacting their men, who had gone on an exercise in Rostov Oblast, near the Russian–Ukrainian border, and were not allowed to use their mobile phones. In some cases, comments revealed enough to find additional profiles on VK. We also found details on Odnoklassniki, another popular social network designed to connect former classmates and friends. The father of one soldier posted photos of his son on 4 July 2014, with the caption '2014 – border'. One of the pictures showed his son before a giant road sign reading MILLEROVO – the last place that the Buk convoy in June had been seen, a short drive from Ukraine.

Rather than scraping up tiny details, our challenge was sifting through such a large volume of material. Imagine checking every post that every soldier had made on social media, then all the posts of their friends, then all the comments everyone had made on all those pages, then all the profiles of all the people who made the comments, and so on. As they progressed, the Investigation Team's techniques sharpened. Social-media searching is a subfield of online investigation. Among the best is Henk van Ess, a Dutch trainer who is constantly finding ways to dredge up valuable clues from Facebook, Twitter and beyond. Most of his tips are technical, but several employ lateral thinking. For instance, if seeking tweets from eyewitnesses to a disaster, one should not just search the relevant hashtags – in a crisis, people are too shocked to worry about tagging posts. Instead, you think up pertinent keywords that someone might type in haste. Another insight of Henk's is that users of Facebook who click 'love' on a post rather than simply 'like' tend to have open personalities: they probably have not locked down their privacy settings. That means you can find out much more about them, from where they are located, to what they do for a living, to who their friends are. Even if the prime target of an investigation is prudent, a friend or a lover or a relative may give them away.

During our social-media research into the 53rd Brigade we learned that a Buk normally required a four-man crew to operate it: a detachment commander, with the rank of lieutenant; a sergeant; and two soldiers, who served as operator and driver. The lieutenant gives the order to fire a missile and the operator hits the button. Above this crew in the chain of command were the 53rd Brigade commander (a colonel); the battalion commander (a lieutenant colonel) who gave instructions to the battery commander (a major or captain), who gave instructions to the lieutenant in the Buk itself. Bit by bit, scrutinising enlisted soldiers' profiles and reading clues left by their families, we pinned down the names of officers and found photos of many, too. These officers also had VK pages and contact lists, and so it went on.

In February 2016 we published a major report, tracing the chain of command upwards, with a detailed chart, including photos and names from top down. Above the 53rd Brigade itself, you had colonels, generals, Defence Ministry officials. Lastly, you had the one person required to condone the transportation of powerful Russian military equipment across the border to stir up separatist violence – and, in this case, inadvertently down a passenger plane. That person was President Vladimir Putin.[43]

Responsibility for this tragedy could be traced all the way to the top, and we had the evidence, presented for all to see: the Kremlin was to blame.

On 28 September 2016, the Joint Investigation Team – the prosecutors and police from various nations leading the MH17 criminal inquiry – conducted a briefing for the public and victims' families, summarising more than two years of its work. They offered fascinating new bits of evidence: another missile-trail photo; an additional snapshot of the suspected Buk in Torez; a full video that, it turned out, the *Paris Match* image had been taken from; intercepted phone calls between separatists planning on transporting the Buk; entry and exit routes in and out of Ukraine and Russia.

Most striking of all was the fact that Bellingcat – without major levers at our disposal, lacking legal powers or much of a budget – had already proved all the key points of the Joint Investigation Team's report, mere months after the downing of the plane.

SLEUTHING AROUND THE GLOBE

The MH17 case helped make Bellingcat, but our new form of investigation could be applied to almost any topic. Every new inquiry – as I had found when moving from the Libya conflict to phone-hacking to the Syrian civil war – connected to a fresh node of obsessives online, expanding the network of crowd-sourced expertise, while spreading word of what digital sleuthing could achieve.

During our first couple of years, Bellingcat conducted cases from Latin America and the United States, to the Arabian Peninsula and Turkey. A French freelancer, Aliaume Leroy, geolocated Mexican cartel hitmen via YouTube videos and produced a study of drug lord bling on social media.[44] We published on the illegal activities of a Detroit street gang, as tracked down via their habit of scrawling graffiti with a hashtag.[45] We delved into the civil war in Yemen,[46] and gave an award-winning glimpse into a Turkish military coup via the plotters' leaked WhatsApp feed. We also engaged the public through the crowd-verification app Checkdesk, where anyone could join an investigative project,[47] as when we geolocated YouTube airstrike videos of the Russian bombing campaign in Syria, which the Kremlin claimed to focus on ISIS terrorists but was actually targeting moderate rebels in a bid to prop up Assad.

To widen the impact of our work we published versions in foreign languages, with online volunteers translating into Arabic, Russian, Spanish, French and German. We also produced explanatory articles on the latest tradecraft. A self-described 'OSINT ninja', Melissa Hanham, took readers through the plethora of online maps.[48] She also explained the value of metadata – how, when a camera or smartphone snaps a picture, extra datapoints such as the time and perhaps location are saved in the file.

Satellite pictures played an increasing role in our work, notably through Chris Biggers, an expert in imagery intelligence, or IMINT, who had worked at the US National Geospatial-Intelligence Agency. He contributed articles with satellite views of Iran building frigates, India constructing its first indigenous aircraft carrier and what looked like a new midget submarine from China. Through satellite images, he showed the spread of drones from Iran to China to Turkey. Spying from the air had once been a technical feat available only to the richest nations, accomplished by flying over a target and taking photos, later augmented by billion-dollar satellites that could snap images from several hundred miles up. But in the 1990s, private companies entered the business, such as DigitalGlobe, which produces aerial imagery seen on Google Earth. Suddenly, any citizen could view what had previously been available only to wealthy militaries and intelligence agencies.

Reverse image search also became a staple of the Bellingcat method. You input an image into a search engine and find out where else that picture has appeared. When rioting broke out in Baltimore in April 2015 after a young African-American man, Freddie Gray, died in police custody, images turned up online, ostensibly shared by looters. One showed a trashed KFC restaurant, posted by someone with the handle @slangincrack. But a reverse image search showed that the image had been taken three years earlier[49] in Pakistan. Reverse image searches are also invaluable for checking the profile photos of suspicious social-media accounts, which often steal images from elsewhere on the internet to falsify a new identity.[50]

While expanding techniques and topics, Bellingcat kept bumping into the issue of criminal justice. Was it sufficient just to publish damning reports, which might sit there on the internet while the guilty enjoyed impunity? Was there more to do? When on 19 August 2014 ISIS posted footage of the execution of the freelance reporter James Foley, I geolocated the video to the hills south of Raqqa. Other hostages were still being held, so it mattered where this beheading had taken place, in case they might yet be rescued.[51] I published the article but had no way of knowing if anything became of it. After the November 2015 attack by ISIS supporters in Paris that killed 131 people, including the mass murder at the Bataclan concert hall, we found a profile of one of the attackers that Facebook had seemingly failed to identify and take down. We wanted to convey our findings to the French authorities.[52] Again, we were unsure how to proceed, so we called a French police tipline. The Facebook page promptly disappeared.

Traditional journalists maintain a certain distance from officials (even if this is regularly violated). We were not traditional journalists. We needed an ethic to suit the internet sleuth. For example, we had noticed that, when we published a report, the guilty often eliminated their online traces. That meant that, if we chose *not* to inform the authorities beforehand, we might jeopardise the chance of justice forever. Our first responsibility, we decided, was to the victims. If our actions might foreseeably harm them, we take steps before publication. We also try to protect those who appear in criminal evidence but do not bear responsibility. For instance, when reporting on the 53rd Brigade, we excluded the identification of the low-ranking Russian soldiers not linked directly to the downing of MH17. On occasion, we were also approached by MH17 witnesses, and could have published their information as Bellingcat scoops. Old-school journalists would have. Instead, we put them in touch with the Joint Investigation Team, so that police and prosecutors could gather the evidence first. Regarding Syria, we have documented numerous crimes but cannot contact the local authorities for obvious reasons. So we work with bodies such as the UN-established inquiry into war crimes in Syria, as well as rights groups and international lawyers mounting legal cases.

However, we wanted something besides the phone numbers of police officers and lawyers. We wanted decision-makers to heed the information available online. I can never forget the woeful debate in parliament over whether to intervene militarily in Syria, when British legislators knew almost nothing of the reams of evidence that any citizen could access. Powerbrokers needed to know of the Bellingcat method, and I saw a way to spread the word.

Maks Czuperski, a young staffer at the Atlantic Council, the influential Washington-based think tank, knew of my work on Syria and Russia, and asked me if Bellingcat would embark on a joint project with them. This, I realised, could provide the boost that we wanted, showing the powerful figures who circulated around the Atlantic Council that we were more than online amateurs. Our first collaboration was a major report in May 2015, 'Hiding in Plain Sight: Putin's War in Ukraine', about Russia's direct military involvement in eastern Ukraine.[53] The work made waves, and soon I was travelling the globe explaining these findings and what exactly Bellingcat did. I spoke at the Ukrainian parliament, in a journalism conference in Norway, the European Parliament in Brussels, to officials of the International Criminal Court in The Hague, in Silicon Valley. As someone from a humble background who had dropped out of college, I had never found myself in such circles. While they learned of Bellingcat, I learned how their world worked.

Two other major Atlantic Council reports followed: 'Distract Deceive Destroy: Putin at War in Syria' (2016), and 'Breaking Aleppo' (2017), about the Assad regime's devastation of the city. Another consequence of my period as a senior fellow at the Atlantic Council was our creation of the Digital Forensic Research Lab, today a leading incubator of open-source innovation, with its annual 'Digital Sherlocks' summit bringing together online sleuths from around the world.

Along the way, people kept asking me to explain our methods, so we conducted global workshops. I was still administering Bellingcat alone, cobbling together just enough funding to keep the operation solvent. At last I could offer a few of the most dedicated Bellingcat contributors payment for teaching workshops. When Google surprised me with a donation to support Bellingcat, I hired Aric as my first fellow staffer, alongside a dozen core volunteer investigators and a small group of occasional collaborators. The next addition to our staff was Hadi Al Khatib, the Syrian activist whom I had met at the Tactical Tech retreat in Italy. After the international community failed to retaliate against Assad's chemical attacks on civilians, Hadi had noticed that Syrians stopped expecting outside help, yet kept filming and posting on social media – it was about preserving this for the next generation, in the hope that some day Syrians might hold the guilty to account. Hadi set up an open-source project based in Berlin, Syrian Archive, which created a cutting-edge methodology for collecting social-media documents for investigators, journalists, activists, human-rights lawyers. He struggled for funding, so we hatched a plan to support the project, with a joint grant from Google's Digital News Initiative Fund.[54] In return, Bellingcat became a platform for Syrian Archive's discoveries.[55] Google funding also allowed us to employ Christiaan Triebert, a young Dutchman whom I taught when lecturing on open-source investigation at King's College London. He had already done a little freelance journalism in Syria, Iraq and Ukraine, but considered that his best chance to break original stories was through the internet. Besides conducting innovative investigations, Christiaan led Bellingcat workshops from Colombia to Lebanon to Poland to Kyrgyzstan to Kenya. We were spreading the Bellingcat method around the world.

I had taken my first stab at geolocation back in 2011, mapping the front lines of a distant war during downtime at an office job. A few years later, I found myself leading the global enterprise that is sure to define my life. When I started, 'online' was synonymous with 'less significant' and 'less valid'. Since then, the very distinction between 'online' and 'offline' has grown foggier. But the rule-smashing transformation that saw the rise of citizen investigators also elevated darker forces.

The Information Wars had arrived. Facts themselves were a target. So was Bellingcat.

3

Firewall of Facts

The fightback against digital dystopia

There's a chance this is a false alarm, but we believe that
government-backed attackers may be trying to trick you
to get your Google Account password. We can't reveal
what tipped us off because these attackers will adapt,
but this happens to less than 0.1% of all Gmail users. If
they succeed, they can spy on you, access your data, or
take other actions using your account. We recommend
change password.

Best,
The Mail Team

You may have noticed the uncomfortable phraseology 'We
recommend change password.' This note – addressed to members
of the Bellingcat Investigation Team in mid-2016, a few months
after our major report on the 53rd Brigade – contained other
suspicious elements. The link to 'change password' went to a
web address that included the words 'google' and 'password'
and 'security' – but had not originated from Google. This was a
spear-phishing attack, where scammers impersonate a legitimate

online request, asking you to change your log-on via a faked webpage, through which hackers can copy your passwords. After that, they can access your account and do anything from leaking private emails, to planting incriminating evidence, to publishing personal photos.

Aric, VP and I had been subjected to such attacks before, and took these messages for commonplace phishing, not a coordinated campaign by a foreign state. But in June 2016, months before the presidential election pitting Hillary Clinton against Donald Trump, news reports emerged that a Russian military intelligence cyber-espionage unit, nicknamed Fancy Bear by security experts, had sought to derail Clinton's election bid. Wikileaks took stolen emails from 'Guccifer 2.0' – purportedly a Romanian hacker but actually Russians[1] – and counselled this Kremlin front operation on how to have the greatest impact on American voters, according to a US indictment.[2] In July 2016, WikiLeaks released tens of thousands of emails before the Democratic National Convention, stirring dissent in the party and undermining Clinton. Cybersecurity companies such as ThreatConnect and CrowdStrike were building a picture of what was going on, explaining how this cyber-espionage unit used fake Google password alerts.[3] The poor syntax of a spoof email caught my attention – *we* had received messages like that, going back more than a year. I forwarded them to Threat Connect, which judged that our attacks had come from Fancy Bear, too.[4]

While trying to hack Bellingcat in private, the Kremlin smeared us in public. Our investigations exposed Moscow, and hostile coverage picked up on the Russian propaganda outlets such as RT and the Sputnik news agency. In October 2015, after we published crowd-sourced geolocations of Russian airstrike footage in Syria,[5] RT posted an article in which I was described as 'a complete fraudster' and an 'unemployed internet addict' who 'is part of a new generation of cyber armchair sleuths who use open-source social media to gather "intelligence" from on the ground'. The source of these insults was cited as 'Defense and security analyst Richard Galustian, who has worked in the Middle East and North African countries for some 40 years'.[6] A LinkedIn page under this name described an employment history of eight years as an unaffiliated consultant in the field of the Middle East and North Africa, along with seventy-eight years with the 'Guyfawkes Corporation', where his position was 'Establishment Anarchist'.[7] The same byline appeared on opinion pieces for conspiratorial online publications, referring, for example, to the Holocaust as 'a brilliant propaganda coup'.[8]

In April 2016, Russian Foreign Ministry spokeswoman Maria Zakharova accused Bellingcat of faking information in cahoots with Ukrainian authorities 'to create quasi-evidence to blame Russia' for the downing of MH17. 'At present, we have information,' she added, 'that leads us to believe that loyal and handy witnesses in this case are being selected and presumably trained.' We asked the Foreign Ministry and Defence Ministry to substantiate these charges. To our surprise, we received an answer. 'It is well known that Bellingcat "expert assessments" has been called into question even by the Western media due to them being unproven and lacking confirmed factual material,' the Foreign Ministry responded. 'You can check it by yourself by googling in the "world wide web", especially since you consider yourself an Internet search professional.'

This sarcastic letter included no substantiation, so we wrote back. The next response was more absurd still, including bogus claims that appear to have been plagiarised, almost verbatim, from the LiveJournal blog posts of a user named 'albert-lex'.[9] The letters were so unprofessional that we wondered if the

Foreign Ministry email account had been hacked. But metadata in documents they had sent us showed these had indeed been produced by people who, identified via Facebook, worked for the Russian Foreign Ministry.

What we were witnessing – both at Bellingcat and in society – went beyond Russian disinformation, though. The effort to distort facts in the digital age implicated swarms of passionate amateurs, opportunistic grifters and violent extremists, too. The resulting 'post-truth' chaos led commentators to despair of what the internet had become. But sane society was not about to surrender its main source of information to the deceitful. The question was whether to accept two parallel information streams, where one part of the public consumed fact-based reports and another was abandoned to dubious viral content; or to fight back. We chose the latter. The stakes were high, as became clear during the Covid-19 pandemic, when lies acquired the potential to kill thousands, perhaps millions, of people.

At Bellingcat, 'emergency prepping' for such information crises had been underway since our inception, as we endured malicious hacking, contended with constant slurs and confronted a thicket of falsehoods online. If our mightiest adversaries had addresses in Russia, our most persistent foes were scattered around the globe, an evidence-denying network that rose like a mirror image of Bellingcat.

THE COUNTERFACTUAL COMMUNITY

Little illustrates how disturbing the Information Wars had become than attempts to portray volunteer rescuers in the Syrian civil war – people who risked their lives to dig innocent victims from the rubble – as murderers, even traffickers in human organs. Accusations against the Syria Civil Defence, better known as the White Helmets, sounded absurd. But scrutiny showed that something sinister was afoot: a leaderless disinformation campaign, with claims leaping from conspiracy theorists to state propagandists to alternative-media outlets and back – an ecosystem I call the Counterfactual Community.

The White Helmets, operating in rebel-held areas where Syrian government services no longer existed, numbered a few thousand volunteers, about 250 of whom died on duty.[10] What made them targets for supporters of Damascus and Moscow were their helmet cams and a practice of uploading clips to social media when attacks harmed civilians: they were documenting war crimes. In April 2017, when Assad forces carried out the Khan Sheikhoun sarin attack, killing at least eighty-three people and wounding hundreds more, the Counterfactual Community spread the fiction that the White Helmets themselves were guilty. The conspiracy site InfoWars dubbed the White Helmets 'an Al-Qaeda affiliated group funded by George Soros and the British government'[11] in an article by Mimi Al-Laham, one of several names used by YouTube broadcaster Maram Susli, also known as Partisan Girl[12] and Syrian Girl. Espousing baseless theories about 9/11 and more,[13] she has appeared on the podcast of former KKK leader David Duke[14] as well as that of Ryan Dawson,[15] who denies many aspects of the Holocaust, calling the gas chambers 'extraordinary bullshit'.[16]

I had encountered characters like Susli for years, ever since I had begun posting in the comments section of the *Guardian* live blog. Even then, I found myself abused for the sin of citing evidence, dubbed a mouthpiece for 'the Deep State', a bought-off tool of NATO, or worse. The hatred for me worsened in August 2013, when I presented Brown Moses evidence about the Ghouta chemical attacks. A week after this war crime, Susli – who hails from Damascus and now lives in Australia[17] – posted a video stating: 'It looks like we're about to see another imperialist war, this time against my own country. The false-flag chemical weapons attack that I said would happen last year has occurred.' She described me as unqualified and biased,[18] adding on Twitter that I was 'a plant'[19] and 'the guy with no military training who makes up crap out of dubious photos and thinks he has proved anything'.[20]

Her comments – paranoiac rants that would have condemned a person to obscurity in another era – gained an audience online, reaching a mutually reinforcing community of fact-deniers. While Bellingcat gained traction by networking among like-minded researchers, a similar process was creating this adversary. Like our network, the Counterfactual Community includes news junkies who seek truth online. They, too, worry that journalistic institutions miss major stories. They, too, have watched politicians make ignorant claims, and hope that technological tools could hold leaders to account. But if our roots share something, our actions do not. While the Bellingcat motto is 'Identify, Verify, Amplify', that of the Counterfactual Community could be 'Believe, Insist, Ignore'. Their practice is to begin with a conclusion, skip verification and shout down contradictory facts. Whereas we search the internet for evidence, they search for confirmation. Although the Counterfactual Community lurks at the political fringes, this ecosystem cannot be discounted – at times, its deranged narratives drift into public discourse.

Studying this community, you find a strange ideological mix: anti-imperialists, the pro-Assad, the pro-Russian, the alt-right, the alt-left. The disparate strands keep drawing closer together, citing more of the same sources, contributing to more of the same alternative-media websites. Their belief system is marked by pathological suspicion of the West, especially the US government. Those who oppose the West and the United States are cast as innocent victims, irrespective of their behaviour. This leads to strange conclusions – for instance, that because Western organisations allege the Assad government uses chemical weapons, then independent proof *must* be part of a conspiracy. A rhetorical reflex of the Counterfactual Community is endless queries, never pausing to absorb the replies. If I direct them to our exhaustive research, they pivot to the next question. This shell game implies that evidence should be disregarded because political manipulation lurks everywhere – an answer-negating tactic pushed by the likes of RT, whose very slogan is 'Question More'.

Of course, scepticism ought to be part of any decent investigation. Too much credulity risks grave errors, as in the acceptance of the US government's WMD allegations before the Iraq War. The defining trait of the Counterfactual Community is not scepticism, though, but cynicism. While sceptics say, 'Prove it,' cynics say, 'Who stands to gain?' Invariably, they already have an answer in mind.

From an online sleuth's perspective, the Counterfactual Community badgering can be irksome – but it is useful, too. Naysaying requires us to justify every scrap of evidence, which sharpens our work. I encourage anyone starting in open-source investigation to analyse what conspiracists say, to check whether they have cited evidence and to see if one can fact-check their claims. An online detective sharpens skills this way and is better prepared to handle the onslaught that will come when you publish strong material. I myself still tweet back and forth with members of the Counterfactual Community, hoping to find someone who will surprise me rather than repeat the same tedious aspersions. As they come from the same ecosystem, I can usually predict their responses. What strikes me most is their lack of dissonance: they fail to prove the previous claim, or the one before, yet make the next with equal certainty.

The Douma chemical attacks of 7 April 2018 provided another chance for the Counterfactual Community to falsely blame the White Helmets. Seven years after the uprising in Syria spiralled into civil war, the Russian intervention had turned the conflict decisively in favour of Assad, and his forces sought to eliminate the final resistance with chemical attacks on rebel-held civilian areas. The West had no will to invade; that had been obvious for years. Yet major chemical attacks still provoked an international reaction, meaning that Assad and his supporters had to conceal them. This event, they claimed, was a false-flag operation conducted by the rescuers themselves in an attempt to frame the Assad regime.

Moscow went further, asserting that it was the British government that had ordered the White Helmets to fake the chemical attack. Russian state TV claimed a major scoop: photos of a White Helmets film set in eastern Ghouta, where they had supposedly falsified evidence. A rack of costumes was visible, as were makeup artists painting dust and bruises onto extras, plus men with the Syria Civil Defence logo on their armbands. An older man dressed as a White Helmet held artificial limbs spattered with fake blood. But, as Bellingcat showed, the photos had been lifted from the Facebook page of a Syrian movie called *Revolution Man*, about a journalist who illegally enters the country 'in search of fame and international prizes, and after failing to reach his goal, he resorts to helping the terrorists to fabricate an incident using chemical materials, with the aim of turning his photos into a global event'.[21] This was a pro-Assad propaganda film.

We identified twenty-two accusations regarding chemical warfare against the White Helmets in 2018, most originating from Russian sources. What was notable is how many were blind charges – they had scarcely even bothered to fabricate evidence, yet accused the White Helmets of conspiring with a farcical number of outside groups, including both US special forces and Islamists militants. Any logical observer saw how absurd it was to imagine this mess of competing groups all conspiring together.[22]

Professor Kate Starbird of the University of Washington, who studies how disinformation spreads on social media, conducted an insightful study on content about the White Helmets. In a previous study of conspiracy theories regarding mass shootings, she had noted how content on 'alternative media' sites did not align with the classic left/right divide. Instead, an anti-globalist bent made alt-right sites appear similar to alt-left ones.[23] The ideological blur was evident again here. Starbird produced a dataset of tweets from late May to early September 2017 that mentioned the White Helmets, then she and her lab sorted through the embedded links, analysing which websites hosted the content. From this, they produced a network graph, visualising how much each source was cited and when an article was repurposed. This recycling was relevant because of 'false triangulation', where readers saw the same assertion in different sources and inferred that it had been substantiated, although what they were seeing was the identical claim.

Two clusters appeared in Starbird's network graph. One depicted the sharing of mainstream media stories, articles by the Associated Press on the ISIS murder of several White Helmet volunteers. This cluster was dwarfed by the second, deriving from the alternative-media ecosystem – a tangle of connections whose largest nodes were 21stCenturyWire.com, MintPressNews.com, GlobalResearch.ca, SputnikNews.com and RT.com, among others. That is to say, a small number of seemingly obscure websites (along with Kremlin sites) played a meaningful role in the public conversation on the White Helmets.

The most-tweeted website, 21stCenturyWire, was founded by a former editor at InfoWars, while its key contributor on the White Helmets was Vanessa Beeley, who in midlife had transformed herself into a pro-Assad blogger.[24] In 2016, Beeley met Assad himself in Syria. Soon after, she was invited to Moscow, where she met Kremlin officials alongside Mother Agnes,[25] the nun notorious for saying that the Syrian opposition had faked the Ghouta chemical attacks of 2013. Beeley is a revealing case study, for she writes mainly for 21stCenturyWire, but also appears on RT and Sputnik, and her work has been republished at the website Global Research, whose title suggests 'think tank' but is actually a clearing house for conspiracy theories, from anti-vaxxers, to 9/11 truthers, to climate-change denial, while also dabbling in anti-Semitic tropes. By 2019, Beeley was making ever more outlandish assertions, claiming 'evidence of White Helmets' involvement in organ trafficking in Syria. The lucrative trade of human body parts, bones, blood and organs is one of the most protected and hidden harvests of war.' This appeared on RT,[26] but also on 21stCenturyWire,[27] on Global Research[28] and other fringe sites.

Recycling also packages content to appeal to different audiences – say, US military veterans, or the anti-Muslim, or the pro-Muslim, or anti-Semites, or the right, or the left. The alternative-media ecosystem includes sites linked to manipulative governments, but it would be a mistake to ascribe this all to paid trolls. Sadly, the Counterfactual Community includes many sincere people.[29]

Our detractors say that Bellingcat itself is the insincere party, that we plot with imperialist front operations and that I have become rich from doing so. This tempts me to show them my modest lifestyle, and to explain our laborious efforts to gather funding. Our strategy is to obtain the widest range of financial sources, so Bellingcat is never beholden to anyone. The main portion comes from foundations (all openly listed on our website), plus one-third more from open-source-investigation workshops that we conduct around the world, in addition to citizen contributions via the crowdfunding site Patreon. We make clear to any donor organisation that they will gain no influence over our editorial content or policies. Adding to our transparency, we submit to an audit every year with the results published on our website, as required by Bellingcat's status as a charitable foundation in the Netherlands, which we gained in 2020. We also have an independent supervisory board to oversee Bellingcat management – if we fail to live up to board members' scrutiny, they may take action against any of us.

Regarding our impartiality, detractors often point to Bellingcat's numerous investigations relating to the Putin government and the Assad regime. This is not because we have a political agenda, but because they have been among the most dishonest and violent administrations of recent years, and left a trail of open-source evidence on the internet. We are equally prepared to apply our investigative tools to Western culpability whenever possible, and have done so, exposing the fraudulent use of corporate rules in Britain; studying Saudi-led coalition airstrikes in Yemen that showed American, and probably British, arms were used in violation of international law; plus a notably complex investigation into the bombardment of a Syrian mosque in Al-Jīnah that killed dozens during evening prayers on 16 March 2017. We concluded that US forces were responsible.

What vexes members of the Counterfactual Community is that nobody respectable takes them seriously. They cannot grasp why the Bellingcat method is treated differently from theirs. After all, they use videos to make points. They cite social-media posts. But they are scorned. To rationalise this, the Counterfactual Community employs a circle of illogic: established organisations trust Bellingcat investigations, therefore we must be working with the establishment, therefore anyone who attends to our findings is an accomplice in this conspiracy, and so on.

Our detractors comb through our reports, desperate to find errors. They struggle for satisfaction. This is not because we are infallible but because our practices diverge from those of the traditional investigative reporter. An old-school journalist cultivates sources, who often insist on anonymity. This obliges the journalist to tell the public: *I trust this, and you need to trust me*. This bargain is fraught with the risk of confirmation bias, manipulation and plain misunderstanding. By contrast, the Bellingcat method is founded on transparency – the 'open' in open-source investigation. We state what we found and where, and do not claim to know the whole story, only the facts that we have discovered. If we come across evidence from a closed source, such as phone metadata that is leaked to us, we always seek to corroborate it through open sources. Everything ought to line up. If we have doubts, we declare them openly, or refrain from publishing.

The Counterfactual Community presumes, given how much Bellingcat has discovered, that intelligence agencies must be feeding us stories. This only reveals ignorance about what is possible with online investigation. Verification stands on its own, not on the reputation of Bellingcat, or America, or Russia, or China. If anyone wants to know where we get our material, they can read our reports, click the links and judge for themselves.

BUILDING THE FIREWALL

Consider the lies that followed the downing of MH17. And consider what happened five years later, when Ukraine International Airlines Flight PS752 was shot down outside Tehran, killing all 176 people on board. Bellingcat and other open-source investigators immediately picked through social media, finding evidence that missiles had brought down the flight of 8 January 2020 and geolocating the probable launch site. After a faltering attempt to deny the facts, Iranian authorities confessed that their forces had inadvertently shot down the civilian airliner. Perhaps they contemplated the fate of the Russian officials who appear to have lied about MH17, and had their reputations called into question as a result. When citizens can see evidence for themselves, lying becomes a fool's mission.

In the early days of Bellingcat I met with executives from Google and Facebook about fact-finding and the disinformation spreading on their platforms. Google wanted to help our work and created a tool to add metadata to clips on YouTube, which it owns. But later, YouTube's relationship with open-source investigation grew more complicated when the video platform came under public pressure to remove violent content, especially that which could radicalise viewers. In the summer of 2017, YouTube introduced an algorithm to flag videos that violated its standards, and hundreds of thousands of Syria videos vanished,[30] wiping out reams of potential evidence. Meantime, Facebook sought partner organisations like ours to provide credibility and quality to its content moderation, preferably for free. Bellingcat was not big enough for such an endeavour, but Facebook pursued its goal elsewhere, persuading a few US organisations, including the Associated Press, Snopes and ABC News, to help debunk false claims. Later, Facebook expanded to more partners in several dozen languages. Yet this fact-checking has never solved the problem. A partner organisation might complete, say, 200 fact-checks per year[31] in response to specific cases. Each demands considerable effort – perhaps days of research – to rightly judge evidence on each side of a heated debate. The respected fact-checking site Snopes ended up pulling out of the project. What Facebook was paying Snopes could not have helped much – just $100,000 in 2017.[32]

Social-media giants have a genuine dilemma. They do not want to promote dangerous material, nor do they want to curb free speech. But they operate with a conflict of interest, running a profit model of 'engagement' that nudges users to emotionally stirring content, which is not necessarily truthful. If social-media giants ever resolve to fight fake news and conspiracy theories in earnest, they will need to change recommendation algorithms and add vast numbers of moderators. Even this would probably not suffice. Imagine a moderator jumping into the middle of an online argument, which could be on any subject. Is hexamine a marker of sarin gas produced by the Assad regime? What about the treatment of members of Falun Gong imprisoned in China? Is France illegally supplying arms used in Saudi airstrikes in Yemen? What a moderator must evaluate could be part of a disinformation campaign or part of a genuine public debate. It could be a genuine debate *based* on disinformation.

The depth of this problem feeds into internet miserabilism, the dread that our tech future is an unfixable mess. At Bellingcat, we recognise that fact-based information will not always prevail. Yet our efforts are making a difference. Open-source investigation does more than inhibit government dishonesty; it weakens false narratives that enter the information system via the Counterfactual Community. A notable case occurred in 2019.

Alternative-media websites were abuzz with charges that the Organisation for the Prohibition of Chemical Weapons, or OPCW, was suppressing information that cleared the Syrian government in the Douma chemical attacks of the year before. Conspiracists trumpeted these allegations, but Bellingcat studied the supposed scandal, found it baseless and major news sources took heed. When they ignored the matter, it hardly penetrated the serious information pool. The firewall was working.

To see how this came about, you need to understand the importance of chemical weapons in the history of open-source sleuthing on the internet. These arms violate humanitarian law, stir moral repugnance and risk retaliation from the international community. Therefore, those who deploy them always hide it, which has made information a key component of any chemical-weapons attack, from Syria to the Skripals. After the Ghouta attacks of 21 August 2013, Assad forces restricted their use of sarin, shifting to munitions filled with chlorine, which kill fewer people but still terrorise a population. By 2019, independent researchers had enumerated 336 chemical-weapons attacks during the Syrian civil war – 98 per cent by the regime.[33]

Another notorious sarin attack took place on 4 April 2017, when Assad forces sought to obliterate remaining pockets of rebel control and targeted the town of Khan Sheikhoun on the main highway between Aleppo and Damascus. In response, the United States fired Tomahawk cruise missiles at Shayrat Airbase in Homs, the suspected origin of the regime strike. We pored through the open-source evidence, notably the work of a network of Syrian volunteers that used a smartphone app to record takeoffs, flight direction and other information about aircraft leaving military airfields, to provide timely warnings in rebel-held areas – a system known as the Syrian 'Sentry'.[34] At 6:26 a.m. local time, a Sukhoi 22 fighter-bomber took off from its airbase in Homs. This Su-22 was marked 'Quds 1', indicating that it was the plane of the squadron commander – notable because he had carried out previous reported chemical attacks.[35] The Syrian Army chief corroborated the squadron commander's role, visiting his airbase (in a YouTube video), thanking the officer (a photo on Twitter) and referring to him as 'the hero who struck the depot' (statements on Facebook). The OPCW analysed samples from victims, living and dead, and found 'exposure to sarin or a sarin-like substance' – results that it called 'incontrovertible'.[36]

Yet it was the next infamous chemical attack that drew the OPCW into a supposed scandal. One year after Khan Sheikhoun, the Assad regime was violently retaking eastern suburbs of the capital. Douma was the last stronghold. The Syrian Network for Human Rights reported at least two separate attacks on 7 April 2018 involving chemical agents, one at 4 p.m. near Sa'da bakery, which afflicted fifteen people, and a second attack at around 7:30 p.m. near al-Shuhada Square, which killed fifty-five and injured 860. Witnesses reported smelling chlorine. A week later, the United States, France and the United Kingdom launched attacks on three Syrian chemical-weapons facilities.

What puzzled many was how chlorine could have produced such severe symptoms, killing dozens and making hundreds ill. Typically, a chlorine bomb releases poisonous gas with a light-green cloud that disperses rapidly. But at the worst-hit site, a gas cylinder had burst into a closed building rather than on the street, so there was no wind to waft the poison away. In war-hardened Syria, civilians know what to look for, aware that chlorine is heavier than air, meaning that the gas sinks. To save yourself, you hurry to higher ground. This knowledge probably increased the death toll because residents correctly detected a chlorine attack and sought higher ground, running upstairs – unaware that the poison was coming from the top of the building itself, and that they were hurrying towards the source.[37] The OPCW carried out various visits to the attack sites, taking samples and interviewing witnesses, and issuing a lengthy final report in March 2019, which confirmed that a chlorine attack had taken place, delivered by gas cylinders dropped from the air. That the cylinders had been designed to fall from the sky was itself evidence of regime responsibility: the rebels have no air force.

But the opponents of fact-based information were not passively accepting this. Within days of the Douma attack, a GRU team was caught trying to hack into the wifi at OPCW headquarters in The Hague, and four spies were expelled from the country. We can only speculate about the extent of Russian penetration into OPCW files. What is certain is that, shortly after Moscow objected to the OPCW final report on Douma, this 'scandal' bubbled up online within the Counterfactual Community. Exhibit A was an internal memo written by an OPCW inspector, Ian Henderson, who objected to elements of the organisation's report. This document turned up[38] on the website of a fringe network of academics and researchers called the Working Group on Syria, Propaganda and Media, known for conspiracy theories about the White Helmets, the Skripal case and chemical-weapons use in Syria.[39] In the document, Henderson argued that it was more likely that two cylinders in question had been 'manually placed at those two locations rather than being delivered from aircraft'. If he was right and the cylinders had been 'manually placed', it suggested a false-flag operation.

This hypothesis seeped into the mainstream press via Peter Hitchens of the *Mail on Sunday*,[40] a columnist known for the ardour of his opinions, including misgivings about the theory of evolution.[41] Another well-known journalist, Robert Fisk of the *Independent*, followed up with an article headlined 'The evidence we were never meant to see about the Douma "gas" attack'.[42] In November 2019, WikiLeaks gradually began releasing more internal documents, including an email from a second employee known by the pseudonym 'Alex', who was a member of the Fact-Finding Mission, the innermost team of the OPCW inquiry. 'Alex' complained that superiors had misrepresented what he and his colleagues had discovered, saying that only trace amounts of chlorine markers had been found, and that these could have come from other sources.[43]

'The revelation appears to be the worst instance of "sexing-up" in support of war since the invasion of Iraq and Tony Blair's doctored dossiers,' Hitchens wrote, playing directly into a tendency in the Counterfactual Community to equate any evidence of weapons of mass destruction to the manipulated intelligence used to justify the US-led attack on Iraq in 2003. But the lesson of that event is not that *any* WMD accusation is a hoax. The lesson is that evidence is mandatory and must be laid out for all to see.

Bellingcat senior investigator Nick Waters, a young former British Army infantry officer who had served in Afghanistan and became involved in open-source research after attending lectures I gave at King's College London, led our inquiry, studying both the leaked documents and the official OPCW reports, while consulting with independent chemists, toxicologists and other experts. His central question was whether the Douma attack could plausibly have been a false-flag operation.

According to the Russian and Syrian governments, rebels had brought dead bodies to the residential building and planted them there. In open-source images, you could count at least thirty-four corpses, including children, many with frothy discharge on their faces. None showed other signs of violence, and they appeared to be recently deceased, their bodies displaying no markers of decomposition. The notion that a large group of civilians had been murdered in some other way at exactly the same time, then deposited on various floors of a residential building, without any known witnesses to this operation, stretched credulity. In a second conspiratorial scenario, the cylinders *had* contained chlorine gas but were manually placed there to frame the Assad government. The context of the Douma attack was a massive Syrian military bombardment of the area, a scene of such mayhem that rebels surrendered the suburb just a day later. Amid this heavy shelling, false-flag conspirators would have had to fill heavily damaged cylinders with poison gas, transport these extremely heavy objects up several flights of stairs in two separate locations, without anyone ever mentioning such an extraordinary scene to independent journalists or to OPCW inspectors.

A further problem with the 'manually placed' theory was that the cylinders showed damage consistent with a fall from several hundred metres. In his leaked critique, Henderson made the assumption that Syrian helicopters would not have dropped them from such a low height. But Syrian military helicopters did sometimes fly low on purpose, which made them harder to target, especially at night, which is when the Douma attack occurred. When you consider what it would involve to take gas cylinders from previous attacks and plant them, the idea falls apart. First, impact damage on the cylinders would need to be exactly consistent with a crash into those specific locations. Also, metal corrodes when exposed to chlorine gas, and the plotters would have had to reproduce this corrosion exactly. You had bomb craters, too, which would need to be perfectly consistent with the cylinders impacting from a height. There was incidental damage to the edge of a terrace wall, visible in footage taken by a Russian media crew. How could false-flag plotters have known to falsify that?

Henderson complained that the Fact-Finding Mission had excluded his opinions. This was hardly surprising. He belonged to the support staff, not the innermost team. In an internal email published by WikiLeaks, a senior OPCW official, Sébastien Braha, seemed nonplussed as to why someone in Henderson's secondary position was even writing such a report. In any case, the Fact-Finding Mission commissioned three independent engineering studies. All contradicted Henderson's views.

An objection of the second complainant, 'Alex', was that only trace amounts of chlorine markers had been found. According to one Counterfactual Community narrative, chlorine traces could have derived from household cleaning products. But Bellingcat contributor Tariq Bhatti, a chemist, pointed out that 'trace' amounts were exactly what you would expect after such an attack.[44] Chlorine gas does not leave a single marker, but a combination that points to its use. In Douma, these chlorinated organic compounds were detected on various floors of the building and on the adjacent street. The highest concentration was beneath where a cylinder had landed on a bed.

Either a stunningly complicated and intricate plan had been carried out to absolute perfection, all while under bombardment, unwitnessed by anybody who ever spoke about it afterwards – or Syrian military helicopters had carried out a much-documented attack that was consistent with scores of previous chlorine attacks by Syrian military helicopters.

Few serious news sources took the false-flag bait, granting this hollow 'scandal' the indifference it deserved. When a *Newsweek* journalist proposed an article on the OPCW scandal, his editors declined, pointing him to a Bellingcat piece debunking the matter. The reporter, who quit the magazine, then failed to bolster his credibility by telling his tale to that bastion of reliable newsgathering, RT.[45]

Later, the OPCW released an independent investigation into the leaks. The head of the organisation, Fernando Arias, commented in February 2020 that 'whistleblower' was the wrong term for the two complainants. The first had circulated an ill-informed personal document, while the second had travelled to Syria in April 2018 but 'never left the command post in Damascus because he had not completed the necessary training required to deploy on-site', and left the OPCW at the end of August 2018, missing the final *seven months* of the Fact-Finding Mission. 'They are individuals who could not accept that their views were not backed by evidence. When their views could not gain traction, they took matters into their own hands and breached their obligations to the organization,' Arias said. 'Their conclusions are erroneous, uninformed, and wrong.'[46]

If Bellingcat helps build a firewall against falsehoods, the Counterfactual Community inadvertently strengthens this firewall. When reputable journalists see that the people sharing a theory are those who spent the past years disputing the exhaustive evidence on MH17, denying every chemical attack in Syria and confabulating conspiracies in the Skripal case, any decent reporter will steer clear.

In certain countries, maintaining the firewall is more challenging. Polarisation in the United States, for example, means that powerful media voices like Fox News often disregard factual findings in favour of spin, polluting the mainstream with false narratives. During the administration of President Trump – a repeated purveyor of claims from the alternative-media ecosystem – the problem worsened. Perhaps most worryingly, the Information Wars were seeping from the internet into the wider world.

Bellingcat had been established to investigate offline news events via online clues, but our mandate needed to expand. The internet had become more than a repository of what occurred in society; it was a Petri dish of what lay ahead. This was especially true for political extremists. Bellingcat investigators had witnessed their proliferation on the internet for years. Suddenly, they were taking to the streets.

ONLINE HATE SPILLS OFFLINE

At home in Kansas, Aric studied images from the Unite the Right rally. Ever since his first geolocation of that Buk missile launcher three years earlier, he had sifted through open sources to explain violent unrest abroad. But on 12 August 2017, violent unrest visited his own country, on the streets of Charlottesville, Virginia. The Ku Klux Klan and those in Nazi uniform were typical for far-right events, but this rally included youths in polo shirts and khakis – young men you'd expect to see on a college campus.

Aric archived social-media feeds, compiling a database of clips from the live-video streaming app Periscope, in addition to those appearing on Twitter, YouTube, Facebook. Posterity needed a record of this day in American history. He ignored clips from major news networks – they archived their footage, so it was not going to disappear. Instead, Aric wanted user-generated content, which could vanish offline without warning. There was much to collect, with alt-right demonstrators, anti-fascists and observers all recording and broadcasting the chaos, several with GoPro HD cameras strapped to their heads.

In one sequence documented with photos on social media, a group of white men surrounded a young African-American in a parking garage, beating him to the ground, swinging planks, breaking his wrist and cutting a deep gash in his head. The photojournalist Zach D. Roberts tweeted his most shocking image: the victim on all fours, under attack, with one assailant pictured head-on – a young man in khakis, open-collar shirt and a white hardhat with stickers on it – wielding a pole in a blur of downward motion.[47] The parking garage was a short walk from a police station, but not a single officer was on the scene. The activist Shaun King tweeted a photo compilation of three images of the attacker in the construction hat, along with a question: 'WHO IS HE?'[48]

Four years earlier, online sleuths had bungled the search for culprits in the Boston Bombings. Much had changed since then. We had the skills to do this and knew caution, too. Aric scrutinised the three images of the suspect: one from the attack itself, two others of him in the same outfit, leering and shouting among fellow far-right protesters. Writing on his hardhat said 'Commie Killer' above gun-sight crosshairs and a sticker of the Nazi SS skull and crossbones. He wore a backpack with camouflage straps and an open-necked shirt. Still, how to determine who this person was in a country of 325 million people?

Within an hour, Aric had identified him.

In addition to the three tweeted images, Aric had found a news photo of what appeared to be the same person during the torchlit march on the eve of the Unite the Right rally,[49] when clean-cut young men chanted: 'You will not replace us! Jews will not replace us!' Verifying a face follows the same principles as verifying a place, but the geography is the person's body, on which one seeks 'landmarks' to match with other images. In both the torchlit-march photo and the close-up hardhat image, Aric noticed that the young man wore a dogtag chain. Both photos gave a clear view of the subject's right ear. They matched. Most conclusive was the man's throat. It was summer, and hot in the South. He had unbuttoned his shirt to the top of his chest, baring a distinctive array of moles at the base of his throat. They lined up identically in the two images. This was the same person.

Another account on Twitter, @YesYoureRacist, which aimed to expose alt-right protesters at the rally, had identified two men in the torchlit photo as Jacob Dix and Ryan Martin of Centerville, Ohio. Some observers raised doubts about doxxing people who had attended a political rally, no matter how detestable their views. If we had tried, Bellingcat could probably have identified every alt-right protester, but we had no such intention. Our ethics revolve around a core question: does our investigation concern people who may have committed a serious crime, or who hold public positions of power and are threatening criminal acts? In the early days of Brown Moses, when I covered the phone-hacking scandal, disgraceful press practices exemplified what I never wanted to do: bullying and targeting people for being in the wrong place or with the wrong person. Information warriors in Ukraine use open-source investigation to attack those who are even tangentially involved with pro-Russian separatists, including journalists who write favourably about Moscow, placing them on a list of undesirables. This is not the Bellingcat approach. For instance, when looking into a GRU agent implicated in the assassination attempt against the Skripals, we found social-media images of the wedding of his boss's daughter. The GRU agent's child was a flower girl, which helped establish the agent's close relationship with the boss of the unit. But we absolutely did not include images of her. We are about seeking accountability, particularly when authorities fail to act. In the Charlottesville case, we had no qualms: the man we sought to identify was a suspect in a violent crime.

Aric proceeded on the hypothesis that protesters tend to go to rallies with friends. Much as when Bellingcat identified officers in the 53rd Brigade through soldiers' social-media postings, he searched the online tracks of the two men beside the suspect in that photo. On Facebook, he searched for 'jacob dix Centerville', and discovered the profile of a blond, athletic young man. The public photos posted on his account were a clear match to the man at the suspect's right in the torchlit march. Next, Aric typed in 'ryan martin centerville' and found a chunky, dark-haired youth with goatee and neck tattoos – a match for the man on the suspect's left in the march. The settings on Ryan Martin's Facebook profile kept his list of friends secret, but Jacob Dix was not as privacy-conscious. In his list was Ryan Martin, plus another young man whose profile photo resembled the suspect, identified as 'Dan Boc Borden (Bigrabbit)' of Mason, Ohio. Aric checked the list of pages Borden had liked. They included Men's Rights Activism Universe, Feminism is Evil and Kekistan, an imaginary country conceived online to deride political correctness and whose emblem is based on a Nazi military flag. Among Borden's friends were Dix and Martin.

Aric sifted through Borden's public photos, looking for images to compare with those of the suspect in the hardhat. He did not need to look far. The Facebook profile picture showed Borden with his chin cocked upwards, exposing his neck: that distinctive pattern of moles again. Aric had it, a chain of visual evidence. This was the man in the torchlit march, who was the man in the hardhat, who was the man in the parking garage in the midst of a violent assault. 'He's Dan Borden,' Aric tweeted. 'Got him.'[50]

We cannot know what role this played in the police investigation, but two weeks later Borden was in custody. The eighteen-year-old had faced accusations before. When he was at school, another student reported that he had pulled a knife, calling him 'Jew boy'. Borden also reportedly gave Nazi salutes. For the Charlottesville assault, he was sentenced to nearly four years.[51]

After the Unite the Right rally, news articles flooded out, decoding a range of far-right organisations: Identity Evropa with its white polo shirts, Nazi-era haircuts and pseudo-intellectualism; the Traditionalist Worker Party, blue-collar Nazis with the look of a motorcycle club; Vanguard America, whose supporters included the twenty-year-old who drove his car into a crowd of counter-protesters in Charlottesville, murdering Heather Heyer.[52] But what had looked like a coming-out for fascists was not quite that, partly because of online investigators like Aric, who showed that extremists could not rampage offline with the same impunity that they enjoyed online. The white nationalist Richard Spencer acknowledged that everything had changed after Charlottesville. 'Let's just admit what happened,' he said. 'We feared to go out in public.'[53] The internet helped spread extremism, but was also the tool to expose it.

Aric archived around 300 videos from Charlottesville, many that would have otherwise vanished from the internet.[54] Some day, one of those men may seek elected office, presumably hiding their participation in this event. Thanks to the internet, voters may learn what he did on 12 August 2017.

DISARMING THE TRAPS

Robert Evans grew up in Oklahoma and Texas around the turn of the millennium, raised in a conservative Christian family whose values he imbibed. During an abortive stint at college, he drifted far from his childhood politics and closer to his childhood passion: the internet. He dabbled in tech journalism, then wrote irreverent newsy pieces for Cracked. com, and did conflict reporting from Ukraine, Iraq and Syria. When he discovered Bellingcat, he became fascinated with this new form of reporting. Soon, he was pitching me articles on an area of his expertise: the far-right online. Robert did not offer technically stunning geolocations or measurements of shadowlines to tell the time. He parsed what fascists actually said to each other on social media. His goal was to explain how a subculture of young men became radicalised on message boards, and to warn the news media against informational traps set by extremist trolls. Robert's explanatory investigations were to become the most read Bellingcat pieces to date.

Back when I frequented the message boards of Something Awful, young men were already devoting hours to photoshopping stock images with captions and producing comical GIF video loops, intended to amuse their peers. A more extreme forum, 4chan, took shape, and meme-making transferred there, sharpened according to its spirit of adolescent cruelty. A faction on 4chan – especially the Politically Incorrect board, known by its abbreviation /pol/ – applied meme skills to promoting the presidential candidacy of Trump in 2016, a project they dubbed 'The Great Meme War'. Many started out considering their efforts as just a troll joke on the public, yet some became seduced by the effect they were having. Anonymous posters popularised the cartoon frog Pepe, an ambiguous symbol that sometimes represented Trump, or the alt-right, or white nationalism. The most successful memes landed on Facebook, viewed by a mass audience.[55]

As with the growth of the Counterfactual Community, bad ideas found company online and intensified there. One difference is that the ordinary citizens who blindly defend Assad or Putin tend to think they are doing good in the world, while 'channers' are rarely concerned with global issues. A form of ironic nihilism prevails on 4chan, underpinned by the idea that life is ugly and pointless. If you take any matter seriously, you become the butt of the joke – even if someone is threatening to shoot you in the face.

Robert went trawling through leaked posts from a gamers' chat app, Discord, that had been infiltrated by neo-fascists. After Charlottesville, a fresh branch of the alt-right rose – groups such as the Proud Boys, Patriot Prayer and Anti-Communist Action, that denied bigotry, characterising themselves as defenders of free speech and old-fashioned values, a bulwark against the radical left. This was not the whole truth.

In leaked private posts, Robert found that some spoke of 'hiding our power levels', meaning disguising their true views to avoid alienating the masses. 'Why not make a nationalist party?' the founder of Anti-Communist Action wrote in one message exchange. 'We can promise strong military spending and border security to win over the conservatives, and promise science funding and space exploration to win over the reddit crowd, as well as universal healthcare to get the lefties onboard. … We just hide our power levels.'[56]

Those Discord chat logs – leaked by a left-wing crowdfunded media collective, Unicorn Riot – proved to be a goldmine. Robert analysed how seventy-five people had become radicalised, a topic that the fascists discussed obsessively, with many recounting exactly when and how they had been 'red-pilled'. This term derives from the 1999 sci-fi movie *The Matrix*, in which the main character must choose whether to take a red pill and see the shocking reality that humans are unknowing slaves, or to take a blue pill and return to blissful ignorance. Supporters of the far right speak of 'taking the red pill' to mean abandoning socially acceptable views, even buying into the narrative that Jews are conspiring to bring about white genocide, described in these circles as 'the Jewish Question' or 'JQ'.[57] A typical progression was from interest in Trump, to engagement in The Great Meme War, to 4chan, to neo-fascism.

One person in the Discord chats said that he had formerly been a male feminist, and used to dismiss Trump as a racist, but had wanted to understand the candidate for himself, after which he judged that the Republican leader was not actually a racist and had good ideas. He proceeded to 'The_Donald' forum on Reddit for the memes produced there, began actively supporting Trump, grew tired of the subreddit, visited 4chan's /pol/ board a month before the election, found the Nazi memes silly but amusing, began using some of their 'ironic' white-supremacist language, and finally came to believe there might be truth in those memes, that there truly *was* an anti-white agenda. By the end, he was a white nationalist.[58]

Overwhelmingly, the red-pilled in these forums were men, along with a small number of women with exceptionally extreme views – a pattern that is consistent with studies of far-right demographics.[59] More than half of the seventy-five fascists reported having been red-pilled online. The most-cited location for this was YouTube, notably the videos of Carl 'Sargon of Akkad' Benjamin, a British man who gained prominence with videos denouncing feminists and went on to rail against immigration and political correctness. Clips of Alex Jones from InfoWars were also influential. What Jones claimed about a globalist world conspiracy appealed to several, although it was not sufficiently anti-Semitic for them. 'Infowars actually did a good job of prepping me for the JQ, as much of their facts are fairly true, they just change the names',[60] one poster wrote.[61]

Nobody could pretend that this radicalisation was limited to social media. On 27 October 2018, a forty-six-year-old opened fire in a Pittsburgh synagogue during Saturday morning services, killing eleven people and wounding six, in the deadliest attack on the Jewish community in American history. He had been writing messages on Gab, an app known as Twitter for the far right. There, he reposted material from Fox News as well as memes that expressed admiration for General Augusto Pinochet, the dictator who ruled Chile from 1973 to 1990 and whose regime was known for throwing political dissidents to their death from helicopters. 'Death flights' have become a meme for neo-fascists, appearing on T-shirts that promise 'free helicopter rides' for leftists.

Online white supremacy looked new, but its digital trail went back decades, Robert discovered. A key figure was Louis Beam, a Texan who joined the US Army during the Vietnam War, serving as a machine-gunner on helicopters and later recalling 'the joys of killing your enemy'. He cultivated a hatred of communists and his own government, and became a member of the Ku Klux Klan. Two of Beam's actions in the 1980s had an enduring effect. First, he wrote about 'leaderless resistance'. Second, he established an online bulletin board, Aryan Liberty Net, set up in 1984, in the days when computer use was extremely limited.[62] In a printed KKK newsletter that year, he said: 'Imagine, if you can, a single computer to which all leaders and strategists of the patriotic movement are connected. Imagine further that any patriot in the country is able to tap into this computer at will in order to reap the benefit of all accumulative knowledge and wisdom of the leaders. "Someday," you may say? How about today?'[63] With this, he announced the Aryan Liberty Net, which was so ahead of its time that it even doxxed people, publishing addresses and phone numbers of Jewish and leftist organisations, along with those deemed traitors to the white race.[64]

Thirty years later, white supremacy gained indirect traction through the Gamergate controversy of 2014, when a faction of male videogamers complained that elites in the industry were favouring women and progressives. This degenerated into harassment of female game developers, prompting 4chan to ban the subject. 4channers who were obsessed with the subject transferred to an even more extreme chat site, 8chan. Robert first visited 8chan around this time, and was taken aback by its misogyny, its doxxing and the 'raids' conducted by its members. As a teenager, Robert had frequented Something Awful, where he and fellow youths launched 'raids' – online swarms – against those they deemed worthy of punishment, such as a company that hosted paedophile websites. Adolescents who were otherwise virtually powerless in their everyday lives found themselves impacting the world when they united on the internet; it was addictive. But Gamergate diverged from what Robert knew of online raids, applying the same harassment but to intimidate women who had simply spoken out.

Ever since Gamergate, Robert had kept an eye on 8chan. On 15 March 2019, he read of horrific attacks at two mosques in Christchurch, New Zealand, and learned that the alleged gunman had posted a manifesto on 8chan's /pol/ board, with links to a videostream of the killings as they happened. On Facebook Live you could watch the twenty-eight-year-old driving his station wagon towards the first mosque, with a carefully selected soundtrack playing in the background. Upon parking, he looked at the passenger seat, laden with three firearms, including an assault rifle covered in messages in white paint. He turned on a strobe light on the rifle – apparently to confuse and distract his victims – then fetched a shotgun.

A worshipper said 'Hello, brother' by the entrance of Al Noor Mosque. The gunman opened fire,[65] killing this person along with others by the entrance. Inside, he shot children and the elderly alike. Midway through this assault, he returned to his station wagon for another rifle. He went from room to room, executing survivors, then left the building, firing at bystanders. Music continued to play as he drove to a second target. To his Facebook Live audience he commented, 'There wasn't even time to aim; there was so many targets.' In six minutes, he had killed more than forty people. The video feed cut out, after which he killed seven more people before the police captured him.[66]

Journalism on mass shootings followed a predictable pattern: reporters established the number of dead and wounded, identified the killer, then tried to figure out why. But mass shooters in the digital age anticipated this, leaving curated manifestos online. The Christchurch killer spent considerable time on his, a seventy-four-page document called 'The Great Replacement', evoking a conspiracy theory of global elites plotting to eliminate those of European Christian descent and supplant them with non-white ethnicities. Written on his rifle was the number '14', referring to a fourteen-word incantation of neo-Nazi bank robber David Lane: 'We must secure the existence of our people and a future for white children.'

In New Zealand, Muslims constituted 1 per cent of the population – hardly the 'mass invaders' that racists bemoaned. But the attack was meant to resonate beyond this country; it was meant for the worldwide audience on 8chan. Scouring the manifesto, Robert realised what few journalists had: this document was a trap.[67] He worked till early the next morning, writing up his findings for a Bellingcat article that warned of the intent of this manifesto, to dupe the news media and manipulate the public. Whereas other Bellingcat investigations trawl heaps of open-source material for buried clues, Robert tried a different form, decoding information that plenty had seen but few understood.

'Well lads,' the killer posted on 8chan when announcing his impending attack, 'it's time to stop shitposting and time to make a real life effort post.' This term, 'shitposting', referred to the practice of posting content designed to distress and mislead less savvy internet users. His manifesto was full of shitposting. For example, he claimed that the African-American conservative political commentator Candace Owens had inspired him, apparently to draw this prominent voice into the news coverage, although she had no connection to the killer's beliefs. His manipulative intent was more obvious when he claimed that a videogame, Spyro the Dragon, 'taught me ethno-nationalism'. This was all bait and intended to make 8chan laugh.

The fact that someone planning mass murder wanted to crack jokes with his online buddies is hard to comprehend. But this brand of 'humour' is familiar to those of us who grew up with message-board culture. The motto of Something Awful was 'The Internet Makes You Stupid', an ironic tagline that had two effects: mocking fretful critics who bewailed the rotting of young minds online; and declaring that we ourselves were not taking anything too seriously. This made for a liberating environment, permitting outsiders to experiment safely and speak openly. But over the years, as power shifted online, the internet was no longer safe for messing around. Nerd flippancy congealed into sadism by 'anons', as users of 4chan and 8chan are known. (All users on the sites are anonymous – a key factor in why people go to extremes there.) For fascists, callous 'humour' had a secondary purpose. It was a way to camouflage transgressive ideas, and edge them into the mainstream. Typical was 'the Happy Merchant' cartoon of a bearded Jew with demonic eyes, wringing his hands with greed – a caricature similar to those printed in Nazi propaganda but today found in 'humorous' far-right memes.

Robert's article – 'Shitposting, Inspirational Terrorism, and the Christchurch Mosque Massacre' – gained a vast audience, forwarded around the world, and shifting the news coverage. With this form of open-source inquiry, Bellingcat helped uphold the firewall against information chaos, and the mainstream media avoided falling into the traps of the gunman's manifesto. The prime minister of New Zealand, Jacinda Ardern, refused to speak his name, avoiding granting him the notoriety such mass murderers crave, and a study of thousands of English-language articles found that only 14 per cent of US publications gave the killer's name – something unthinkable in previous cases.[68] The *Daily Mail*'s online operation posted images from the killer's helmet-cam video along with a PDF of the entire manifesto. But people were more informed by now, and public outrage led MailOnline to take it down.[69]

By contrast, the 8chan /pol/ community considered the Christchurch killer its new idol, photoshopped into 'ironic' pictures as a saint with a halo. Others translated his manifesto into French, Bulgarian, Russian, German, Dutch. Anons discussed further attacks. When one asked for suggestions, the first reply was: 'Shoot up a Synagogue. Be a hero.' Less than a month later, an 8channer carried out just such an attack. 'It's been real dudes,' he posted. 'From the bottom of my heart thank you for everything. Keep up the infographic redpill threads. I've only been lurking for a year and a half, yet what I've learned here is priceless. It's been an honor.' He left a link to his own manifesto, and to a Facebook livestream of the attack he was about to launch in the Poway synagogue, outside San Diego, which left one person dead and wounded three others. Again, the manifesto was full of shitposting to confuse the authorities and prank the news media, alongside anti-Semitic screeds and 8chan in-jokes. Before, the public was just working out what 'shitposting' meant. Now, the concern turned to 8chan itself.

Robert spent hours in that cesspit so that the public did not have to. The site contained varied discussion groups, the most disturbing of which was the /pol/ hangout, dominated by neo-Nazis. You would find memes of Pepe the Frog tweaked to look like Hitler, or a smiling Pepe the Frog holding a rifle with his scope targeting 'the Happy Merchant'. You also saw more traditional expressions of Nazism – discussions about the best translation of *Mein Kampf*, for example. If there was a theme, it was the desire to exterminate imagined enemies, be they Jews, Muslims, members of the LGBT community, or others. 'Red-pilling' had brought them here, but /pol/ was the next stage of radicalisation, with anons goading each other to carry out 'real-life effortposting', meaning offline violence. Part of this involved a strategy called 'siege-posting' whereby terror attacks were supposed to break apart American society, leading to a civil war and opening the way to a Nazi takeover. Both the Christchurch and the Poway attackers hoped their shootings would provoke gun control that would spark a new American civil war.[70]

Clearly, the wider public – horrified by the terrorist culture emerging from the internet underbelly – wanted to know more, for Robert's next explanatory investigation surpassed his previous article as Bellingcat's most viewed; the two pieces drew more than a million page views combined. His next subject was a third shooting announced on 8chan, which left twenty-two dead at a Walmart in El Paso, Texas. The first 8chan response to the gunman's post and manifesto was another anon describing the site as a 'board of peace'. That itself was a meme, mocking assertions that Islam is a religion of peace. The next 8chan response to the killer's announcement was 'Every shabbat', ironically using the Hebrew word for Saturday to augur more violence. Nobody could call this the work of a lone gunman anymore.

An element of neo-fascist terrorism that 8chan stirred is what Robert called 'the gamification' of mass violence.[71] While billions of people have played videogames, and almost none are moved to harm others, elements of gaming culture have become incorporated into attacks. Livestreaming on a helmet cam showed the Christchurch gunman's perspective with a weapon in hand – eerily like the view in shoot-em-up videogames. He and the Poway killer carefully chose musical soundtracks to go along with their live streams, as in a videogame. When the Poway synagogue gunman announced on 8chan that he was about to kill innocent people, the first reply was 'get the high score' – murder more people than previous mass-shooters.[72] Online, you find 'high-score' leader boards, including categories related to different videogames, such as a Microsoft Flight Simulator list for those who have carried out mass killings involving aeroplanes. On the site Encyclopedia Dramatica, which is like Wikipedia for trolls, the 'high-score' entry cites 'difficulty levels' of various attacks. It deems lone-gunman attacks to be the 'gold standard of murder'. Although the list cites massacres going back to 1835, almost all of the highest murder counts have been in the past few years.[73]

After the third shooting announced on 8chan, its founder, Fredrick Brennan, who had already cut ties with the site, called for it to be shut down.[74] For a while, it went offline[75] – only to return as 8kun.[76] Whatever its eventual fate, the radicalisation of many users had already taken place.

Yet the message is not discouraging. Nobody will ever 'fix' the internet, just as nobody will ever fix the world. But this has never justified giving in to miserabilism about life offline. The internet has given us immense new powers, and it is time to marshal them.

INVOLVING THE PUBLIC

We always seek ways to engage citizens in open-source investigation, and a striking case emerged due to Islamic State. One of the extremist group's media outlets, known for the release of beheading videos and audio messages from its leaders[77], [78] was about to make an announcement in May 2016. The group spread word via the encrypted-messaging app Telegram, and its clandestine supporters uploaded handwritten notes of allegiance to the extremist group from various European cities, as if to brag that its secret foot soldiers were legion and had reached the West.

The reporter Jenan Moussa of pan-Arab satellite channel Al Aan posted one such photo that an ISIS supporter had purportedly taken in the German city of Münster, holding up a note and showing a traffic intersection in the fuzzy background.[79] Other handwritten-note images included backgrounds of a suburban road in Amsterdam, a view from a window in Paris, a red double-decker bus in London, among others. Recent ISIS terrorist attacks in Brussels and Paris had killed scores and wounded hundreds more, so fear of the organisation was acute. This latest social-media campaign sought to intimidate the public further.

'There's a geolocation challenge for ya,' I wrote, reposting the Münster photo to the tens of thousands of people who by that stage followed me on Twitter. Resourceful amateurs noted an advertising column in the background, and discovered that a marketing-company website mapped all of these in the German city. Now, they needed only to find advertising columns near traffic intersections and check the locations on Google Street View to see which matched the photo. Soon, they had it. This was not a fruitless exercise. The ISIS supporter had taken the photo in the preceding few hours. If CCTV cameras recorded that well-trodden area, police could check the location and identify a terrorist supporter in their midst. All this in less than an hour.

Members of the public had similar success with the London photo including a red double-decker bus in the background. They could not decipher its number, but did notice a bus stop marked with the code K and a bridge with the word 'GROVE' emblazoned on it in large letters. A simple web search for 'bus stop k grove london' gave an answer: the 149 bus. They found its route online, and the stop lettered K, near Bruce Grove station in north London. A visit to Google Street View pinpointed the precise location, equidistant between Tottenham police station and Tottenham magistrates court – places that the photographer might have soon become familiar with, given that the local authorities picked up the lead.

By this point, ISIS supporters were warning each other to *stop* putting out photos identifying their cities. They were too late. Other members of the public geolocated an image in a town near Amsterdam Schiphol Airport, tracing the photographer to a particular set of balconies in a specific building. The photo overlooking a Paris street carelessly included part of a shop sign, a stylised red 'S' that amateur sleuths identified as the logo of Suzuki motorcycles. About half a dozen Suzuki dealerships existed in Paris. It was just a matter of checking each on Google Street View to find the match: rue Championnet. They even determined which building the photographer had taken it from, and which window he had stood at.

Police forces chased down our leads, and the ISIS social-media effort dissolved. Rather than circulating fear, those who had outed themselves were mocked online as 'ISIS fanboys' and 'wannabe jihadis'. As for the Islamic State media release, it turned out to be a half-hour audio statement by a spokesman and nobody much cared.[80] Islamic State had developed a reputation for exploiting social media to radicalise youths, mobilise sympathisers and scare off resistance. Yet the vast bulk of humanity considered ISIS repugnant, and we did not need to sit back and cede the internet to war criminals and their supporters.

A year after the ISIS social-media failure, we mobilised members of the public again, to help investigations into another of the most reprehensible online subcultures: those who sexually abuse children. Europol, the agency that coordinates criminal intelligence among European police forces, has forty million captured images of child sexual abuse that can offer clues to where crimes took place and who was responsible. In many cases, the police are stumped yet they cannot circulate illegal and traumatising images to seek help from the public. So they had another idea: to crop the abuse photos, removing the victims and showing only the background, in the hope that someone might recognise something and help identify the location. In June 2017 they launched Trace an Object, canvassing help from the public. By this time, Bellingcat had a base of thousands of amateur sleuths reachable instantly via Twitter, so we tweeted the Europol images to our followers. Often the picture showed a piece of clothing, or perhaps a building, or an advertising flyer. We set up pages devoted to various images on the collaborative verification app Check, the successor software to Checkdesk, which we had previously used to crowd-source geolocations of airstrikes in the Middle East.

Within days, we had initial identifications. One user, who goes by the handle 'Bo', was especially effective, tracking down one item after another. Usually, volunteers' techniques were basic – little more than reverse image searches. But even elementary methods can produce results. Also, crowd investigations benefit from a broad knowledge base. In just two weeks, Europol had 10,000 contributions to Trace an Object.[81] During its first year, Europol published images of 119 objects, of which 79 were identified.[82] Tips kept coming in, exceeding 24,000 by January 2020,[83] leading to the identification of at least ten children and the prosecution of two offenders.[84]

In more countries than ever, citizens are mobilising to fight disinformation and push back against the Counterfactual Community. The Baltic states – Estonia, Latvia, Lithuania – have been especially active. These three nations, sandwiched between Russia and the Baltic Sea, were once part of the Soviet Union and the Kremlin still views them being within its sphere of influence, also because each has an ethnic-Russian minority, amounting to about 900,000 people across the three countries.[85] Moscow has previously used the pretext of protecting ethnic Russians to justify military action, notably against Ukraine, so the Baltic states are tense about their powerful neighbour. They are also subjected to much Russian disinformation, via Kremlin-funded news operations and on social media. In response to Russian trolls, they came up with 'the elves', volunteers who combat falsehoods online. When trolls divert the online conversation, inserting manipulative content to inflame naïve users on Facebook and in comments section under news articles, the elves retaliate. 'We don't try to be propagandists in reverse,' one Lithuanian elf – a thirtysomething advertising executive – explained to the *Daily Beast*. 'We only want to expose the bullshit.'[86]

Finland is another northern European nation with a long border with Russia. After the Russian occupation of Crimea in 2014, the Finnish government stepped up its defences against false news reports and online manipulation, establishing courses on disinformation for members of the public. In the first few years, thousands attended.[87] Sweden, too, launched campaigns to tackle disinformation and has worked on a new government agency for the psychological defence of the country.[88]

We all need to stay alert to disinformation techniques. If you imagine that digital natives, those who grew up with the internet, are equipped to handle this environment, you are wrong. A Stanford study from 2016, which tested thousands of American students' ability to spot fakery online, reported that 'young people's ability to reason about the information on the Internet can be summed up in one word: *bleak*. ... In every case and at every level, we were taken aback by students' lack of preparation.'[89] Some 82 per cent of middle-school students could not tell a news story from an advertisement.

The Swedes have developed teaching materials to educate kids about fake news, online propaganda and doctored imagery. Teenagers in Ukraine – perhaps the country most assaulted by propaganda trolls – are taking classes on media literacy to good effect: students who participated in a pilot programme were twice as alert to hate speech and 18 per cent better at spotting fake news.[90] In Denmark, 'Trolls in Your Feed' is a publication for high-school kids, part of a push there against Russian disinformation.[91] Classes, including cautionary study of false news reports, are working their way into school curricula in parts of the United States.[92]

In parallel, fact-checking projects have also taken off. Fewer than fifty existed worldwide in 2014. Two years later, the number had doubled. By mid-2020, there were at least 290 fact-checking projects across Africa, Asia, Australia, Europe, North America and South America,[93] according to the Reporters' Lab at Duke University. Some of the most prominent initiatives were hatched by legacy-news organisations, such as Les Décodeurs (affiliated with *Le Monde* newspaper in France) or Faktenfinder (from German broadcaster ARD). Others were independent, such as Pagella Politica (Italy) or Newtral (Spain). There was also the old stalwart Snopes, founded in 1994, along with newcomers with global ambitions such as First Draft News, of which Bellingcat was a founding partner. First Draft seeks to support reporters and academics with verifications, especially when it comes to elections, leading projects from Brazil to the United States to Nigeria[94] and beyond.

Still, fact-checking projects are minuscule compared with the reach of disinformation. An intriguing essay, published by the British fact-checking organisation Full Fact, contended that a first generation of online fact-checkers followed a 'publish and pray' approach that still applies too widely. A second iteration sought to affect public debate more directly, confronting the sources of fakery, demanding corrections in print, complaining to standards bodies, while pressuring institutions to take action. A third iteration of fact-checkers, Full Fact argued, must meet the scale of the internet, probably through massive collaborations that disregard national frontiers.[95] We are pushing for exactly that.

More than ever, news events prompt people to scour the internet for immediate insights, and we are seeking to mobilise this public in the push for credible evidence. For example, within a month of the World Health Organization designating Covid-19 a pandemic in March 2020, Bellingcat produced a range of material to involve citizens in online sleuthing on the subject, including a guide to debunking coronavirus disinformation;

an article on scammers exploiting the disease on Facebook and YouTube; and a video segment on applying open-source tools to studying a world gone still during lockdown.[96] When a police officer in Minneapolis killed an African-American suspect, George Floyd, setting off protests across the United States and beyond, we produced an explanatory article on the Boogalo movement that hoped unrest would degenerate into a second American civil war; we compiled an exhaustive list of attacks on journalists, geolocated and plotted onto an interactive map to involve the public in absorbing the dimensions of the efforts to suppress information; and we sought to inform citizens of our techniques via a new podcast, BellingChat.

More crises are inevitable, especially given the climate emergency. A fundamental part of all future disaster responses must be countering misinformation. Crisis readiness cannot begin only when disaster hits. Prepping means awareness that manipulators seek advantage in every news event, even global catastrophes; that the Counterfactual Community churns out fresh conspiracy theories; and that extremists devour it all. Bellingcat is erecting firewalls, but we must maintain them together. Nor is it just huge events that merit attention. Indeed, they already draw wide coverage from the news media. A practice of Bellingcat is to dig out the stories that major outlets are overlooking. This is something anyone can do.

The Bellingcat alumnus Christiaan Triebert once appeared on a Dutch talk show, *De Wereld Draait Door*, explaining how he unearthed the workings of a Turkish coup by studying a leaked WhatsApp thread of plotters and piecing it together with additional open-source evidence. Among those watching was an eleven-year-old boy. His mother got in touch, saying that her son wanted to interview Christiaan for a school project. They met up and chatted. In conclusion, the boy asked, 'Why do you focus only on war?' He was more passionate about environmental damage and animal welfare. Why not investigate topics like that? He and Christiaan agreed to find a project together. The boy had concerns about the illegal hunting of sharks, which are killed to make soup and other commodities. Looking into this, we got in touch with the World Wildlife Fund, and linked up with its research arm, TRAFFIC. In turn, this led to Christiaan flying out to South Africa, conducting local training and working on an investigation related to rhino poaching. All this from the initiative of an eleven-year-old.

4

Mice Catch Cat

A spy story turns into a landmark case

Two Russian intelligence officers allegedly carried the chemical weapon in a backpack, strolling through the heart of a peaceful English cathedral city on 4 March 2018. Upon reaching Sergei Skripal's house in Salisbury, they allegedly drew out a container, aimed its nozzle at the front door and sprayed.

Inside the house a family reunion was taking place. Yulia had travelled from Moscow the day before for a two-week holiday with her father. Her mother had died of cancer a few years earlier, while her older brother had passed away just a few months before, apparently of liver disease, aged only forty-three. His birthday was this very weekend. Yulia and Sergei went out to commemorate the two, closing the contaminated door after them.

During the 1990s, Sergei Skripal had worked as a GRU officer, while also feeding secrets to the British. In 2004, the Russian authorities caught him. He received thirteen years for treason, but the sentence was cut short in 2010 as a result of a spy swap with the Americans. He was offered resettlement in a few British cities, and chose Salisbury, settling down at

47 Christie Miller Road. Not long after, his wife died. This Sunday, he and Yulia visited her grave.[1] Afterwards they drove to the city centre, stopped for a drink in a pub and went to an Italian restaurant for lunch.[2] Neither felt quite right. They paid and went outside. Soon, both were slumped on a bench, incapacitated by Novichok.

The Skripal case contains so many elements that have marked the story of Bellingcat: a chemical-weapons crime; an authoritarian government apparently lying to the world and expecting impunity; a campaign of online disinformation; the Counterfactual Community piling on; Western authorities struggling to solve the case; and citizen investigators stepping in, united by a conviction that facts still matter, that evidence exists online, verification is mandatory and accountability is still possible. More than any case yet, our Skripal investigations showed the world what Bellingcat was, how much we can achieve as a collective and that the sway of the internet is not limited to warping public debate. Ordinary citizens can pursue justice and truth there, too.

A common theme runs from the first defining Bellingcat case – our MH17 reports – to our identification of the GRU officers allegedly behind the assassination attempt in Salisbury. By 2017, months before the Skripal attack, we had already explained much about the MH17 tragedy. But we were still looking to pin down the decision-makers on the ground, those whose voices appeared on the intercepted phone calls of pro-Russian separatists. In December 2017, we released a major report on the identity of one such person. A key partner in this investigation was Roman Dobrokhotov, who was to become central to our Skripal discoveries.

Based in Moscow, Roman is the editor of The Insider, an online news outlet of exceptional bravery, working to expose corruption in a country where the murder of journalists is hardly unknown. Roman, a former dissident activist, has been detained more than a hundred times[3] by his count. On one famous occasion in 2008 he interrupted a speech of the Russian president Dmitri Medvedev, shouting to the gathered audience, 'Why listen to him? He has broken all our human rights and freedoms!' Security dragged Roman out. He shifted from activism to investigative journalism, earning global attention for The Insider's work in exposing the hacking attack on Emmanuel Macron's political party and an email dump just before the 2017 presidential election runoff in France. While the official French cybersecurity agency failed to trace it to Russian operatives, The Insider turned up the name Georgy Petrovich Roshka in metadata of hacked emails, then obtained a list of participants at a conference this person had attended. He was listed as a specialist in Military Unit 26165[4] – part of the GRU, and implicated in hacking to manipulate the 2016 US presidential election.[5]

We first teamed up with Roman on stories about Kremlin involvement in an attempted coup in Montenegro, after he and Bellingcat contributor Christo Grozev found each other via Twitter discussions. Christo is a Vienna-based media executive who worked in Russia during the 1990s and had always wanted to produce journalism himself. He found an opportunity in 2014, setting up a blog that focused on Kremlin media deception.[6] However, he was taking a risk as a lone blogger writing about dangerous men, so decided to align himself with a journalistic organisation. He reached out to us. Christo's language skills, gifts of reportage and insights into Kremlin bureaucracy have made him a mainstay of our investigations. But he had also been banned from Russia since teaching a media seminar in Moscow, so needed someone to help conduct on-the-ground reporting.

This led him to Roman. Today, he and Christo speak several times a day, brainstorming ideas and new ways to crack stories.

Back in 2017, the Joint Investigation Team of police and prosecutors seeking culprits in the MH17 tragedy had been struggling to identity two men – known by the call signs 'Delfin' and 'Orion' – whom the Ukrainian security services had recorded. The Joint Investigation Team issued a public call for information on the pair, and we started looking for answers.

Our identification of Delfin came first, in collaboration with The Insider and an American news organisation, McClatchy DC Bureau. We realised that Delfin – also referred to as 'Nikolai Fedorovich' – seemed to be a commanding officer, partly because others referred to him using the respectful Russian plural (*vy*). Reading through pro-Russian-insurgent sources online, we found mentions of Delfin, alluded to as a Russian general involved in managing separatists in Krasnodon, south-eastern Ukraine. At the time in the summer of 2014, both the FSB and the GRU had their high-ranking representatives in Donbass, so we looked for matches both among the Russian military and special services officers, especially those with *Spetsnaz* backgrounds.

We discovered two possible matches. In open sources, we discovered a living Russian Army general with the same name and patronymic, Nikolai Fedorovich Tkachev. We needed voice samples to compare with Delfin on the audio intercepts, but all we could find of Tkachev online were brief videos of a ceremony at the Yekaterinburg Suvorov Military School. Christo noticed that Tkachev had served as chairman of an advisory board at the Yekaterinburg cadet school and looked up the board members in an online company database; this included a contact number. Roman phoned it and confirmed that he had reached Tkachev, then asked for an interview, claiming he had official permission to speak with him for an article on the school in an official Russian Defence

Ministry publication. From this, we obtained audio samples of his voice, and submitted them for two independent analyses. The Forensic Science Centre of Lithuania deemed the match of audio snippets 'highly probable', while the National Center for Media Forensics at the University of Colorado at Denver rendered a likelihood ratio of 428 – meaning that the audio samples were 428 times more likely to be the same speaker than another person. Tkachev had told The Insider by phone that he had not been an independent operator at the time of the downing in July 2014: he was still serving in the Russian armed forces, and we had found a photo of him acting as Russia's military adviser in Syria, making him the most senior Russian officer yet potentially linked to the case.[7] Tkachev responded to our investigation by stating: 'I don't know what it is they are saying but it is obvious stupidity.'[8]

The second possible match was an FSB colonel, Vladimir Makarenko, whose telephone number we had discovered among call records of another Russian colonel (Igor Egorov – 'Elbrus') whom we had identified as a key figure in Russian clandestine operations in eastern Ukraine in 2014. Colonel Makarenko's father was named Nikolay Fedorovich, and had been a Soviet-era general. It was not a rare occurrence for undercover Russian operatives to use their decorated father or brother's names as an alias. We could not obtain a voice sample for the very reclusive Colonel Makarenko – he had given no interviews, and his phone was set to reject calls from unknown numbers. We provided both identities to the JIT as possible matches for the famed Delfin and published a 'high likelihood' identification report on the only one of the two for whom we had obtained a forensic voice comparison.

Next came Orion, an identification again pursued with The Insider and McClatchy. The man who went by this call sign was also referred to as 'Andrey Ivanovich' in the intercepts, and boasted of obtaining a Buk missile launcher, pledging that

Ukrainian military planes would soon be shot down. A blog post from a former separatist combatant mentioned a Russian adviser in Luhansk named 'Andrey Ivanych'. The blog post also noted that the man had a strikingly high voice – something true of Orion in the intercepted recordings.

At first, we tried to replicate our success in exposing Delfin, narrowing down the possible candidates, acquiring voice samples and matching these. But 'Andrey Ivanovich' was too common a name among Russians. Also, we had doubts that a GRU officer would use his true name and patronymic in communications on the phone. Fortunately, the Ukrainian security services had, in addition to releasing the recording, published the phone numbers of those talking. The Orion number had been disconnected, but we searched for it in phone-number-sharing apps popular with Russians, such as TrueCaller. These apps amalgamate the contact lists of all their users, granting them a crowd-sourced caller ID. Names do not appear as phone owners choose to identify themselves, but how they happen to be listed in another person's 'Contacts', which explains the many anomalous spellings. In this open source, we found the number listed as 'Oreon'. During an unrelated project regarding Ukraine, we had obtained cell phone-usage metadata, including for this number, which showed four Russian phones had held calls with Oreon. We took these four numbers and plugged them into the contacts-sharing apps. One came up as 'Ivannikov' and then, amazingly, as 'Andrey Ivanovich GRU – from Husky'.

We searched the internet for combinations of this Russian phone number and the last name 'Ivannikov', and had two hits: a Russian open-source phone database; and a defunct e-commerce site whose database of customers and orders had been leaked online. The phone database gave the owner's full name as 'Oleg Vladimirovich Ivannikov', plus a birthdate and a Moscow address, which happened to be across the street from the Russian Military Academy. The e-commerce database contained a 2017 order for an elevation training mask, delivered to a different Moscow address. Google Maps and Yandex Maps both indicated that the number in this delivery address did not exist on that street. A reporter from The Insider visited the location and found that the street morphed into a highway, where the number did exist. When the reporter reached it, he found himself standing before the headquarters of the GRU.

Our hypothesis was that the name cited in the intercepts, 'Andrey Ivanovich', was the cover of Oleg Vladimirovich Ivannikov. Under what we suspected was his true name, we found address registration details and discovered that he had been a military officer with a specialisation in rocket systems. We also obtained a 2012 photo of Ivannikov, but still lacked his voice. So we picked up the phone, calling a landline at the reported home address of Oleg Ivannikov. A relative answered, saying Oleg wasn't there. We tried later. This time the relative shouted to Oleg, 'Is it convenient now to take the call?' In the background, he could be heard replying, 'No, it is not convenient now' – speaking in a strikingly high-pitched voice, much like Orion in the intercepted calls. However, we still did not have the audio quality for a forensic analysis.

We spent months monitoring his mobile number on messenger apps, hoping for a ping if ever that number went back online. In March 2018 it did. Our plan was to pretend we were seeking a different Oleg Vladimirovich Ivannikov, coincidentally the name of an unrelated public figure. The Oleg Ivannikov whom we suspected answered his phone, speaking with that distinctive high-pitched voice. We had audio now, and we had Orion – the first link to a senior Russian officer operating inside Ukraine to the downing of MH17.[9]

We had also gained experience in identifying Russian officers who wished to remain anonymous. This was soon to prove invaluable. The very month we detected that ping from the phone of Orion was when Sergei Skripal and his daughter collapsed in Salisbury. With the British authorities struggling to identify their suspects, they decided to present their clues in public. We were ready to pick up the case.

PUSHING THE BOUNDARIES OF OPEN SOURCE

After the Skripal assassination attempt, the Kremlin disinformation apparatus kicked into action, with RT and Sputnik pumping out 735 articles in just four weeks, including a staggering 138 contradictory narratives with a range of conspiracy theories. In some versions, the Skripals were never poisoned. Or perhaps they had ties with organised crime. Or Yulia had brought the Novichok to Salisbury. Or 'Russophobia' was behind the British response. Or the Americans may have supplied the nerve agent, or the Ukrainians, or the Iranians, or a number of other countries.[10] When asked about this, RT responded, 'We are amazed that it took some in the UK this long to jump on the tried-and-true bandwagon: blame RT for journalistic audacity to demand facts and ask questions.'[11] The Counterfactual Community amplified Kremlin disinformation, both parroting Russian talking points and supplying additional baseless claims.

We just got down to work, especially after the British police released those images of the two unidentified Skripal suspects in September 2018. At first, we uploaded pictures of 'Alexander Petrov' and 'Ruslan Boshirov' onto search engines, seeking reverse image matches. Nothing came back. We searched through Skype handles, seeking variants of their supposed names. Nothing. We scanned Russian news reports for clues and dredged Twitter for insights. Christo led the Bellingcat Investigation Team with Daniel Romein, a key contributor in the MH17 investigations, along with the close collaboration of Roman at The Insider. Aric oversaw their efforts, providing the extra set of eyes that is invaluable when undertaking a complex investigation.

Unable to track the suspects through standard open-source methods, we went deeper, digging into a stash of leaked databases. Over the past twenty years, hundreds of these have ended up on Russian torrent sites – the kind of webpages that illegally share copyrighted movies, allowing people to download files in digital segments from a multitude of users, thereby preventing the authorities from shutting down any single source. The leaked Russian databases included passport data, residential address data, car ownership data, often on a city-by-city basis. Rarely were these databases up to date. We might find something from, say, 2012, and another from 2014. Originally, the databases had been sold legally, intended for Russian corporations that wanted to run background checks on job applicants. Other buyers were criminals who sought addresses of victims. When the databases become outdated, they ended up on Russian torrent sites. What Bellingcat has done is download as many as we can. By the time of the Skripal investigation, we had about 100 gigabytes on file – approximately a thousand separate databases.

Among these were leaked databases of Russian flight manifests, including the check-in details of who was aboard a plane. However, we lacked March 2018, when 'Petrov' and 'Boshirov' had travelled from Moscow to London. On the Russian internet, on-demand queries are possible, too – a black market for personal information. Going down that route pushed the boundaries of the Bellingcat method. We always prefer open sources; usually, that is all we need. Previously, we had crowd-sourced the purchase of satellite imagery in our MH17 investigations, buying material from an established vendor and posting the results online for all to see. Yet the source of this flight manifest would not be an established retailer. We found ourselves staring at a locked door, and knew where to buy the key.

We have had internal debates about such dilemmas before, and they help demarcate the ethical edges of the Bellingcat method. All our investigations, we believe, must be founded on open-source information. But in carefully judged situations we will build upon that base. Collaborations have always been essential for us, from back when our online community first took shape via Twitter, up to the most complex joint investigations of today. Our partners – rights activists, independent researchers, news organisations – employ more traditional techniques, including anonymising imperiled sources. We do not ignore such closed-source input. But when we go beyond open sources, we are careful never to assume that such information – because secretive – is more likely to be true. On the contrary, we employ heightened scepticism about such material, demanding an extra layer of corroboration.

In the case of the passenger manifest for the Moscow–London flight, we found somebody online with access to the Russian airlines' booking-data system and paid about €200 for the file. The flight manifest added two crucial datapoints: the suspects' purported birthdates and passport numbers. Suspiciously, these were only three digits apart. From here, we needed to cross-reference the data against identification documents that the Russian state holds on every citizen. As part of the Orion case, we had come across someone else online who boasted of accessing such dossiers through a personal connection at a government agency. In our Slack chats, we joked that the online braggart's 'personal connection' was probably his grandmother working in a dismal ministry office, riffling through filing cabinets after hours. From this, we came to nickname our source 'the Babushka', Russian for 'Granny'. Yet the Babushka was not helping for free. We would need to pay about €100 per identification dossier.

Before paying, we could check whether the Babushka even had what we sought. However, the name Boshirov is so odd in Russian that it would have drawn instant suspicion if we had requested that identification file, possibly prompting the Babushka to do an online search and realise the dangerous nature of the material we sought. By contrast, the other suspect's purported name, Alexander Petrov, was common. From the Aeroflot passenger list, we also had the claimed birthdate of Alexander Petrov. So we asked the Babushka if the government system contained files on anyone with this combination of name and birthdate. Four matches came back. To see the dossiers themselves meant paying yet again, which Aric called 'the nuclear option'. We hesitated. But the Kremlin disinformation machine provoked us – namely, that RT interview of the two supposed sports-nutrition salesmen, claiming rather stiltedly that they had visited Salisbury Cathedral to admire its spire.

Christo was in a business meeting, furtively checking his phone under the conference table, awaiting the four dossiers he had ordered. The Babushka must have been in the office, because all four arrived fast. Christo clicked on the first dossier of a Russian citizen called Alexander Petrov with the specified birthdate. He scanned down, seeking the ID photo. No, this was not our Petrov. Christo clicked the second dossier. Down he scrolled. Hurriedly, he thumbed in the words 'Found him' onto our Slack chat and uploaded the ID photo. Unmistakable: this was him. 'There are two odd things on his file,' Christo messaged us, uploading an official stamp found in the Petrov dossier: *Do Not Provide Any Information*. Also, the page of biographical data was blank, except for a handwritten note stating, 'There is a letter. S.S.' – an abbreviation for '*Sovershenno Sekretno*', Russian for 'Top Secret'.

'This shouts SPY,' Christo messaged us. 'This person's EXISTENCE begins in 2009. This is a fake identity … I think we have the story.'

According to the dossier, this man in his late thirties, 'Alexander Yevgeniyevich Petrov', had appeared in official files only in 2009. The office that issued his ID was not just another dusty bureaucratic outpost, but the special Moscow office that grants papers to Kremlin insiders and intelligence agents.

Putin had said of the suspects: 'They are civilians, of course … I can assure you that there is nothing special, nothing criminal here.'[12] He had lied, and we could prove it.

Bellingcat investigations often take months. But mere minutes had passed since the RT interview of 13 September 2018 had aired. 'Probably good to start writing on this now,' I messaged the others. 'It needs to be quick.'

BLOWING THEIR COVER

In Washington DC it was morning and our newest staff employee, editor Natalia Antonova, was sleepily reading Twitter. Until recently, Bellingcat had only half a dozen employees, supplemented by many volunteer contributors. However, we were on the cusp of a major expansion, converting our investigative hub from fledgling concept into a veritable organisation. Within a year, the staff would have tripled, allowing me to step back from an overabundance of roles (chief investigator, chief spokesman, chief editor, chief administrator, chief fundraiser).

Everyone, she discovered that morning, was abuzz about the suspects' interview on RT. Natalia had known Russian military officers like these. Though raised mostly in North Carolina, she had been born in Kiev with a grandfather who was a Soviet general. Natalia recognised immediately that 'Petrov' and 'Boshirov' did *not* want to be talking on TV like this. When the RT interviewer suggested an innocent explanation for their trip – perhaps they were just a gay couple on vacation together? – 'Petrov' and 'Boshirov' seemed barely able to contain their indignation. Natalia had to pause the video, she was laughing so hard.

The shameless fakery of that RT interview stirred memories of the Russian generals' press conference after the downing of MH17. Little motivates an open-source investigator as much as blatant lies. In this case, they spoke of the trip to Salisbury as long planned. Yet the Aeroflot passenger manifest showed they had booked their tickets and checked in online at 10 p.m. Moscow time the night before their flight.

The Petrov dossier contained other suspicious features, too. When we ordered dossiers for the four Russian men with that name and birthdate, the other three all had what any normal ID dossier would have contained: a full history of previous expired documents, including passports and previous addresses. But not the 'Alexander Petrov' who popped into existence in November 2009. And if he had no passport, why was there a passport number listed for him on the Aeroflot passenger manifest?[13]

Our first published piece on the Skripal suspects caused news organisations around the world to cover our work, sending a flood of readers to our website and stirring renewed concern about Moscow's lawless actions abroad. We expected the Russian media to gloss over it, but we were wrong. Both pro-Kremlin and anti-Kremlin media jumped on the case. This was blowing up faster than we had expected. One Russian news outlet acquired the dossier of the other suspect, 'Ruslan Timurovich Boshirov', and it included a photo of the anxious fair-haired man with the goatee from the RT interview. His dossier had suspicious markings, too, with the *Do Not Provide Any Information* stamp, plus the handwritten 'Top Secret' annotation with reference to an explanatory letter. Again, an issuing authority reserved for state VIPs and intelligence officers had created the identification – this time, in 2010.

Beneath the *Do Not Provide Any Information* stamp was a series of digits that looked like a phone number. Russian reporters called it. The Russian Defence Ministry answered, seemingly GRU headquarters. The Insider acquired border-crossing data for 'Petrov' and 'Boshirov', showing their travels in various countries in Europe from mid-2016 to September 2018, around the time we first published our article on the dubious Petrov identity. The two men had taken numerous flights, including to London, Paris, Amsterdam, Frankfurt, Geneva and Tel Aviv. European news media outlets reported in spring 2018 that two unidentified Russian spies had been briefly detained in Dutch territory, apparently linked to attempts to hack into the Speiz laboratory in Switzerland, which investigated chemical attacks in Syria and had looked into the nerve agent used against the Skripals.[14]

These were not sports-nutrition salesmen, and Petrov and Boshirov were not their names. Our hypothesis was that they were GRU officers, carrying out clandestine acts in Western Europe, so we reached out to former Russian military officers to ask where future GRU agents might have been trained fifteen to twenty years earlier, when 'Boshirov' and 'Petrov' would probably have started their careers. During that period, the Far Eastern Military Command Academy had an excellent reputation for training overseas covert operatives. On social media, we found incomplete yearbook photos and reunion galleries from the time, but no certain matches. A 2018 article on the history of the academy mentioned seven graduates who had gone on to receive the prestigious Hero of the Russian Federation Award. We also found a photo of graduates, deployed on snowy ground in Chechnya. In the top row, there was one man who looked a little like 'Boshirov'. The resemblance was not enough to go on, but it inspired us to try adding 'Chechnya' into online searches for the Russian acronym of the Far Eastern Military Command Academy, 'DVOKU', along with 'Hero of the Russian Federation'. This landed us on the website of a state-run civil-defence force, which mentioned a colonel by the name of Anatoliy Chepiga. We ran his name through Google as well as two Russian search engines, but found nothing. No social-media profiles. No images. The Hero of the Russian Federation is the country's highest state award, personally decreed by the president. Most are presented in public. The man's online invisibility was suspicious.

We went through our collection of leaked Russian databases and found references to Anatoliy Chepiga twice: in Khabarovsk, far south-eastern Russia, near the border with China (2003); and Moscow (2012). His contact information in Khabarovsk was listed as 'в/ч 20662' – a Russian abbreviation for Military Unit 20662, the *Spetsnaz* unit of GRU's 14th Brigade. The elite *Spetsnaz* unit under GRU command played a role in the Second Chechen War, and was recorded near Ukraine in late 2014. The website of the military volunteer organisation stated that Chepiga's Hero of Russia prize had been awarded 'for conducting a peacekeeping mission' – intriguing because, in 2014, there were no military activities in Chechnya, nor was Russia yet directly involved in the Syrian conflict, leaving only one active theatre: eastern Ukraine. The database listing from 2012 showed Anatoliy Vladimirovich Chepiga, born 5 April 1979, residing in Moscow. What we needed was an image of Chepiga to see if he was 'Ruslan Boshirov'. No matter how we searched, no picture of the man appeared in open sources. We had not wanted to ask the Babushka for a dossier in the unusual name Boshirov because it would have set off alarm bells, but as yet the public associated nothing with the name Chepiga. So we took the chance; we bought his ID dossier. And we had him: his photo, dated around 2003. 'Boshirov' was Colonel Anatoliy Chepiga.[15]

When we published it caused the biggest stir of any Bellingcat article to date, with headlines around the world trumpeting our findings while marvelling that a bunch of citizen investigators had somehow outed a Russian 'hit team'. Online, the Counterfactual Community raged against us with predictable nonsense. Putin's spokesman Dmitry Peskov insisted there was 'no data' that anyone called Anatoliy Chepiga had ever received the Hero of Russia award. He also denied that 'Boshirov' and Chepiga looked identical, claiming that any similarity was mere coincidence. Five separate news outlets tracked down people who had known Chepiga – they confirmed that the Boshirov who appeared in the RT interview was indeed Anatoliy Chepiga.

Reporters from Radio Svoboda in Prague went through social-media photos and videos of those who had visited or attended the Far Eastern Military Command Academy, seeking a high-resolution image of the school's Wall of Heroes, which featured graduates who had won the highest state honour. A portrait at the far end of the wall, which went up at some point between July 2014 and March 2016, might have been Chepiga, but the image resolution was not clear enough to say for sure. We picked up the trail, finding on the Russian social network Odnoklassniki a visitor's image of the school from June 2017, clearly displaying a new entry on the wall of heroes, including his name: Colonel Anatoly Chepiga.[16]

Putin issued a foul-tempered denial, not sounding terribly innocent when he called Skripal 'a scumbag' and 'a traitor to the motherland'. Later, the Russian foreign minister, Sergey Lavrov, added his disapproval. 'Bellingcat is closely connected with the intelligence services, which use it to channel information intended to influence public opinion,' he said.

While the media storm engulfed us, British and Dutch authorities were disclosing the identities of those four other Russians, believed to be part of the GRU's cyberwarfare division, who had visited the Netherlands in April 2018, aiming to hack into the Organisation for the Prohibition of Chemical Weapons. One of the men's names turned up in a leaked Russian database on vehicle ownership. The address where he had registered his Lada was Komsomolsky Prospekt 20, the GRU's cyberwarfare department. This prompted us to try a reverse search of the vehicle database for this same address, revealing 305 people who had registered their cars to this address, including full names, ages, passport numbers, mobile phone numbers. We had stumbled onto one of the most extraordinary breaches of covert-officer IDs in espionage history.

This was only a jaw-dropping diversion from the Skripal case. For now, we focused on finding the true name of the remaining Skripal suspect, 'Alexander Petrov'. Our starting point was photos of this person from three sources: the RT interview; the initial press release of the British police; and the Petrov identity dossier. We got nowhere trying reverse image searches, so pored over social-media photos and videos of graduates of the Far Eastern Military School, in case he had attended like the other suspect. No luck. So we checked group photos of the *Spetsnaz* unit that Chepiga once belonged to. Again, nothing.

In the Petrov dossier, there was a reference to a previous identity document, issued in St Petersburg in 1999. We searched dozens of leaked databases, but found no sign of the supposed document number, so concluded that this was a faked corroboration. But why was St Petersburg mentioned? When we had previously identified a GRU officer involved in a Montenegro coup plot, we found that his undercover persona retained his true first name, birthdate and birthplace, changing only his surname. Perhaps the same was true for 'Petrov', whose first name and patronymic were given as Alexander Yevgeniyevich and whose cover birthdate was 13 July 1979. We took those details and punched them into leaked databases from St Petersburg that listed residents, phone subscribers, vehicle owners. The only matches were from 2003 and 2006, someone with the first name and patronymic of Alexander Yevgeniyevich plus the birthdate. His last name was Mishkin. The database included a phone number that was out of service. But this was still a possible datapoint. We searched our leaked St Petersburg databases for the phone number, seeking other residents who had once been linked to it. Eight people came up in the 2003 and 2006 databases, suggesting a shared apartment of the type common during Soviet times and later used by students. We checked the address on Yandex Maps. It was across from the Military Medical Academy.

The Petrov identity dossier was registered in Moscow, so we sought traces of this new name, Alexander Yevgenyevich Mishkin, in the Russian capital. An open-source phone database turned up a mobile number. We fed this number, with his name, into the leaked Moscow databases and found a match to car insurance from 2013 for a Volvo XC90. From an official Russian database of registration histories, we learned that it had been imported, registered first in St Petersburg in 2012, then transferred to the Khoroshevsky District of Moscow — the district of the GRU headquarters. That was tantalising but not conclusive. We found a website selling a more recent car insurance database, dated 2014. This had a precise registration address for Alexander Mishkin's Volvo: Khoroshevskoye Shosse 76B, also known as GRU headquarters.

On Russian social-media networks we contacted hundreds of graduates who had attended the same medical academy in the early years of the century, coinciding with the presumptive period of Mishkin's study there. Most never responded. Many said they were not aware of anyone named Mishkin. But one person, who insisted on anonymity, confirmed that Alexander Mishkin had graduated from the academy, and that he was the man posing as 'Petrov' in the RT interview. The source explained that Russian security services had been contacting those from Mishkin's class, telling them not to divulge his identity.

With the Kremlin security apparatus clamping down, we could not risk pressing the Babushka for more identity dossiers without endangering the person. But we did manage to obtain from another source a scanned copy of Mishkin's 2001 identity document. The source did not want us to reveal the slightest description of them, making this information about as closed-source as you could get. But the document included a photo of Mishkin, and it was the man from the RT interview. To verify the picture, we contacted an expert in simulated age progression; this was Hassan Ugail, professor of visual computing at the University of Bradford. He conducted a forensic facial-similarity analysis between the Mishkin ID photo from 2001 and the 'Petrov' passport photo from 2016 and confirmed unequivocally: they were the same person.

The Insider took one last step. Just before publication of our exposé on Mishkin, Roman dispatched a reporter to the birthplace mentioned in the 2001 identity document: Loyga, a village in northern Russia of about a thousand residents so remote it had no access by road, reached only by narrow-gauge railway. The reporter spoke to various locals there, and all recognised 'Petrov' from the RT interview as local boy Mishkin. Several described him as a military doctor who had received the Hero of Russia award a few years earlier. One person said that Mishkin's grandmother – an elderly former doctor revered in the village – cherished a photo of Putin bestowing the award on Mishkin and shaking his hand. This same person said the reason for the honour had been secret but that locals understood it pertained either to the Russian annexation of Crimea in 2014, or to helping the former Ukrainian president Viktor Yanukovych, presumably assisting him to flee to Russia that same year.

We published our investigation, and the story blew up again.[17] We had now identified the two-man 'hit squad': a war-hardened GRU colonel, Anatoliy Chepiga, along with a Russian military doctor, Alexander Mishkin, who perhaps attended to maintain their safety around the nerve agent. Yet this, we discovered, was not the entire 'kill team'.

THE THIRD MAN

British counter-terrorism police and security services reportedly believed that another Russian officer had undertaken a reconnaissance mission before the poisoning.[18] The Russian news site Fontanka wrote that a forty-five-year-old, travelling as 'Sergey Fedotov', had flown to London the same day as the two suspects but on a different flight – and with a passport number suspiciously close to theirs.[19] With The Insider, we obtained the travel records of a forty-five-year-old using the name Sergey Vyacheslavovich Fedotov. His ID had come into existence in 2010. This 'Fedotov' happened to have visited Bulgaria days before a prominent local businessman, his son and a third person had been mysteriously poisoned a few years earlier.[20]

For months we tried to crack the identity of 'Fedotov'. It proved harder than Chepiga and Mishkin, whose photos the British authorities had provided, and who RT exposed in the television interview. This time, we had little besides a fake name. In collaboration with The Insider, the Czech news organisation Respekt and the Finnish newspaper *Helsingin Sanomat*, we searched online for clues, but the Kremlin was eliminating details on all three men from public records.

Picking up the reporting of Fontanka, we obtained passenger records of 'Sergey Fedotov', whose flight from Russia had left a few hours before that of the two suspects, landing at Heathrow Airport rather than Gatwick. We ran his name and birthdate through our hundreds of leaked databases, finding four possible matches, including one Moscow address under 'Sergey Vyacheslavovich Fedotov'. Right away, there were peculiarities. The Moscow residential databases gave the person's birthplace as Apushka, a small village in north-eastern Russia. But in that region's databases, no such person appeared. Supposedly, 'Fedotov' worked for a company called Business-Courier that existed between 2004 and 2008, yet it showed no sign of ever having operated. Also, his registered address pointed to an apartment owned by an entirely different family named Fedotov.

At this point, Christo reached out to a contact with access to the police travel-tracking database who gave us details from the Fedotov passport file. As with 'Petrov' and 'Boshirov', the issuing office was the same one known to grant travel documents and passports to VIPs and intelligence officers. What we needed was a picture of 'Fedotov'. For this, we sought to acquire a copy of his domestic ID from a source with access to the central Russian database, RosPassport. But no such record existed. We knew that such an ID file had existed at some point – the police travel-tracking database contained details of his passport. The only explanation was that the Russian authorities were wiping Fedotov files. We were not going to find his picture in Russian records, so tried to think where else he might have left his image. We checked border-crossing authorities in various countries that he had visited, even hotels where he had stayed. Finally, a source sent us a photo of his scanned passport, and we had the man's face.

We still did not have his true name. Knowing that GRU officers sometimes adopt a fake identity based on their own, we searched hundreds of residential databases for the 'Fedotov' first name and patronymic, alongside the claimed birthdate. We got nowhere, so we tried the first name 'Sergey' and his birthdate. This brought up too many results, none of them suspicious. We tried just the birthdate and patronymic, 'Vyacheslavovich'. This presented fifteen hits in the Moscow residential database of 2012. One stood out. The person had an address at Narodnoe Opolchenie 50, the dormitory of the Military Diplomatic Academy, known in Russia as the GRU Conservatory, a place that turns out a hundred elite intelligence officers every year. His full name was Denis Vyacheslavovich Sergeev.

We plugged that back into the other leaked databases, getting more hits, some citing his address as Military Unit 22177 – again, the GRU Conservatory. From leaked domestic-travel databases, we found records of train journeys between Moscow and St Petersburg in joint bookings with people whose residences or cars had been registered to Khoroshevskoye Shosse 76B, the GRU headquarters. Yet finding a photo of Denis Sergeev to compare with the passport photo of 'Fedotov' proved all but impossible. The Russian authorities had purged him from public records.

We worked backwards from a hypothesis. The GRU Conservatory was most likely to recruit from special-forces units, especially those with fighting experience. As it happened, the name Denis Sergeev turned up in a book describing 1999 fighting in the Russian republic of Dagestan. That year, an Islamist group from neighbouring Chechnya had invaded Dagestan. The Russian military soon regained control, driving back the Islamists, but the fighting led to the Second Chechen War. In 1999, Sergeev was a paratroop commander who had been wounded in a bid to recapture territory from Chechen fighters. We discovered a documentary from the time, detailing the battle and including interviews with Sergeev.

We provided a screen grab from the documentary and the passport photo of 'Fedotov' to Professor Ugail, who had conducted the facial-similarity analysis of the Mishkin photos. In this case, the scanned passport photo of 'Fedotov' was low-resolution while the documentary image was from nearly twenty years earlier. Ugail used a machine-learning algorithm that had been trained on millions of faces. A result above 70 per cent is deemed sufficient to confirm identify. The match was 78.2 per cent.[21]

The remaining question was what Sergeev's role might have been. We teamed up with BBC's *Newsnight*, whose sources said that Sergeev held the rank of major general, meaning he would have outranked Chepiga and Mishkin, so may have been their commanding officer, overseeing the operation. A contact at a Russian mobile operator provided us with metadata from a phone number registered under Sergeev's cover persona, Fedotov. This showed all movements of Sergeev's phone over the course of two years, from May 2017 to May 2019, including the date of the Skripal attack. In Russia, his daily routine involved commuting from his residence to GRU offices, including the headquarters on Khoroshevskoye Shosse. One unexpected call to 'Fedotov' confirmed the link: it came from Sergeev's wife.

We were able to recreate Sergeev's movements on the days around the Skripal poisoning, starting with his purchase the evening before his flight of a ticket to London. He turned up early at the airport, but the Aeroflot flight was delayed by two hours. While waiting, he communicated using Telegram, Viber, WhatsApp and Facebook Messenger, and also received a call from someone whose number we identified via the phone-number sharing app GetContact as 'Amir – Moscow'. This person was a key contact throughout the London trip.

Sergeev landed at Heathrow Airport at 10:33 a.m. local time, and made his way to central London, reaching a hotel near Paddington Station. He hardly left his room for the next two days, spending considerable time on his smartphone. Nor did Sergeev seem to trust the wifi, expending more than a gigabyte of cellular data in two days. We do not know whether he was using encrypted messaging apps like Telegram to communicate with the 'hit team', but his usage seemed to include file transfers, some the size of high-resolution photos and some large enough to be videos. Otherwise, he exchanged mobile calls with only one number, 'Amir – Moscow', with whom he communicated eleven times from London. The Amir number lacked the normal owner-identification details and metadata footprint, meaning it was probably a special unregistered number available only to Russian security services.

When the two-man 'hit squad' undertook their first brief foray to Salisbury, probably for reconnaissance, Sergeev remained in London, venturing once from his hotel, his smartphone pinging a cell phone tower near Oxford Circus around midday, then connecting again near the Embankment several times between noon and 1:30 p.m. According to the British police timeline, Chepiga and Mishkin left for Salisbury at 12:50 p.m. that day from Waterloo Station, a ten-minute walk from the Embankment. Might their suspected minder have met the 'hit team' in person, conveying instructions, even an object? We can only guess.

That evening, after Chepiga and Mishkin returned from their first trip to Salisbury, Sergeev again spoke by phone twice with 'Amir – Moscow'. On the morning of the poisonings, Sergeev was at his Paddington hotel, once again communicating with 'Amir – Moscow'. Next, Sergeev hurried to Heathrow for his scheduled flight back to Russia, arriving at Terminal 4 around the time that the 'hit squad' reached Skripal's home in Salisbury. By the time Sergeev's Aeroflot flight was cruising back to Moscow,[22] Sergei and Yulia were near death.

UNIT 29155 AND 'THE LABORATORY'

Covert operations took place around Europe, from attempted murder to the sabotage of nations that failed to align with Moscow. And the same operatives kept turning up. GRU officers appeared in Bellingcat investigations into the annexation of Crimea (2014); the destabilisation of Moldova (2014); an assassination attempt against a Bulgarian arms manufacturer (2015); a failed coup in Montenegro (2016); attempts to target the World Anti-Doping

Agency in Switzerland (2016–17); the destabilisation of Spain during the Catalonia independence referendum (2017); and the Skripal poisonings (2018). The assassination attempt in Salisbury looked like part of something far larger.

To delve into this we returned to the three confirmed identities of the alleged Skripal attackers: Anatoliy Chepiga aka 'Ruslan Boshirov', Dr Alexander Mishkin aka 'Alexander Petrov' and Denis Sergeev aka 'Sergey Fedotov'. Those names we plugged into leaked travel records, studying where they had travelled and with whom. Bit by bit, we compiled a list of names, each of which we fed back into our leaked databases, seeking tell-tale signs of GRU fakery, such as passport numbers in sequence with other known operatives.

In parallel, we scrutinised phone metadata obtained on 'the third man' in the Skripal operation to see which numbers he had contacted. Each name that came up we plugged into reverse phone directory searches, discovering fresh names which we fed back into our leaked databases of addresses, car registrations and other identity documents. One phone number that kept appearing belonged to someone called Andrey Averyanov. We searched for this name on social media, but found no profiles. So we sought his phone metadata, too. You might expect anyone with access to Russian mobile-phone records to be fearful of cooperating with Bellingcat after we had published high-profile articles about operatives trying to murder Kremlin opponents. Yet our findings had troubled enough people that Christo was able to develop a small network of contacts at various Russian mobile operators who were willing to share data. We obtained phone records on several more suspected GRU officers in this group, and conducted a correlation analysis, learning which numbers had been called by all or most of the others.

Combining our research into the leaked travel records and the phone metadata, we compiled a list of names, which stopped expanding at about thirty officers, twenty of whom worked internationally, each with combat experience alongside skills ranging from signals intelligence (intercepting and deciphering communications) to medicine. What stood out in Averyanov's phone records was how much contact he had made with nearly all of them. Somehow, this man connected to everyone else. He himself had travelled undercover a couple of times – once to Vienna, another time to Lisbon, and once – coincidentally, just a few weeks after the MH17 downing – to Amsterdam. But relative to the other team members, he seemed to prefer to stay in Moscow.

On 8 October 2019, while we were still working out Averyanov's exact role, the *New York Times* disclosed his name, citing unidentified intelligence sources as saying that he led Unit 29155, described in the article as a secret team behind the assassination attempts and destabilisation that Bellingcat had detailed.[23] We fact-checked the *Times* article via open sources and leaked databases, and found a few inaccuracies. Public registries confirmed that the Unit 29155 commander was indeed Major General Andrey Vladimirovich Averyanov, a man of around fifty at the time of the Skripal attack. Yet the unit comprised about 300 officers and, according to Russian military chat forums, it served as a training unit for GRU special ops.[24] In other words, 29155 was not the murder and subversion team but a larger unit that *contained* this elite group of about thirty officers, some twenty of whom travelled around Europe carrying out undercover operations. Another small inaccuracy was the *Times*' assertion that Averyanov 'lives in a run-down Soviet-era building a few blocks from the unit's headquarters and drives a 1996 VAZ 21053, a rattletrap Russia-made sedan'. According to our leaked databases, his lifestyle was not so humble. The general owned desirable Western cars,[25] and his true residence was an exclusive closed compound in the Moscow suburbs.

A tantalising clue in the *Times* article was its reference to a 2017 photograph, which purportedly showed Chepiga at the wedding of Averyanov's daughter. The *New York Times* did not publish the photo, showing only a cropped image of the general at the ceremony. A Bellingcat Investigation Team – led by Christo, with Aric, Daniel Romein and Pieter van Huis – set out to find the cited image, scouring social media for postings about such a wedding. Since Averyanov had no social-media presence, we sought out his family circle. In residential databases, we searched his address for the female version of his last name, Averyanova, finding his wife's identity. She had no evident social-media accounts either. Broader searches for the name Averyanov turned up accounts of a man with a resemblance to the GRU general – his brother, it turned out. Bit by bit, we were closing in, finding cousins and uncles, charting a family tree and finally learning the name of the newly married daughter.

She had Instagram and VK accounts, and we shared these with colleagues at Radio Free Europe/Radio Liberty, who were working on the same investigation. In her 'friends' lists, they noticed, was a videographer at a wedding-planning company, which marketed its services with high-resolution images on its website. Among these was a lavish wedding held during the summer of 2017 in Senezh, a small town outside Moscow notable as the training base of Unit 29155. We identified other guests at this wedding who had posted videos on Instagram and YouTube, including images of Chepiga. The wedding planners' website even included a picture of the seating plan. Chepiga – according to the Kremlin an innocent sports-nutrition salesman with no link to Russian covert operations – was seated at the table of General Averyanov[26] of the GRU.

When we analysed the phone metadata of members of Unit 29155, one number stood out, belonging to someone named Sergey Chepur, with whom Averyanov had exchanged at least sixty-five calls and text messages between May 2017 and September 2019. A web search showed that Chepur was a chemistry professor and director of the State Experimental Institute for Scientific Research in Military Medicine, at Lesoparkovaya Street No. 4 in St Petersburg. Our investigative partners at The Insider sent a journalist to this site on the sleepy outskirts of the city, discovering a drab complex of buildings at the edge of a forested area. When the journalist tried to take pictures, soldiers blocked him.

We pored over academic papers, textbooks, patent applications and public procurements, seeking to understand Chepur's career and the institute he led, which we nicknamed The Laboratory. Its structure and purpose were not public, but we did find a dissertation from 2016 that it had certified, listing its leading scientists and their fields of expertise: 'extreme toxicology' and 'neurochemistry'. Chepur joined with colleagues to register a patent in 2010 for an invention 'intended for inhalation of the introduction of pharmacologically active substances into the body' that would affect 'the central nervous system, peripheral neurotransmitter processes, the cardiovascular system'. Another scientist at The Laboratory, G. A. Sofronov, worked on a textbook called *Extreme Toxicology*, defined as 'dealing with the toxicity of chemical compounds able to inflict massive damage on a human population in extraordinary situations and military operations'. The Laboratory's deputy director, V. N. Bikov, along with other affiliated scientists, and with Chepur himself, had published articles on the inhalation of chemical compounds and related to 'poisoning by organophosphate compounds'. One notable organophosphate poison[27] is the nerve agent used against the Skripals: Novichok.

According to Chepur's phone metadata, he was in regular contact with Averyanov long before the attack. On 30 December 2017, Chepur contacted Dr Mishkin, too. In the weeks leading up to the 4 March 2018 assassination attempt, Chepur held several more conversations with Averyanov and Mishkin, and also communicated with the suspected third man in the Skripal 'hit team', Sergeev. Chepur was especially busy on 23 February 2018, which is Defender of the Fatherland Day, when members of the Russian military exchange celebratory greetings. He engaged in more than 600 phone calls or texts that day, including to Averyanov, Mishkin and another medical officer of the elite murder and subversion team. On 27 February 2018, three days before the Skripal 'hit squad' departed for London, Chepur was in Moscow, according to his phone metadata, visiting the district where GRU headquarters is located at Khoroshevskoye Shosse 76B.

Another notable number with which Chepur communicated belonged to Sergey Kuhotkin, director of the 33rd Central Experimental Institute for Scientific Research in the small town of Shikhany, about 500 miles south-east of Moscow on the Volga River. According to weapons experts, this town contained military units during Soviet times involved in chemical, biological and radiation warfare, and it was where scientists developed Novichok[28] in the 1970s. In 2008, Kuhotkin told the official newspaper of the Russian Defence Ministry that the institute still employed more than 100 scientists working in forty laboratories, 'conducting research in the interest of all military divisions and units'.[29] On a single day in the leadup to the Skripal attack, 13 January 2018, Chepur was in communication with Kuhotkin, Averyanov and Mishkin. Three months after the failed Skripal attack, Kuhotkin stepped down as head of the Shikhany institute. In response to our investigation, Mr Sergey Chepur said he had never spoken to any of Alexander Mishkin, Denis Sergeev or Andrey Averyanov.

He also appeared to clearly remember that he did not visit the GRU headquarters on 27 February 2018. Before hanging up, he advised us to 'stop lying to everyone, including to yourselves'. Two and a half years later, after the Novichok poisoning of Russian opposition leader Alexey Navalny, the US placed sanctions on the Shikhany institute, suggesting its intelligence saw a link between it and the substance used in that attack.

The phone metadata also revealed an intriguing absence: call records of Averyanov and members of the elite murder and subversion team had been cleansed immediately around the time of the Skripal attack, so you cannot see what interactions took place just before and after the crime. Yet something remarkable is evident a few months later. In September and October 2018 – right after we had disclosed the identities of the Skripal suspects – Averyanov placed six calls to the office of Sergey Lavrov, the foreign minister and one of President Vladimir Putin's most loyal allies, followed by several calls to and from FSB's director of counter-intelligence. Soon thereafter, Lavrov began publicly maligning Bellingcat.[30]

As for the elite murder and subversion team, we suspect that our investigations led to its disbandment. Since our reports, we have tracked members' locations and found several reassigned to remote areas, given important-sounding administrative jobs but with all signs pointing to them being demoted. What we cannot say is whether the GRU has since created a replacement.

Some observers look upon these exposed operations and suggest that the elite team was a failed enterprise. More likely, what we uncovered was just a fraction of its operations, the few that slipped into public view. Either way, these operations present a glimpse of how brazen Moscow had become about committing violent crimes on foreign soil. With Bellingcat exposing such brutality, people began asking whether we ourselves were in danger.

THE RISKS

After the TV interview in which the alleged Skripal 'hit team' claimed to have been tourists at Salisbury Cathedral, RT sent out its annual Christmas present. That year, the gift was a chocolate cathedral. It seemed peculiar to joke about an assassination attempt that killed an innocent civilian – unless you wanted to pretend that nothing is serious, everything is questionable and blame is impossible.

Bellingcat represents the opposite conviction, which is why Moscow holds us in contempt. While its media mouthpieces make jokes, the military wing of the Kremlin is deadly serious. Even before the Skripal attack, US intelligence believed that Russian agents and mobsters had assassinated fourteen people on British soil in recent years, according to a BuzzFeed News investigation. Some died of suspicious 'suicides'; others had dubious heart attacks.[31]

Christo has faced Twitter diatribes that veered into specific threats. He informed the police and remains determined. Roman has courage that outstrips us all, residing in Russia while exposing the misdeeds of its upper echelon. He aims to keep safe by staying in the spotlight, especially joining forces with foreign organisations like Bellingcat. Eliminating one person would not silence the reporting. It would only amplify it, as was the case with the murdered Saudi journalist Jamal Khashoggi.

The biggest danger, in my view, is not a state actor. It is the troubled individual, someone who has bought into the most virulent falsehoods of the Counterfactual Community and decides that we should be taken out. I frequently receive anonymous messages containing violent threats. It is difficult to know how to react: you're probably just dealing with an idiot who wants to upset you, but the person could intend to harm you.

Robert Evans, after writing about the shitposting in the Christchurch gunman's manifesto, found a post on 8chan of his own face photoshopped into a 'Wanted' poster, with a bullet hole in his forehead and the promise of a fifteen-bitcoin bounty – approximately $60,000 at the time. The one-word message was 'bump'. Another 8chan poster responded: 'Unironically? For that much it can be done.' This was probably an empty boast. But 8chan 'pranks' have a way of turning into real bloodshed.

In another instance, we were investigating Ukrainian neo-Nazis through the Bellingcat Anti-Equality Monitoring group, which studies fascist movements targeting the LGBT community, feminists and ethnic minorities in Ukraine, Armenia and Kyrgyzstan. One of these reports told of how Ukrainian neo-Nazis were publishing the Christchurch manifesto in bound form.[32] They emailed death threats to two of our investigators, warning that the 'Day Of The Rope is close, nigger.' The emails included a video titled 'Fuck the kikes' in which photos of our team members and other journalists were placed in a forest and shot. We informed the authorities, and kept working. We still had more to say about the rise of the Ukrainian extreme right, and kept saying it.

Cyberattack is another persistent danger. I have already described the attempt of the Russian military intelligence group Fancy Bear to hack us in 2015 and 2016, but a further phishing campaign came to light in 2019, targeting more than thirty users of the encrypted email service ProtonMail, including Christo and Roman, as well as journalists from the *Guardian* and the BBC, employees of NGOs, private investigators and academics. All of those targeted had a common trait: they were studying Russia. In parallel, Roman faced an offline attack on his communications, when his mobile phone stopped working in August 2019. Roman contacted his mobile provider, MTS, but they told him that he had picked up a replacement SIM card that day. He had not. To obtain a replacement SIM, you have to visit an MTS service centre and present your passport. Someone had either impersonated Roman with a fake passport, or had otherwise compromised the security of MTS, the leading mobile operator in Russia.[33]

The danger to open-source investigators goes beyond physical and digital threats; there is also the psychological damage. After the Christchurch mosque shootings, Andy Carvin – by then a senior fellow at the Atlantic Council's Digital Forensic Research Lab – wrote a powerful warning. Like me, he had watched hours and hours of violent imagery online, from the Columbine massacre, to the Boston bombings, to the Libyan conflict, to the Syrian civil war. How else to gather open-source evidence, if not by looking unsparingly? After each story, Carvin moved to the next. Until, walking down a street in Washington, he noticed a head of cauliflower squashed on the road. His chest pounded and he started hyperventilating: he was experiencing a panic attack, triggered by a visual echo of online footage that he had seen of battle wounds, including a skull smashed apart.

'Over time, the panic attacks were complemented by nightmares and intrusive imagery,' Carvin recounted. 'I imagined seeing my kids playing at home, then suddenly caught in a war zone or terrorist attack. The imagery would pop into my head during meetings, at dinner, hanging out with friends, taking out the trash. There was no obvious way for me to mitigate them. Eventually, I began to feel a fight-or-flight response when out in public, especially with my family. On one occasion we attended a July 4th parade, and I found myself scrutinizing cars parked across the road. For some reason, I was making a mental note of which direction they faced in case there was a mass shooting and we needed to duck behind a car's engine block for safety.'

He sought help and was diagnosed with post-traumatic stress disorder, PTSD[34] – the condition long associated with soldiers haunted by horrors on the battlefield. Psychologists have come to identify another variety of PTSD, 'vicarious trauma' or 'secondary trauma'. Gavin Rees, of the Columbia School of Journalism's Dart Center on trauma, explains that the intellect and body can get out of sync. We know that the horrifying events on video happened far away but the nervous system kicks in as if it were close at hand. 'The reason we're coming across it more and more now is because of the surfeit of traumatic imagery that is flooding into people's newsrooms and also through social media – so particularly thinking of things like beheading videos made by ISIS or the carnage and horror of barrel bombs exploding in Syria. It's this kind of footage that is coming in the newsroom in a raw and unmediated form,'[35] he says.

Passing exposure to traumatic imagery may cause only fleeting distress. The serious problems come from a slow-drip effect of repeated exposure.[36] At Bellingcat, most staff investigators have spent hours staring at strewn body parts, and we have learned to compartmentalise, to separate what we watch from our own existence. But consider Carvin, who seemed fine, then was struck down. You believe you can handle it, until you abruptly cannot. Nor can you forget all that you have seen and heard. The worst impact is from the material that catches you unprepared. In my own experience, when watching conflict footage, I expected to see people shot and dying, and I braced myself for it. But when sifting through MH17 wreckage photos, I glimpsed a child's toy exactly like one belonging to my daughter, and it shook me.

Storyful, which has dedicated itself to poring over social-media content for years, has set up sensible practices for dealing with the psychological burden, cycling people out of assignments where they are subjected to troubling material, and holding group sessions to debrief. By contrast, I have heard troubling stories about a prominent rights organisation where staffers were told to suck it up, that it was simply part of the job. Much negative behaviour ensued, including substance abuse, sexual problems and inappropriate behaviour at work.

To address the problem of vicarious trauma, we published a Bellingcat guide to identifying and preventing it, by an experienced open-source investigator, Hannah Ellis, who noted that personal connections to material intensify your emotional response: the victim resembles someone you know, or it is from a part of the world you are familiar with. This means that intimate knowledge of a subject – that which makes you expert – also makes you vulnerable. In our years of investigating the downing of MH17, I always avoided engaging with family members of the victims. In hindsight, I realise why: it was an instinctive need to block an emotional connection with the imagery I studied. To carry out the work, I must see objects as evidence, not be distracted by their emotional weight.

Citizen investigators should investigate themselves now and then. We must pay attention to shifts in our behaviour, if we are sleeping more than normal or less, suffering nightmares, losing our appetite or eating to excess, becoming more isolated and pushing people away, drinking more or using drugs[37] to self-medicate. Taking breaks from the screen makes a difference. And social support – opening up to others who are viewing similar material – builds resilience. Lastly, we must ask ourselves: do we need to see everything that is out there? The internet makes it so easy. That does not mean we should click, as I regrettably did on the Christchurch shooting video. Nobody needs that footage lodged in their memory.

Back to the question of physical safety, I stay as careful as I believe necessary. There are certain countries I do not visit; you can probably guess which. But beyond sensible precautions, I find no reason to panic. Our opponents could try to harm me. Yet Bellingcat has become far more than a single person. In the year after our first Skripal investigations, Bellingcat opened our first office, a proper workspace in The Hague added to the mailing address in Leicester. We hired a business director, a data scientist and administrative experts, too, nearing twenty staffers – still nimble and innovative but with the heft of an established enterprise. While it's true that I could do little to stop an attack, our opponents could do nothing to stop what we are becoming.

5

Next Steps

The future of justice and the power of AI

Eighteen men in orange jumpsuits knelt on the ground, hands tied behind their backs, hoods over their heads. Standing beside them, a bearded Libyan man read in Arabic from a piece of paper, informing the prisoners of what awaited. Five gunmen raised their assault rifles, fired and five hooded victims fell forward. Next a second row, then a third. Lastly, a trio of kneeling men remained. The gunshots sounded. According to text posted alongside this Facebook video, the victims were 'terrorists' executed on 17 July 2017, in Benghazi.

Back in 2011, Libya had been the source of my first attempts at online sleuthing. Six years later, I found myself studying conflict from the country again. But much had changed. The endeavour was not just fact-finding anymore; it had become a question of justice.

The case of Mahmoud al-Werfalli, the bearded Libyan whose death squad carried out those summary executions and posted them to Facebook, marked a turning point in the history of open-source investigation. Libya suffered years of violence after the fall of Gaddafi. A dominant armed group was the Libyan National Army, led by the ageing General Khalifa Haftar and with a brutal special-forces unit, Al-Saiqa Brigade, which included Werfalli. In August 2017, the International Criminal Court issued an arrest warrant, accusing Werfalli of thirty-three murders over the previous year in the Benghazi area.[1] For the first time in history, nearly all the evidence came from social-media postings.

Back in March 2015 I had participated in a panel discussion in Istanbul about activism and the social-media videos pouring out of Syria.[2] A soft-spoken Syrian in the audience, who had worked for an organisation filming protests, said that he and his colleagues initially believed that broadcasting would inhibit Assad forces from committing atrocities akin to the notorious Hama massacre from 1982, when the regime had murderously crushed an uprising far from public view. Yet the world *had* watched this time, and the violence had not stopped. What was the value,[3] the Syrian activist asked, of risking one's life for this stuff? The question never left me. They risked death, and we studied footage. A Bellingcat article might follow, plus a brief spurt of attention on Twitter, and a smattering of news reports. But was that destined to be the end? The Werfalli case suggested that Bellingcat had prospects beyond uncovering newsworthy facts. Whether we considered it or not, we dealt in legal evidence now, often the first in the world to discover it, and the only ones archiving it. Our responsibilities had grown considerably.

We decided to dig into the seven videos cited in the Werfalli arrest warrant, to see exactly what the footage exposed, explain it to the public and lend our expertise to prosecutors so that they might understand better what they had. Our first step was to geolocate as many of the seven videos as possible, and we invited the public to join through the crowd-verification platform Check.[4] In the Facebook footage of that mass murder on the dusty lot in Benghazi, Werfalli mentioned the date when reeling off the execution decree. From this, we could measure shadows with the SunCalc app, and establish the war crime as taking place at 6:37 a.m. Geolocation proved harder because the sequence had been filmed slightly from above, meaning that you saw little of the surrounding landmarks. What dominated the frame was the dusty open area with faint vehicle tracks in two paths through the sand, plus a few hills and patches of scrub. Briefly, the camera angle rose, showing a fence in the distance and a few blurry buildings.

We took screen grabs and stitched the stills together into a panoramic view, which aggregated as much visual information as possible in a single picture. The fuzzy grey concrete buildings in the background seemed to lack doors, as if part of an unfinished construction project. Finding where buildings were under construction in Benghazi was not easy, for it is a large city dealing with years of structural damage. But a Twitter user, @ROELart, provided a tip, suggesting that this could be south-western Benghazi. Satellite imagery showed that the sand there was notably greyer than in other areas; this matched up. Wikimapia contained mention of what locals dubbed 'the Chinese Buildings' area, a property development initiated in around 2009 but halted two years later when the civil war erupted. The Libyan National Army had captured parts of this area in January 2017. Online, we found a photo of the Chinese Buildings that resembled those in the execution video. Aerial images on Google Earth looked promising, too. The problem was, there were hundreds of identical unfinished buildings.

Social-media videos from June 2017 showed Werfalli and his soldiers using a bulldozer to dig up weapons buried by their opponents around the skeletal building zone. In the background, we noticed a fence much like that glimpsed briefly in the execution footage. On Google Earth, we found that just such a fence led to an open area with patches of vegetation. In satellite imagery, the patches seemed to match the scrub in the execution video. A top-down view also displayed vehicle tracks in the sand, along with buildings. Comparing aerial images from 14 July 2017 with those from the day of the murders, 17 July 2017, we discovered something remarkable: dark spots on the ground, detectable on TerraServer imagery, the highest resolution available to consumers. These dark spots matched exactly where fifteen of the victims knelt in that video. We had found bloodstains.[5]

In wartime, legal accountability never comes quickly. Years after the arrest warrant, Werfalli remained free in Libya – he even appeared in another social-media video, murdering more prisoners. Yet his case was not a discouragement. Justice may be slow, but we must think long term. I still recall cases from years back such as the 'Caesar' pictures, involving a vast archive leaked by a Syrian military photographer. He had worked for Assad's forces photographing the bodies of those murdered in regime dungeons: men stripped naked, their ribcages visible and collarbones protruding from starvation, a detainee number sometimes written on the skin. The photographer, codenamed 'Caesar', began copying images and smuggling them from work. When he defected in August 2013, he brought with him 53,275 photos on memory sticks. Sometimes, victims' families learned what had happened to a disappeared relative only through a Caesar photo, as in the case of fourteen-year-old Ahmad al-Musalmani, who had been travelling to his mother's funeral by minibus when a soldier found an anti-Assad song on his phone.[6] After years of searching, his uncle saw the boy's body in a Caesar photo.

In March 2015, Twitter user @ArtWendeley alerted us to a notable photo in the archive, showing corpses strewn around what looked like an open-air garage. It displayed at least nine dead men, stripped naked, laid on their backs in a dusty courtyard with a covered parking area behind and hills with a few trees and buildings behind. Another Twitter user, @pfc_joker, said the tallest hill might be Mount Qasioun, which overlooks the Syrian capital. We searched locations around there, seeking army sites, finally discovering one that seemed to line up, Military Hospital 601, which had a vehicle-maintenance bay that was visible on Google Maps. We did a geolocation, matching every notable feature in the photo with the satellite imagery. We had it. On Google Earth, you saw that the location was a short walk downhill from the presidential palace – Assad could have stood at the edge of his property and gazed towards bodies rotting under the sun.[7]

Someday, open-source evidence like this may appear in court. But this raises a question: if you were a prosecutor in 2035, considering Syrian war-crime allegations from 2020, where would you look? You might scour YouTube (or its future equivalents). But will everything that was once posted still be available? Will it have been verified? Will the clips be findable? I think about those who saved the diaries of Second World War survivors. Today, equally valuable documentation exists in video form. We have a duty to preserve it.

A paradox about the internet is that the online world seems both enduring and ephemeral. You see a tweet, forget it almost immediately, but assume it will be there later. Not necessarily. Consider the case of Bambuser, a live-streaming app that was popular early in the Syrian uprising, through which protesters used to broadcast demonstrations. Once the regime cut off the internet in rebel-held areas, live-streaming halted but Bambuser retained an archive of those protest videos. Until Bambuser itself closed. Even those who filmed the protests did not own their footage anymore. Cases abound of vital material on YouTube or Twitter that was taken down without warning because it violated the platforms' terms and conditions. In the summer of 2019, Facebook – facing intense criticism for exploiting users' personal data – abruptly restricted Graph Search, which had allowed experts to search public content, cross-referencing locations and 'likes' and employers, for example. This was invaluable both in building charts of suspects in crimes[8] and rights abuses, and in finding video evidence from witnesses. But the tool just stopped working.

In parallel, repressive states became more careful about what appeared in open sources. The Kremlin has banned Russian soldiers from sharing details of their military service on social media, and cracked down on data leaks.[9] (Moscow is quick to dismiss Bellingcat, yet these restrictions – apparently in direct response to our investigations – indirectly confirm our work.) Some observers worry that a golden age of open-source investigation may be coming to an end.[10] This does not worry us. Bellingcat is busier than ever today; our problem is never too little information, but too little time. Also, obstacles can produce advances. After YouTube removed important video evidence in 2017, open-source investigators finally took archiving seriously. Those takedowns also led to direct discussions on the subject with YouTube and Facebook, where we were able to make clear that they, like it or not, played a pivotal role in criminal accountability.

We have had to scrutinise our own practices, too. In court, evidence is admissible only if chain-of-custody is documented to a high standard, and this would apply to social-media content. Perhaps an investigator found a video on Facebook, then contacted the page where it appeared and asked for more footage. Or perhaps we came across the clip on YouTube. What did we know about who had posted it there, and how to document all this to the appropriate standard? Separately, there was digital media collected on the ground, such as someone filming an airstrike, then smuggling the content out of the country. All of this had to be explicit for judges. Rights organisations keep archives, too, each varying in how they collect and store material – perhaps disorganised, or ordered in different ways, using varied file types. If judges are not aware of how to appraise digital material, they might dismiss vital evidence.

Advances in technology have shaped international criminal law going back to the Nuremberg trials after the Second World War. The scale of Nazi murders precluded comprehensive witness testimony. But the perpetrators had kept detailed records, even tracking names on early IBM computers. Documentary evidence became key, including military records and footage and images by war correspondents. The next technological shift came with the international tribunals in the early 1990s on the conflicts in the Balkans and Rwanda, incorporating forensic advances such as DNA profiling, along with computers to analyse data and satellite imagery to identify mass graves. A third phase came with the permanent International Criminal Court in The Hague, founded in 2002,[11] just as digital changes were transforming human communication and documentation. Today, I am a member of the International Criminal Court's technology advisory board, helping judicial officials understand how open-source investigation can apply to their cases.

A key player in the intersection between online sleuthing and the law is the Human Rights Center at the University of California, Berkeley,[12] which became involved in the subject back in 2011 after noticing that cases at the International Criminal Court kept falling apart at the early stages of prosecution. Judges, they found, believed that prosecutors were relying too much on NGO reports and witness testimony, rather than gathering evidence of their own. Also, because of the passage of time between an allegation and a trial, witnesses did not necessarily want to show up – they wanted to move on, or had been scared into silence. Meanwhile, the volume of social-media content grew every day. Here was an opportunity.

Reaching the scene of a war crime may be impossible, but social-media records are available anywhere. Digital content corroborates survivor testimony, affirming or debunking sources, while adding context to physical evidence. Social media also helps to map networks of relationships among suspects, invaluable for tribunals that want to prosecute the highest level responsible.[13] We demonstrated this in our MH17 inquiry, when delving into the social-media profiles and posts of the 53rd Brigade, connecting soldiers up the command structure to senior officers.

The Human Rights Center has been working on a Protocol on Open Source Investigations, led by Lindsay Freeman, Alexa Koenig and Eric Stover, and drawing in many of the keenest minds in justice and accountability. When students kept asking Koenig, who directs the Berkeley centre, about a code of ethics for online sleuthing, she and her team decided to produce one, reviewing the best practices of older fields including journalism, law and social-science research. Three core values emerged: 1) safety (both physical and psychological) of investigators, uploaders, those depicted, and those who possess data; 2) protecting faith in facts through transparent methods along with the testing of varied hypotheses and peer review; 3) respecting the dignity of those involved, from acknowledging authorship of source material, to attributing others' detective work, to conducting risk assessments on who is made vulnerable[14] by an investigation.

Bellingcat and other open-source sleuths operate in the fast-evolving online world, yet today's investigations must hold up for years. 'The pressure will build, and if Assad lives a few more decades, there will come a day when he'll be under an international arrest warrant,' says the former international-tribunal prosecutor Stephen Rapp. 'With these kinds of crimes, the message has to be: there is no escape in this life.'[15]

Many activists working on Syria are less confident, but they have other reasons for impeccable detective work. Their hopes have shifted to the long game, to rebuilding their country someday, at which point the story of the past will be critical. Hadi, our partner at Syrian Archive, points out that the Assad regime is already seeking to alter the history of what it has wrought, setting up a pseudo-academic documentation project on the Syrian civil war.[16] If any meaningful national memory is to exist, it cannot derive from war-crimes deniers.

A BLUEPRINT FOR FUTURE WARS

To many in the West the conflict in Yemen seemed like another confusing war in another failed state in another obscure part of the world, unrelated to their lives. But this war had global implications. First, it was a proxy conflict pitting Saudi Arabia against Iran. Second, it was the worst humanitarian catastrophe on the planet, the United Nations said in 2019. Twenty-four million people there needed assistance and protection, about 80 per cent of the population. Since the country fell into civil war four years before, tens of thousands had been killed, including more than 17,000 civilians.[17] Another reason for Westerners to care was that arms and intelligence underpinning the conflict had come from the United States, Britain, France, Canada and other nations. This was not a distant tragedy with no relation to anybody else.

When it comes to Bellingcat, the Yemen conflict has had special relevance. This was where we began implementing our most cutting-edge practices, testing higher standards of collection than ever, creating impeccable archives from the outset and establishing a blueprint for open-source investigation of the wars ahead.

Even before its conflict, Yemen was among the poorest countries in the Middle East – per capita GDP of $2,400, compared with $135,000 in Qatar[18] on the same Arabian Peninsula. Yemen was also among the most heavily armed nations in the world, second only to the United States in a recent[19] survey. During the Arab Spring of 2011, protests broke out against decades of kleptocracy by the regime of President Ali Abdullah Saleh. After his ousting, Abdrabbuh Mansur Hadi took over but faced insurgencies, including from rebels known as the Houthis. This group, affiliated with a Shia sect, seized the capital, Sana'a, in September 2014. The neighbouring Sunni powerhouse, Saudi Arabia, was not going to allow this. A Saudi-led coalition – supported by intelligence and arms sales from Western allies – carried out airstrikes to support the Hadi government. This campaign, which routinely impacted citizens and civilian infrastructure, was, according to the Armed Conflict Location & Event Data Project, responsible for two-thirds of Yemeni civilian deaths.[20] The Saudi-led coalition also imposed a naval blockade, stopping food and medicine from reaching areas controlled by Houthi rebels. This contributed to the worst cholera outbreak in recorded history – more than a million cases.[21, 22] The Houthis, too, carried out human-rights abuses, including torture and 'disappearances', indiscriminately shelling civilians, planting thousands of landmines and conscripting children to fight.[23]

One reason Yemen was known as 'the forgotten war' was because traditional news reporting had been nearly impossible. The government resisted granting visas to journalists, and those who got them were often stopped from entering by the Saudi-led coalition. Even when reporters gained access, they were saddled with official minders, curtailing their ability to hear honest views from locals. One journalist who managed to bypass these obstacles was Rawan Shaif, who based herself in Yemen during the early years of the conflict and ended up jointly leading our first massive open-source investigative project on the war along with Bellingcat senior investigator Nick Waters.

Rawan, who grew up in London, had always wanted to understand the Yemeni side of her family better, so moved there in 2013 while in her twenties. She freelanced for Unicef, then moved into journalism when the civil war broke out, working as a fixer for the BBC, contributing to *Foreign Policy*, stringing for the *New York Times* and others. As the Saudi-led bombing campaign intensified, she acquired a speciality: analysing airstrikes, combining on-the-ground reporting with open-source satellite imagery and social-media videos. In August 2017, after a friend was shot and killed in the centre of Sana'a, she left the country. A year later, Rawan attended a meeting in London with the Global Legal Action Network, or GLAN, which pursues legal action to block arms exports to Yemen. When British munitions are dropped abroad, arms-export agreements state that they must not be used on civilian targets. But GLAN kept finding cases in which they had been. These were scattered cases; they had no proven pattern of illegal use.

Working with GLAN lawyers, Rawan helped set up a data-collection protocol and methodology to parse the open-source evidence on aerial bombardments in Yemen. This process began with collecting source material, moved to verifying and analysing, then integrating this with supporting evidence from NGO reports and the news media. For example, investigators would identify an alleged airstrike on a civilian area in Yemen, and categorise and evaluate primary and secondary sources of evidence, then seek to answer six basic questions: where, when, what, how, who, why. Absolute rigour was the key, with evidence graded from 'confirmed' (cross-referenced with at least three sources), to 'likely', 'weak', 'other cause to explosion', 'unsubstantiated', or 'unknown'. Our data collection used a cutting-edge software platform, Hunchly, which tracks what the investigator clicks and views, preserving every page, so that we retain the entire process, in case another researcher or a prosecutor wants to consult it in the future.

Bellingcat tested the new methodology at a four-day hackathon in January 2019 that also initiated our Yemen project led by Rawan and Nick.[24] The joint Bellingcat/GLAN event attracted a who's who of open-source investigation, with news reporters, technologists and lawyers analysing a hundred airstrikes in the Yemeni conflict.[25] From this collaboration, we sought to ensure that our research met the standards for triple use: investigative journalism, academic study and legal cases. We also shared the work with the newly established Yemeni Archive, run by the preservation experts at Syrian Archive, who had broadened their work under a new name, Mnemonic. They have already collected more than 150,000 pieces of digital content on the Yemeni war.[26] Eventually, anyone should be able to call up a map, draw a circle around an area, set date parameters and find geotagged social-media posts for that area. Or they could search by munitions documented, or seek only attacks implicating a particular type of bomb, or a manufacturer of bombs, or a specific country.

Mnemonic aims to add archives on other conflicts, which would permit even more expansive searches – for example, every attack targeting water sources across the whole Middle East. Eventually, you could study, say, demonstrations in oppressive regimes around the world, and check what munitions are used by riot police, thereby figuring out who is selling the weaponry that supports despots. Or if a human-rights organisation needs to establish the truth about a specific violation, and has a witness statement but does not want to identify that vulnerable person, it could run pinpoint searches, pulling up digital data on this event. Journalists would find a bounty of investigative pieces awaiting their attention, too, all based on verified open-source material. Equally, prosecutors building war-crimes cases could pull up evidence gathered and preserved to judicial standards. With the click of a few buttons, they would save themselves years of research.

The Yemen project also shows how investigators can proceed when future conflicts break out. Imagine that violent clashes break out in Venezuela. Or more ethnic cleansing in Myanmar. Or abuses in Congo. We have established a system and a process, know how much it all costs and are not proprietary about it. We ourselves cannot investigate every conflict in the world. Instead, Bellingcat tries to judge where we have both the resources and a chance of making an impact. We studied airstrikes in Yemen, for instance, because exposure of what was happening there could help legal challenges. But we only have so many open-source investigators who know only so many languages. That is why our training courses around the world are so important. As with every aspect of Bellingcat, we want others to join in, and are ready to explain. Nor is this methodology limited to war. It could be used to document environmental degradation, or acts of political extremism, or police brutality. It is a flexible system, applicable anywhere.

I never forgot what that Syrian activist asked me during the 2015 panel discussion in Istanbul, when he questioned the point of filming human-rights violations at the risk of one's life, when nothing ever seemed to come of it. Then, I had no reply. A few years late, this is an answer.

THE PERILS AND OPPORTUNITIES OF ARTIFICIAL INTELLIGENCE

You never forget your first glimpse of a 'deepfake'. Partly, you are awed by the power of technology – that video footage can so convincingly be falsified. Partly, you are filled with dread at what this tool will wreak. As a public warning in 2018, the comedian Jordan Peele put out a deepfake showing Barack Obama in a video address, calling Trump 'a total and complete dipshit'.[27] The former Democratic president had said no such thing, of course. Information chaos online was already frightening enough. Now, it looked as though deepfakes were about to demolish legitimate discourse, and perhaps undermine the verification techniques that serve as our best defence. Another alarm sounded in 2019, when video circulated of House Speaker Nancy Pelosi slurring her speech. Here was a 'shallow fake' – genuine footage that had been manipulated, in this case to slow it and adjust the pitch of her voice, giving the impression that she was drunk[28] or mentally incapacitated. If a low-grade tweak reverberated so widely, many dreaded what might happen in five years, or ten.

Doctored images have a long history, notably in the twentieth-century propaganda of the Soviet Union, when enemies of Stalin disappeared into prison cells, then disappeared from the photographic record. Such work required darkroom expertise, and its distribution demanded obedient publications. Today, manipulations of far greater technical complexity can be done on a smartphone, while distribution is effortless and global.

The term 'deepfake' encompasses more than video. Artificial intelligence, AI, can conjure photographic portraits of people who never existed. The website Which Face Is Real demonstrates this, placing a computer-generated portrait beside a real photo.[29] They are frighteningly hard to distinguish. Audio deepfakes have already been put to malicious use, with scammers using speech samples of a CEO to replicate his voice digitally, with which they ordered a junior employee to urgently transfer €220,000 into the con artists' account.[30] A research company backed by Elon Musk, OpenAI, created an algorithm that writes coherent text independently, creating the prospect of automated trolls able to do more than just spam; they could engage people in argument, push conspiracy theories and dilute meaningful public discussion. Fearful of misuse, OpenAI decided not release the research.[31, 32]

While deepfakes are a threat, we can inform ourselves, prepare and respond. To become paranoid about deepfakes would itself have disastrous consequences, leading people to judge all documentation cynically. What quicker way to discredit a conclusive open-source investigation than to claim that nothing is to be believed? I am certain this tactic will soon become routine in disinformation campaigns. I already see tweets dismissing videos from Syria, saying, *But how do you know this isn't a deepfake?* The uninformed give this technology powers beyond its current capabilities.

A leading expert on synthetic media and its possible misuse, Sam Gregory of the human-rights organisation WITNESS, contends that we still have the chance to do better against this threat than we did in society's recent online collision with disinformation. First, we must grasp what kinds of trickery are possible.[33] You can already remove a person or an object from a video. You can change weather in a video. You can 'face swap' and edit body movements, converting footage of real people into a puppet show whose subjects say and do what the operator wants. Next, we must consider the consequences of 'synthetic media'. These include undermining legitimate reporting and investigations; the purposeful tainting of reputations of politicians and members of civil society; and the deception of voters. Video archives could become targets, too, allowing bad actors to meddle with the historical record. Third, we must think about where this technology is heading. Deepfakes are improving. The AI technology that underlies it is a topic of vast and competitive research, and software companies are commercialising what had been academic research, lowering barriers to entry. The amount of training data (that is, the number of images or audio samples that an algorithm needs to convincingly mimic something) keeps dropping. Fourth, we must beware that synthetic media will spread through the same disinformation routes that we are battling already, from microtargeting on social media, to mass-spamming, to dissemination through deceitful alternative-media outlets.

Part of the response is media literacy. The difficulty is keeping up to date. This technology moves so quickly that the flaws that give away a deepfake tend to be resolved soon after they are recognised. Another part of the response, Gregory argues, is closer coordination between major news sources and open-source researchers, who are best positioned to evaluate and debunk. Also, companies that produce media-manipulation software must consider their ethical responsibilities, building detection tools alongside deception tools.[34] One possibility is to have verification data built in, so that each time a video or a photo is taken, metadata is uploaded for easy checks by forensic specialists or social-media platforms.[35] The Research & Development team at the *New York Times* set up a News

Provenance Project, testing the possibility of including context and metadata within images, perhaps with a watermark that affirms that the content was verified. They also experimented with publishing photos using blockchain, the technology made famous by cryptocurrencies, where a shared online ledger is updated at each transaction, which prevents tampering.[36] Facebook also encouraged researchers to work on the problem, launching a $10 million Deepfake Detection Challenge, whose goal was to find how best to identify synthetic media.[37]

Deepfakes do not trouble me too much for now. A photo or a video is not a free-floating entity; it is part of a nexus of information. Take that Obama video. Imagine that it had appeared one day on YouTube without explanation and went viral. Immediately, Bellingcat and many others would have checked what else had been posted on that same YouTube feed. What was the credibility and origin of the source? Had the footage appeared elsewhere first? Who immediately shared it around Twitter or Facebook? Which pages had those users liked? And so on. Also, real events happen in context. When did Obama say that? Where? Is there proof that he was at the alleged location at the supposed time? If anything about a video seems dubious, you dig deep. The most likely outcome for a viral deepfake video is that we would end up exposing it, to the discredit of whoever created the clip. If people become sceptical (rather than cynical) about what they see online, that is a public good. Instead of believing that Pelosi video, or accepting whatever auto-plays on Facebook, the public should demand that imagery is vetted by organisations with a record of truthfulness.

AI is also a cause for optimism when it comes to open-source investigation. Machine-learning, or using datasets to train a computer to 'learn' independently, provides a way to process the volume of information online. The Syrian war has left in its wake more hours of footage than hours in the conflict itself.[38] So far, Syrian Archive has preserved about 3.5 million pieces of digital content (approximately 1.5 million YouTube videos, plus two million clips and images from Twitter and Facebook). They have a core team of three people, with another four or five collaborators. Together, they have verified more than 8,000 pieces from this collection – an impressive achievement that still leaves more than 99 per cent unverified.[39] The only realistic answer is to employ machines to watch the videos on their behalf.

Since 2017, Syrian Archive has been working with artificial intelligence to sift through its collection for instances of cluster-munitions use, training it with images of unexploded ordnance and the blasts themselves, which produce a distinctive explosive pattern that algorithms can learn. Eventually, the AI will be able to work alone, tagging all instances of cluster-munitions footage among millions of clips, allowing humans to check just those cases and perhaps gain insight into how the munitions were used over time in the war. Additionally, Syrian Archive hopes to apply AI to identify attacks on rescuers and hospitals; the use of incendiary munitions; and the presence of tanks or helicopters.

Forensic Architecture, a pioneering group of researchers at the University of London that uses digital modelling to document human-rights violations, has applied machine-learning to expose Russia's role in the fighting in eastern Ukraine, specifically at the Battle of Ilovaysk in August 2014, which occurred weeks after the downing of MH17. The AI churned through 2,500 hours of YouTube footage from the region at the time of the fighting, seeking frames in which tanks appeared. Researchers checked the results, confirming the presence of a kind of tank only used by the Russians at the time.[40]

Benetech, a non-profit organisation that seeks to apply technology for social good, had a serendipitous discovery when tackling a recurrent investigative problem: the same video gets downloaded by various people, then re-uploaded repeatedly in slightly different versions, confusing matters and wasting time. The organisation developed a machine-learning tool to sift through this undifferentiated mass, plucking out versions of the same video, creating a unique fingerprint of up to 500 numbers and letters that identified each clip. Each fingerprint could be compared with others, with any two clips earning a score based on the degree of similarity. This led to a serendipitous discovery: if you checked clips that scored just below the threshold of a match, the AI was somehow identifying different footage of the same event. This inadvertently created a way to automatically find related videos, which holds immense promise for investigators.

At Bellingcat, we often discuss with computer scientists ways to work through massive datasets, such as the hundreds of leaked Russian databases we have downloaded. This could allow us to take what we learned about how the GRU produces false identities, then train artificial intelligence to look for similar profiles within the entire population of the Russian Federation as recorded in those databases. Rather than manually digging through this vast pile, AI would do the grunt work, identifying suspicious identities lurking in the data. Another tool that open-source investigators yearn for is a reverse image search for videos, which would allow us to instantly check if footage had appeared elsewhere – a critical question when judging the authenticity and originality of digital content. We also hope for a way to trawl automatically through social-media postings. During our MH17 investigation, when ascertaining the movements of the 53rd Brigade, two Bellingcat investigators spent a year clicking social-media profiles and studying posted photos to learn who belonged to the unit. Someday, we could automate such work – train a computer to, say, detect people in uniform, or those wearing specific military colours, or search social-media posts for mentions of a military unit, and compile the results for review by humans, including a network map of how everyone is connected, identifying high-status individuals whom we should study most closely. With this, we could monitor the actions of military forces suspected of wrongdoing. One complication is that such a tool would be desirable to every government intelligence agency in the world. For us, the major question becomes this: once we develop such tools, do we want to publicise them?

Besides providing answers, technology helps ask the right questions. Peter de Kock served in an undercover unit of the Dutch police during the MH17 investigation. While the security services had sixty staffers struggling to advance their investigation, he watched Bellingcat swiftly pull together the route of the Buk launcher from open sources alone. When he pointed this out to colleagues, some were receptive. But the police force was conservative and preferred traditional methods of investigation. Soon thereafter, he completed a Ph.D. on anticipating criminal behaviour; with ambitions to use data science for better policing, he quit and founded his own company, Pandora Intelligence. One of its notable projects revamps the emergency-dispatch call using OSINT. In the traditional scenario, a dispatcher answers, notes down what is deemed significant, then forwards a briefing to an emergency service unit. But the Pandora Intelligence system transcribes the words of the caller in real time, extracting relevant datapoints: address, phone number, licence plate, for example. Automatically, these details are fed back into open sources such as social media, along with closed police databases.

This produces fresh datapoints, which are fed into further searches, building a cascade of clues, fed in real time to the dispatcher, who can pose more directed questions to the caller, gathering timely evidence that might otherwise be overlooked.

Virtual reality presents intriguing possibilities, too. Our graphical expert Timmi Allen has experimented with strapping on goggles to investigate scenes in three dimensions – for example, creating a virtual model of the site of a market bombing in Syria. Another promising concept is 'digital memories', where virtual-reality software combines multiple images of a location into a photorealistic 3D computer model. Witnesses don goggles and 'enter' the reconstructed scene – perhaps a location they cannot return to, either for practical or emotional reasons. Our hope is that this could jog memories, contributing evidence to the existing open-source record.

Forensic Architecture used this technology in a February 2020 report, recreating a human-rights violation in the occupied West Bank city of Hebron. A former Israeli Army officer, Dean Issacharoff – who had become spokesman for an organisation of reservists speaking out against Israeli military violations – confessed to having assaulted a Palestinian man in the city during his service there in 2014. He wanted the authorities to investigate him, but prosecutors accused Issacharoff of lying. So his organisation, Breaking the Silence, approached Forensic Architecture to produce a photorealistic 3D model of the event, including the alley where the beating occurred; the Hebron street down which arrested Palestinians were led; and a checkpoint where they were detained. With virtual-reality goggles, Issacharoff and two Palestinian witnesses separately 'walked' through the locations, situating soldiers, civilians and vehicles, which allowed their visualised memories to be superimposed and compared.[41] This has great potential for future cases, helping witnesses render more accurate testimony, while permitting investigators and lawyers to better parse conflicting accounts. Immersive virtual memories seem like the start of something incredible.

To nurture more cutting-edge techniques, Bellingcat is jointly establishing an innovation lab in Berlin, along with Forensic Architecture, Syrian Archive and the European Center for Constitutional and Human Rights, or ECCHR, a non-governmental organisation that uses litigation to hold the guilty responsible for rights violations. This collaborative workspace aspires to become a centre of development and excellence for open-source techniques, as applied to justice and accountability. The expertise of our four organisations is complementary: Bellingcat in online investigations, Forensic Architecture applying tech tools to visualising and expanding evidence, Syrian Archive preserving digital records to the highest standard, and the ECCHR ensuring that such material helps to enforce human rights.

Online sleuthing emerged from the untapped powers of tech, and its future will follow this same course, expanding in parallel with the standard uses of digital inventions. Environmental damage is an obvious area for future scrutiny as the climate emergency produces ever more visible effects. Open-source investigation only hits a limit with events that happen off the grid – bombings in remote parts of Afghanistan, for example, are hard to study. An extreme example came in March 2014, with the disappearance of Malaysian Airlines Flight 370 somewhere in the Indian Ocean. Unless a fisherman had taken a photo that day and caught the plane going down in the background, we would never find anything. But societies are only becoming more connected. Humans share more of their experiences online for the world to see. The blank zones are shrinking.

WHERE WE GO FROM HERE

The past, present and future of open-source investigation is collaboration.

Disinformation operatives have greater tools than ever, and the aggressively misinformed find huge audiences online. Against this, we must act in numbers, and cooperatively, not with the bruising jealousy that infused old-school journalism. Thankfully, legacy news organisations are now recognising the value of this new field, and rushing to join in. The *New York Times* – where I had my early break with that front-page story of February 2013 on Syrian arms-smuggling – has established a Visual Investigations Team of online-investigative virtuosos, including Bellingcat veterans such as Christiaan Triebert, plus our early contributor Christoph Koettl, previously of Amnesty International, and open-source pioneer Malachy Browne, formerly of Storyful. This team is already conducting many of the most powerful reports of the hallowed news organisation, explaining chemical weapons attacks in Syria, the 2017 Las Vegas mass shootings, the 2018 murder of Jamal Khashoggi, and working parallel with Bellingcat to explain the Iranian downing of Flight PS752 in January 2020. In only their first few years, they were recipients of a Pulitzer Prize, two Emmys and an Overseas Press Club award.

After Bellingcat conducted a workshop for the BBC, the Corporation decided to establish an open-source investigative unit, too, focusing on Africa, which is largely untapped when it comes to online sleuthing. The BBC *Africa Eye* team employed another Bellingcat contributor, Aliaume Leroy, and was promptly acclaimed for a harrowing piece in September 2018, 'Anatomy of a Killing', which studied a YouTube video showing soldiers in Cameroon executing two women and two young children at a roadside. The Cameroonian government initially denied that the atrocity had even taken place in the country, dubbing it 'fake news'.[42] But the BBC team, with help from Amnesty and Bellingcat, identified the culprits. Finally, Cameroon acknowledged that the men had been soldiers, and put seven from the video on trial. The BBC investigation won a Peabody Award.

Elsewhere in the news world, verification teams and disinformation squads are increasingly common. The *Wall Street Journal* established a 'deepfake' committee of staffers from across the newsroom to help reporters judge whether content is authentic.[43] Reuters trained staff to spot fake content while employing a growing team of video-verifiers.[44] Given how much information derives from social media, serious news organisations that are *not* practising online verification are dangerously exposed, while those that fail to develop open-source investigators among their staff will keep missing major scoops. Yet at the executive level, many organisations – in the news media, human-rights activism, humanitarian law and beyond – still do not realise what is possible.

In order to seed these powers among the younger generation, Bellingcat has launched a pilot training programme for university students in the Netherlands, attempting to build a grassroots movement among those studying journalism, data science and visualisation. With Dutch government funding, we conducted our first project in Utrecht, instructing a score of university students aged eighteen to twenty-five. The programme proved so successful that we expanded to five bootcamps. Each involved five days of training, spread over several weeks, allowing students to consolidate and practise the Bellingcat method: geolocation, chronolocation, social-media trawling, and so on. Once they have the basics, we oversee their projects. We present the best research to local news outlets. In the Utrecht test programme, we immediately had results, including the reconstruction of a March 2019 terrorist attack in that city, when a man opened fire on a tram, killing three people and wounding seven. From open sources, the students discovered details about the suspect that Dutch law enforcement itself had not figured out.

We hope to set up college bootcamps in Britain, Germany and France, then the United States and beyond. The demand is there; all we need is enough trainers to sate the appetite. Later, we will look at instructing younger students, too. Such education must be carefully handled – we cannot expose teenagers to traumatising material. But a well-crafted training programme teaching verification skills to those entering adult society ought to be among the basic skills of the twenty-first century. We know that most people who study online verification will not pursue this intense work day to day, but if we teach a class of, say, twenty-five students and three take it up afterwards, that is plenty, given what a single dedicated investigator can achieve. Those who never pursue the discipline themselves will realise what is possible, and will know to expect verification from their information sources.

For anyone curious about testing how this works, we maintain a free Bellingcat Online Investigation Toolkit, including links to everything from satellite maps to video verification to company registries to flight trackers. You could seek digital clues to the origins of a new political group, say, or take up smaller local concerns such as documenting how rubbish bins are overflowing in your neighbourhood, spilling rotting waste across the streets and attracting rats, while an adjacent area is pristine. You could take photos, have your phone geotag the image and send it to a centralised server. If you engaged your neighbourhood community, you could compile a dataset and supply a readymade story to journalists and officials, exposing a public health hazard. Local news organisations can jump into this field, too. They have been among the hardest hit by the industrial collapse of the news business, and struggle to justify their existence and pay their way. They would regain a unique role with local investigative work.

Citizens' projects sound less impressive than war coverage, but they could have an international impact. Each such inquiry – whether documenting a health hazard, or chronicling wildlife migration, or exposing environmental degradation – could inspire others elsewhere. From this, you could see an international community of engaged citizens, with the best investigations in one location replicated in others.

Social media offered refuge to the disenchanted and frustrated, and this benefited some; you could consider Bellingcat a product of this development. But destructive online communities formed, too, spreading lies, provoking violence and dividing societies. Local investigative projects could show citizens that they are not powerless, nor are they alone – we still have common interests that unite us.

One abiding concern I have had since the early days of open-source investigation is that the field lacks diversity, with women notably unrepresented. I had observed similar disparities elsewhere on the internet, especially during my years of intensive gaming, when I led a group of forty players of whom thirty-nine were male. It is not good enough to claim that women are not interested in swords and magic contests; there was a larger issue. From early on, young men colonised the internet, finding company and amusement there. Gaming became so central to their lives that some came to expect that human relationships operated by similar rules: if you meet the objectives, you can have what you want. Once life proved more complicated, a faction grew resentful, twisting online camaraderie into a self-pitying fraternity that vented its spite through digital bullying. Already by the early 2000s, I was witnessing warped comments in message boards regarding women.

Fortunately, the open-source community does not share that mindset. However, investigators are routinely attacked online by the Counterfactual Community, and abuse can be particularly aggressive towards women. Natalia, Bellingcat's former editor, cites this atmosphere as a reason why open-source investigation attracted far more men in the early days. Also, the online misogyny related to Gamergate emerged at exactly the same time as Bellingcat was founded in the summer of 2014. Women who raised their heads above the parapet were attacked, Natalia recalled.

Bellingcat has sought to push back against this trend. In 2015, we published a call to action for the open-source community, advocating more opportunities and higher-profile roles for women. Our contributor Rayna Stamboliyska, a Parisian risk-management consultant who writes about cybersecurity, produced a list of thirty female pioneers then involved in open-source sleuthing, from the BBC, Reuters, ProPublica, Channel 4 News, Storyful, First Draft News, Columbia University, MIT and other organisations.[45] Merely by producing that list, Rayna was making a point, exhorting news producers, think tanks and others to remember these names when booking TV guests, making invitations to conferences and hiring open-source investigators of their own.

In the beginning, I hadn't the resources to employ anyone, so had to rely on whoever offered their time. But after Bellingcat gained funding I sought to build an increasingly diverse staff – by our fifth anniversary in 2019, we had achieved male–female parity. We intend to keep broadening our staffing geographically, too, hiring in Asia, Africa and Latin America.

A question often put to me is whether Bellingcat could be overshadowed by groups that replicate our methods, particularly big-budget news organisations. We are not worried; Bellingcat never sought to compete with huge media companies. From the outset, we have had two goals: find evidence and spread this field. We have gone a distance in both respects. And we still enjoy advantages, serving as a connective hub among experts and observers and rights activists and university scholars and citizens, all ready to launch themselves into investigations.

I often receive emails from people asking how they can volunteer for Bellingcat. Sometimes, we issue calls to action on a specific project, such as when identifying photos that could lead to the arrest of child abusers. Our ambition is to integrate more citizen volunteers into Bellingcat work each year. Other organisations have taken impressive steps in this direction, notably Amnesty International, which has both a Digital Verification Corps – in which university students collaborate on open-source investigations – and a Decoders platform, which is open to any member of the public. In future, we hope to combine the efforts of volunteers with the might of machine-learning. For instance, if Bellingcat identified a YouTube video containing a valuable piece of evidence – for example, troops marching into territory where military officials deny they are operating – AI might comb through a vast dataset of other videos for similar footage, producing a list of several hundred clips. We could present these in a volunteers' section of the Bellingcat website, and our community could crowd-investigate. Besides allowing us to verify large amounts of material, a volunteer corps would help us identify skilled investigators to involve in more complex cases. Above all, we encourage participants to take what they learn and pursue their own inquiries, publishing in their own right or bringing their findings back to us.

Today, Bellingcat finds itself in an unusual position. We are not exactly journalists, nor human-rights activists, nor computer scientists, nor archivists, nor academic researchers, nor criminal investigators, but at the nexus of all those disciplines. The Bellingcat method has expanded far beyond the foundational principles of 'Identify, Verify, Amplify', encompassing an ethic, a social mission and a drive for accountability. We will remain at the vanguard of open-source investigation. We will break major stories. We will present evidence and insist on the primacy of fact. We will act as a firewall against disinformation. And we will encourage as many people to join us as possible.

I started off doing a blog in my spare time. Now we are Bellingcat. This is only the start.

Afterword

Confronting Killers

Bellingcat dials up a hit squad

The Russian opposition leader Alexey Navalny, known for his scathing criticism of Putin, was heading home after a trip to Siberia, where he'd been supporting local politicians. Once the commercial flight took off on the morning of 20 August 2020, Navalny settled into his seat, planning to watch a bit of TV and relax until reaching Moscow. But something felt wrong.

He grew chilly yet was sweating. Navalny looked around, struggling to concentrate. He turned to his spokeswoman, seated beside him, and asked her to say something, as if this might yank him from the fog. The flight attendants appeared, offering refreshments. He pushed past them, hastening into a cramped toilet stall, splashing cold water on himself. He was suffering no pain; this was worse. A sense of impending death pervaded him.

He exited the toilet stall and sought a crew member. 'I've been poisoned,' he said. 'I'm dying.' Navalny lay down on the floor of the plane, his vision and hearing fading. His howls of distress sounded down the aisles.[1]

The pilot diverted for an emergency landing in the town of Omsk, and paramedics rushed on board, loading Navalny into an ambulance, his face as grey as his T-shirt. Medics injected him with atropine, which counteracts nerve agents, but he was still close to death. In a local hospital, they hooked him to a ventilator, and doctors spoke of a presumed poisoning – until police filled the corridor outside Navalny's room. Now the medical staff adjusted its views. Moscow labs, they said, had found no trace of toxins.[2] Perhaps this was just a drop in blood-sugar levels. The pro-Kremlin media added to the disinformation, suggesting that Navalny had drunk himself into a coma, consuming too much moonshine.[3] After tense negotiations, his wife and personal doctor got permission to evacuate Navalny to Germany, and a chartered plane jetted him to Berlin. Outside Russian territory, independent experts confirmed that poison was found in his system – a form of Novichok.

We, and many others, watched this with perplexity. Yes, the Kremlin loathed Navalny. But to attempt to murder its most prominent foe seemed mad, certain to damage Putin's reputation while elevating Navalny's. Bellingcat contributor Christo Grozev figured the culprits would not be the GRU – those operatives specialised in overseas operations. And while the FSB (the successor agency to the KGB) operated within Russia, taking out Navalny seemed too brazen even for them.

Perhaps, Christo reckoned, this was the work of a Kremlin proxy, like the ex-convict businessman Yevgeny Prigozhin. He had carried out many illicit activities for the pleasure of Moscow, including interfering in the 2016 US elections with his fake-news troll factory, the Internet Research Agency; supporting a mercenary outfit, the Wagner Group, in Syria and Ukraine; and intimidating political opponents of Putin. We would probably never know, Christo reasoned. Evidence in Russia 'disappears' more readily than in, say, Salisbury, England.

Anyway, Christo had no time to delve into it. He was engaged on another investigation, showing that the Kremlin lied when claiming to have ended its chemical-poison operations. Instead, its experts had been moved to other research entities, notably the State Experimental Institute for Scientific Research in Military Medicine (GNII VM) outside St Petersburg, which purported merely to seek antidotes for such weapons; and the Scientific Center Signal (SC Signal) in Moscow, which claimed to carry out wholesome projects like developing sports-nutrition drinks.[4]

Two months after the Navalny poisoning, Bellingcat published that investigation, showing how the two institutes had worked with the GRU assassination team inside Unit 29155, as implicated in the Skripal poisoning. Whenever Christo produces a Bellingcat scoop, he relishes the adrenaline rush from watching all the international media coverage. Then days pass, the news moves on, and he hankers for the next breakthrough. No one had yet cracked the Navalny poisoning. Time to try. He reached out to his closest collaborator, Roman Dobrokhotov, of our Russian partner publication *The Insider*. They began digging.

At that time, I had just finished working on this book, and restored full attention to the ever-expanding project of Bellingcat. We were transforming month by month, professionalising, growing in number. From what I understood, this Navalny investigation would be a long shot. But we had pursued long shots before.

Luckily, Russian journalists had done vital groundwork, putting together a timeline of when and where Navalny had been during his Siberia trip. Christo and Roman cross-referenced that information against two sources: 1) call data from those implicated in the chemical-poison institutes; 2) leaked travel records. As noted earlier, the Russian-speaking internet has privacy lapses, to put it mildly, ranging from the open availability of personal information on social media to black-market sources for confidential state records. We needed all we could obtain.

Our investigation team guessed that Navalny's poisoners would not have been so foolish as to take the same flight as him to Moscow, where they could be exposed. So we checked records of flights around the time of his travel, both leaving Moscow for Novosibirsk on 14 August, and returning 20 August from Tomsk to Moscow (though Navalny's plane diverted when he fell ill). Had any passengers shadowed his movements? Yes, they had.

A man calling himself 'Aleksey Frolov' had both a ticket to Novosibirsk the day before Navalny's, and a flight leaving Tomsk for Moscow a day after the opposition leader's planned return. But 'Frolov' never boarded that return flight. If he were following Navalny, he'd have no need to, with his victim in hospital. The return ticket, our investigative team found, was bought with tickets for two other men: 'Vladimir Panyaev' and 'Ivan Spiridonov'.

We sought these three in the Bellingcat repository of past leaked Russian databases. Regarding 'Frolov' and 'Spirodonov', official records told us nearly nothing – which told us much. They had no taxpayer numbers, not even registered residences. You could not exist in Russia without official records. Unless you didn't exist at all. The third person in their booking, Panyaev, had a genuine identity trail. So we fed his details into the GetContact crowdsourcing app, which presents numbers and names as they appear in others' contact lists. One person had him listed as 'FSB Vladimir Alexandrovich Panyaev'.

Christo and Roman were on to something, yet had not uncovered the full story. So Christo had an idea to privately approach Navalny, then recuperating in Germany, via a direct message on Twitter. *I think we may have found them*, Christo wrote. *We need to talk.*

Understandably, the opposition leader – so recently targeted with death – was wary. He insisted on talking via Zoom, with cameras on, so he could see whom he spoke with. An hour later, Christo was explaining what the investigations team had uncovered, and what we lacked. To expose further shadowing by Russian operatives, we could use Navalny's detailed itinerary for the past few years. But we did not want the victim himself participating in our research, which felt like a conflict. So Navalny assigned a member of his anti-corruption team to assist us, on the understanding that she inform him of nothing. This proved tantalising, as Navalny kept hearing rumours of our progress in the coming weeks – we knew of the culprits before he did. 'Tell me, please!' he joked. 'You must tell me!'

The investigative team compared travel records for 'FSB Vladimir Alexandrovich Panyaev' with Navalny's itineraries going back to 2017, weeks after he announced his run for the Russian presidency. Panyaev was clearly trailing the candidate, often travelling with another person, Aleksey Alexandrov, the genuine identity of a military doctor who had joined the FSB in 2013. As we looked into his connections, we realised that Aleksey Alexandrov was none other than 'Aleksey Frolov', one of the three who followed Navalny to Siberia. We revealed this through an absurdly basic pattern that the FSB used to create false personas: an operative's real first name, plus the last name of his wife or girlfriend, and his birthday up or down by a year. The maiden name of Alexandrov's wife, we found on social media, was Frolova – hence he became 'Aleksey Frolov'. His real birthday, 16 June, matched that of 'Frolov' too, just switched from 1981 to 1980.

We sifted through leaked vehicle registrations, checked addresses on Google Maps, even studied paid-parking records online, discovering more and more FSB operatives employed to follow Navalny. Eight men made up the core team, including those three in Tomsk around the time of his poisoning. Our investigation had happened upon a specialised unit within the FSB Criminalistics Institute; some operatives held medical degrees, others had special-ops backgrounds, and a few hailed directly from the world of military chemical weapons. All reported to a scientist, Colonel Stanislav Makshakov, who had previously worked in the military chemical-weapons programme in Shikhany, where Novichok was created.

We identified thirty-seven trips where FSB unit members had tailed Navalny. Usually, two or three men would fly ahead to his destination. For a while, Navalny seemed to be the unit's primary target – its members engaged in only one trip in 2017 that did not overlap with his, and that was a flight Navalny had intended to take but cancelled when someone threw a corrosive substance into his face, forcing him to undergo eye surgery. At the end of 2017, the Russian electoral committee blocked Navalny's application to run as a presidential candidate. The FSB unit's trailing of Navalny fell away. But by 2019, the unit's attention returned. He suffered a suspected poisoning that year too, but the data we acquired was clearer about the unit's actions in 2020, including phone logs of several operatives. From this, we could see not only whom they had communicated with and when, but where each person had been, as shown through cell-tower geolocation.

Call records from officials at the SC Signal institute included a surge of communication with FSB-linked numbers around the time Navalny's wife, Yuliya, fell ill in yet another previous suspected poisoning. The Navalnys had flown to Kaliningrad – a Baltic Sea enclave between Lithuania and Poland – for a five-day break at a beach spa in early July 2020. They expected a romantic getaway, but had company: three FSB operatives, each exchanging calls with Colonel Makshakov. Four days into the break, the Navalnys strolled down the beach, then stopped for a late lunch at a café. Yuliya became weak, and soon 'felt sicker than I had ever felt in my life', she later recalled.[5] She headed for the hotel but had to rest on a bench along the way, then struggled to stand again. Finally, she staggered into their hotel room and collapsed into bed, recovering the following day.

In the shadows, much had been going on. The morning of her illness, 6 July 2020, a flurry of calls was underway. Besides the three FSB operatives' communication with Colonel Makshakov, he was in touch with two key superiors: director of the FSB Criminalistics Institute, General Kirill Vasilyev, a chemical engineer whose name appeared on studies for SC Signal, and General Vladimir Bogdanov, who reported to the director of the FSB. Amid this, Bogdanov flew to Kaliningrad, spending several days there at the FSB offices, talking with Makshakov and other Signal chemists by phone.

A month later, the poison squad had another opportunity, with Navalny heading to Siberia. As with the Kaliningrad operations, the operatives turned off their regular phones when leaving Moscow. Alexandrov (aka 'Frolov'), a portly, moustachioed doctor with a red birthmark on his chin, flew to Novosibirsk on 12 August 2020, along with two fellow operatives: another stout, middle-aged medic, 'Ivan Spiridonov', actually Ivan Osipov, who had vanished off social media in 2012, likely when he entered Russian clandestine services; and Panyaev, the aforementioned FSB operative exposed on GetContact, who had also been present during the presumed poisoning in Kaliningrad.

Tracking the FSB squad members in Siberia was tough, since they were likely using burner phones whose numbers we did not immediately know. But we did have call data from other unit members, which showed a surge in communications on Navalny's last full day in Novosibirsk and a second surge overnight to 20 August, the morning when Navalny collapsed aboard the flight. Senior officials in the FSB unit, including the commander, Makshakov, his superior Bogdanov, and other squad members, were texting each other right through that night.

Alexandrov was sloppy, though, bringing his regular phone along on the mission, and twice revealing his location when it pinged cell towers in Novosibirsk (where Navalny landed) and Tomsk not long before the poisoning (his location was a mere six-minute drive from Navalny's hotel). When Navalny arrived for his 6 a.m. taxi to the airport – a little after 2 a.m. Moscow time – the FSB operatives were texting again. Not long after, Navalny was in mid-air, deathly ill, and the pilot was descending to safety.

When Navalny was later evacuated to Germany, his clothing and personal effects remained behind in the Omsk hospital. These belongings could have contained evidence in the form of poison residue. But everything went missing. At just this time, a member of the FSB squad, Konstantin Kudryavtsev, who had served in a chemical-warfare military unit in Shikhany, flew from Moscow to Omsk, spending a mere ten hours in the town before returning. This hurried visit did not prove that he had tampered with the evidence. But that proof was coming.

By mid-December 2020, we were almost ready to publish, triple-checking our facts along with our media partners on this release, CNN and the German magazine *Der Spiegel*. After Navalny's tantalising wait for answers, he was about to learn what we knew. For that final week of investigation, Christo holed up at an Airbnb in a small German village in the Black Forest, near where Navalny was recuperating. They met and ran over the findings. As part of Bellingcat's new editorial rigour, we wanted the accused to have a right of reply. We had their phone numbers, so planned to call before publication.

What if Navalny phoned them? After all, Christo reasoned, it was he who had nearly lost his life, yet would never have a chance to confront his would-be murderers. Let's give him that, Christo thought. CNN and *Der Spiegel* were on board, as long as the accused had a chance to respond.

With mere hours before the story appeared, Christo began dialling the assassination team members on his mobile, put it on speaker, and handed it to Navalny,[6] with a video team filming. We needed to reach the FSB operatives before they went into the office, so this meant calling in the early morning. Since Moscow is two hours ahead of Germany, reaching them at 6.30 a.m. meant 4.30 a.m. in Germany. None of the investigative team had more than the briefest sleep because they had only finished fact-checking at 1.30 a.m., after which Navalny had driven back to his place, returning just three hours later.

Many of the suspects picked up – only to hear Navalny identify himself and ask for comment on their plot to assassinate him. One after another, they hung up.[7] So Navalny had a thought. What if he posed as a Russian official? Perhaps they'd be truthful then.

Christo was against this. These men had just tried to murder Russia's most prominent opposition politician; surely they'd know what he sounded like. But Navalny was determined, and history shows he is a determined man. Of those left, he asked Christo, which do you think is the dumbest?

The FSB scientists might be less versed in politics, so perhaps would be less likely to recognise Navalny's voice. Still, it seemed unlikely. Reluctantly, Christo set up a number-spoofing app that allowed his phone to present a false caller ID, making it show up as an FSB landline that had been in touch with members of the squad. With two operatives left, Navalny posed as a high-ranking bureaucrat, 'Maxim Ustinov', claiming he had been assigned to write a report on the failed poisoning.

The first FSB operative did not fall for it. 'I know exactly who you are,' he said, and put down the phone.

The last chance was Kudryavtsev, the man who travelled after the poisoning to Omsk, when Navalny's belongings went missing from the hospital. He answered the phone, and Navalny addressed him in the tone of an impatient official, applying the haughty manner that his own father, a lieutenant colonel, once used with subordinates.

Kudryavtsev – quarantining at home with Covid-19 – was cagey at first. Should they be speaking on an open line? Navalny reassured him that all had been authorised. The man started to talk. Listening on speakerphone, Christo half-wondered if Kudryavtsev was just keeping Navalny on the line until an FSB team busted down the door. Was a clandestine FSB operative really going to confess on a prank call? Five minutes of conversation passed, then ten. Jittery from nerves and coffee, Christo could barely contain himself, hearing this unfold. He clapped his hand over his mouth in amazement, and leapt to his feet, pacing around. Navalny kept his cool, authoritative in tone, cajoling and prodding the man into admissions.

In the end, they spoke for forty-nine minutes, during which Kudryavtsev confirmed that Colonel Makshakov was the squad commander, while Alexandrov and Osipov had been the main perpetrators in Tomsk. He also detailed his efforts to clean poison from the clothing. Navalny asked where the highest concentration of poison was. The underpants, Kudryavtsev replied. The goal, he made clear, had been to murder Navalny, not just harm him.

> Navalny [in character]: How come the operation failed?
> Kudryavtsev: Well, I have been wondering myself about that, not once or twice ... They made an emergency landing, the situation developed ... not in our favour. This is what I think: if it was a bit longer, I think things would have turned the other way.[8]

We had an internal debate about the ethics of gaining information this way. Eventually, we judged that a situation this extraordinary – a major political figure exposing a state assassination attempt against him – justified itself on grounds of public interest. The public seemed to agree, for the response was huge. CNN correspondent Clarissa Ward amplified the report further when she boldly knocked on the front door of an FSB squad member at his run-down apartment building on the outskirts of Moscow. He opened briefly – then shut the door in her face.[9]

Putin had an annual press conference coming up, so we published our first story on the FSB squad – but withheld our recording of Navalny speaking directly to the operative. First we would see how the Russian president responded. Asked about the Bellingcat report, Putin admitted that Russian operatives had been tracking Navalny, but he offered a scoffing denial of the murder attempt.[10] 'The intelligence agencies of course need to keep an eye on him. But that does not mean that he needs to be poisoned – who needs him?' Putin told reporters. 'If they had really wanted to, they would have probably finished the job.'

Contradicting this, we released our recording of the FSB operative's confession. Meantime, we had not stopped digging into the travel data. Summoning the power of crowdsourcing, we released the itineraries of ten operatives from the FSB chemical-weapons unit, asking whether any of those dates and places related to unexplained deaths and illnesses. Hundreds of responses came in, and we sifted through them all, carrying out our own corroboration under criteria that were strict enough to rule out coincidences.

Eventually, we identified three cases in which activists had been killed in dubious circumstances in Russia, each dying of supposed 'heart failure'.[11] We also found signs of FSB involvement in the attempted assassinations of two high-profile opponents of Putin who had survived poisoning: the activist Vladimir Kara-Murza,[12] nearly killed by noxious substances twice, in 2015 and 2017, and the outspoken poet Dmitry Bykov,[13] who fell gravely ill from a mysterious toxin in 2019. There was a pattern here: clandestine operatives from an FSB anti-extremism department tailed the victim, then the poison squad from the FSB Criminalistics Institute joined them for the attack itself. They seemed to prefer provincial locations, where proper treatment would be harder to obtain in haste.

When hearing of the Navalny attack, we had initially been sceptical that the Kremlin security apparatus would be so extreme as to seek to assassinate Putin's most famous rival. We had no doubts anymore. The Navalny murder attempt was not a one-off. Poisoning was customary business.

With immense courage, Navalny flew from Germany back to Moscow in January 2021, knowing his probable fate. He was immediately arrested, then imprisoned in a labour camp,[14] where he has since complained of serious abuse. In other signs of worsening oppression in Russia, our close collaborator there, Roman, had his home searched in July 2021, after his publication, *The Insider*, was declared a 'foreign agent'. In parallel, a preposterous libel case was launched against him.[15]

One of our sources in the Navalny investigation – a 'data broker' in the small western Russian republic of Chuvashia, who was a conduit between corrupt officials willing to leak records and those online willing to pay for them – reached out to Christo to explain how our disclosures had affected him. When he was visiting a business partner, he found the man's door broken down. He messaged Christo as this was going on, describing a car with no licence plate idling in front of the building. Abruptly, the source stopped texting.

The following day, he appeared online again, explaining what had happened: officers in balaclavas appeared, bundling his business partner into a vehicle. They abducted our source, too, and drove both outside the city, halting along the way to throw our source into the street. They kept his partner, however, and handed him over to thugs in a forest, who carried out a mock execution before returning him, emotionally broken, to the officers. By then, the business partner admitted to anything they wanted; he faces a long prison sentence now. Our source fled Russia, and this former black-marketeer – convinced of our cause – volunteered to help Bellingcat for nothing.

OUR 'TEAM' BECOMES A TEAM

The Navalny report, which won us two Emmys alongside CNN,[16] was a unique investigation in unique times, carried out against the background of Covid-19. As for Bellingcat's other operations in this period, we found ourselves well positioned to cope with a pandemic – 'work from home' was not a radical change for us. Indeed, we grew larger than ever during this period. As we entered 2022, the core Bellingcat team consisted of about forty people, including staff and our closest contributors.[17]

Covid-19 did force us to move our workshops online, but this had an upside, allowing us to include anyone, anywhere. In 2020, this amounted to more than 800 new trainees, including rights activists and reporters without the funds to pay, whom we granted free access. The pandemic period also saw us develop more partnerships and donors than ever. We were clocking millions of unique website visitors annually, and our Twitter following (including both Bellingcat's account and my own) grew to exceed half a million people.

We took measures to sharpen our articles too, hiring new chief editors, Eoghan Macguire and Maxim Edwards, and adding legal reviews and a right-of-reply. In parallel, we issued *Bellingcat Editorial Standards & Practices*,[18] codifying our rules regarding evidence and transparency, both to guide our staff and for other open-source investigators.

A new tech team took shape, focusing on cutting-edge tools via a Bellingcat GitHub (a collaborative platform for software developers) – for example, a way to find Instagram postings in specific locations, a tool to extract the upload date of TikTok videos, and a way to search Google Earth for cloud-free satellite pictures. The bigger picture, though, was an overhaul of the Bellingcat structure itself. Nobody could call us 'ragtag' anymore.

The leader of this transformation was our new chief operating officer, Dessi Lange-Damianova, who lent media-industry experience and boundless energy to professionalising what we did. Dessi, who joined in March 2019, came from a journalism background, having worked at the BBC World Service as an editor in London and a correspondent in Amsterdam before helping develop news outfits from South Asia to Eastern Europe to Latin America.

What Dessi noticed about Bellingcat was that we had reversed the standard order of things. Typically, an organisation builds its structure, then looks to have an impact. We had already had a vast impact – but hadn't got to the structure part yet. Her challenge was to get Bellingcat in shape, while retaining what worked so well about our freewheeling ways.

In November 2019 she arranged a three-day staff retreat in the Netherlands. Many members of our team had never met in person, and some seemed uneasy about the coming changes. Previously, investigators worked on their own projects, following their own schedules. Was everything about to become corporate?

Dessi consolidated Bellingcat's status as a charitable foundation in the Netherlands, established a clear system of admin and HR, and improved the fundraising process too. We set up a board of directors – Dessi, Aric, and me – plus a solid financial system, with sharper roles and communication. But throughout, we were careful to allow everyone to ferret away at their projects with no 'big boss', but an egalitarian ethos encouraging all to get involved, all to have their say.

Previously, Bellingcat existed on Slack channels. Now we were gathering in regular video conferences: a weekly chat on research and training; an editorial call every two weeks, asserting ethical standards and journalistic procedures; biweekly safety and security talks to ensure the team was properly protected; and an all-staff meeting every three weeks. Everyone – whether they are gobbling cereal or squinting at their laptop on a beach – needs to have their cameras on, ensuring we are all engaged and interacting. Whether your job is catching spies or meeting donors, everyone at Bellingcat must understand how the pieces fit together.

In September 2021, after skipping a Bellingcat retreat the previous year for Covid-19-safety reasons, we held our second in-person meeting. The difference from 2019 was remarkable. 'The team is really a team now,' Dessi said.

My own role has shifted too, especially with the July 2021 establishment of Bellingcat Productions, where I became creative director, overseeing plans for a podcast network and filmed documentaries. This has not meant a slowdown of our investigations. Those are more wide-ranging than ever and attuned to breaking news.

A day before the riot in the US Capitol on 6 January 2021, we published a piece[19] on the alliance between Trumpists and insurgents on the streets of Washington DC. When the breach of the building was underway, we were compiling an archive of open-source material for the historical record, much as we had done for the 2017 Unite the Right rally in Charlottesville. A new initiative was born, too: The Q Origins Project, in which we sought those behind the cultish QAnon conspiracy theory, whose fantasies of Satanic cannibalistic paedophiles stirred many of the rioters to action.

Beyond the United States' political chaos, we drew widespread attention for an investigation by Bellingcat researcher and trainer Foeke Postma[20] into celebrities' and social-media stars' complicity in promoting the illegal trade of exotic animals in Dubai. We were also expanding into Latin America, led by our Toronto-based staffer Giancarlo Fiorella, who had followed my work since the Brown Moses days. In 2014, he noticed how little coverage there was of protests in his native Venezuela, though much raw footage appeared online. He began verifying content on a blog, much as I once had. We eventually connected, leading to his teaching Bellingcat workshops in Latin America and linking up with news organisations there. Among the notable results was his team's identification[21] through video clips of a Colombian police officer who shot and killed an eighteen-year-old student during a protest; the officer was later arrested. We also began delving into open-source ways to study the destruction of the Latin American rainforest, and to chronicle threats against environmental activists there.

Our investigator Nick Waters responded to the developments in Afghanistan, archiving open-source material after the fall of Kabul in August 2021, when the Taliban was still seeking to present itself to the world as a reasonable government. With many Afghans fleeing to Europe and the United States, our plan was to solicit their expertise in the verification and scrutiny of material emerging from post-occupation Afghanistan.

Nick's own research helped expose how Greek security forces had fired live rounds at refugees and migrants trying to break through a border fence with Turkey, in a study produced with Lighthouse Reports, a non-profit Dutch investigative news source that applies both traditional and open-source techniques, plus the pioneering digital researchers at Forensic Architecture, and *Der Spiegel*.[22] This linked to another collaborative piece, showing that the European coastguard agency, Frontex, had been complicit in illegal pushbacks of migrants crossing the Mediterranean to reach the European Union. Some migrants in flimsy dinghies found themselves harassed by coastguard ships, even dragged to the middle of the sea and abandoned there, all in violation of international law.

On a lighter note, the Bellingcat method even proved effective as a dog catcher. A woman was taking her spaniel, Coco, for a walk near Birmingham on 1 October 2020, when the pooch leapt from her vehicle and approached a parked car. The driver opened his door, snatched Coco, and drove off. The price of dogs had shot up during the pandemic, and thefts followed. The police could not drop everything to hunt for a floppy-eared abductee, so this seemed like a hopeless case. But a dog-rescue group reached out to me with a two-second CCTV clip, showing the car. The police had already said that nobody could decipher the licence plate from these images. I called on our graphics expert Timmi Allen, who had honed his skills identifying those military vehicles implicated in the downing of MH17. Minutes later, he sent me an enhanced image, with the licence plate legible. The police connected this to an address, and rescued the dog. The owners recorded their glee on social media, posting a photo of a young boy hugging little Coco.[23]

I mention this minor case to make a point. The Bellingcat method has endless applications. What unifies our work is a drive for accountability. We take scattered facts online and try to turn them into justice.

Slowly, our work is trickling into justice systems themselves. The findings on the downing of MH17 underpinned prosecutors' cases during the Dutch trial of suspects. In Cameroon, four soldiers were sentenced to prison for the murder of women and children, as evidenced by footage analysed in a BBC report we collaborated on.[24] And British prosecutors finally authorised charges in September 2021 against the third suspect in the Skripal poisoning, Denis Sergeev,[25] whom Bellingcat had exposed as the operation commander more than two years earlier.[26]

Amid this, a trial with widespread ramifications for open-source evidence was underway in Germany, after a brawny middle-aged Russian approached an ethnic Chechen asylum seeker in a Berlin park on 23 August 2019, and shot him dead.[27] When German police arrested the suspect, he identified himself as 'Vadim Sokolov'. But Christo and his investigative partners found no sign in Russian state records that any such person existed. Even so, 'Sokolov' possessed an official Russian passport. German prosecutors suspected that he was a Kremlin assassin.

But to prove this, someone had to show who 'Sokolov' truly was. Soon, our investigative team had cracked it.[28]

The man in German custody, we found, was Vadim Krasikov, a suspect in two possible contract killings in Russia that, a few years earlier, had prompted the authorities there to seek his arrest. But mysteriously, Russian investigations into Krasikov appeared to have dissolved away. Our hypothesis[29] was that the authorities there had detained Krasikov, and that he – with an elite military background and facing life in prison – was recruited as a hitman for the state. By tracing the cell-tower connections of his phone, we even demonstrated that Krasikov had repeatedly spent periods at secure FSB training facilities shortly before the Berlin assassination.

The key witness in the court case was none other than Christo, whom elite German police flew by helicopter to Berlin so he could testify as protected witness 'G'. Since the prosecutors' case rested on proving that 'Sokolov' was not just an innocent tourist, our findings proved central, helping determine how other court systems consider digital evidence in the future.

When it comes to Bellingcat's own future, we plan to keep growing. Dessi has already strategised ahead to 2030, when we aim to have expanded across Latin America, into Africa, Asia and the Middle East, publishing not just in English but Arabic, Mandarin, Russian, Spanish and French. By that time, we expect a hundred-strong Bellingcat team, half of them staff members, half regular contributors.

We hope to bring in thousands more volunteers, too – 'Bellingcatters' around the globe, pursuing online facts and offline accountability. To achieve these numbers, we will expand our training at universities and among a new generation of journalists, while establishing annual summits for our community to gather. The crux of our global expansion is a new concept, BellingcatX, far-flung cells of investigators who apply our techniques and standards but operate independently. The Bellingcat method will keep seeding itself throughout journalism, law enforcement and the courts – always in the service of transparency, clear thinking and justice.

When Christo was holed up at that Airbnb in the Black Forest, working on the final details of his Navalny investigation, he offered the opposition leader a chance to confront his attackers for a reason: the man would never enjoy such an opportunity in court. Christo was probably right to think that. But the era of total impunity is dwindling.

As more citizens learn how online evidence is uncovered, we will all expect more from our news sources, our elected officials, our prosecutors. As for tyrants and their henchman, they too must consider the clips, postings and geolocations that expose their crimes. Someday soon they may be considering such evidence from the inside of a courtroom.

Notes

INTRODUCTION

1 (9 March) www.ft.com/content/6a344cf4-2381-11e8-ae48-60d3531b7d11

2 Mark Urban, *The Skripal Files: The Life and Near Death of a Russian Spy*, Henry Holt, 2018, p. 248.

3 www.gov.uk/government/speeches/pm-commons-statement-on-salisbury-incident-12-march-2018

4 www.aljazeera.com/indepth/interactive/2018/04/skripal-case-diplomatic-expulsions-numbers-180402121217839.html

5 Urban, op. cit. pp. 255–60.

6 web.archive.org/web/20180906040259/ news.met.police.uk/news/counter-terrorism-police-release-images-of-two-suspects-in-connection-with-salisbury-attack-320534

7 Skripal BBC documentary: 'Salisbury nerve agent attack: the inside story', *Panorama*, 22 November 2018.

8 Counter-terrorism police release images of two suspects in connection with Salisbury attack: web.archive.org/web/20180906040259/http://news.met.police.uk/news/counter-terrorism-police-release-images-of-two-suspects-in-connection-with-salisbury-attack-320534

9 www.bbc.co.uk/news/world-europe-45494627

10 Full Skripal interview: https://www.youtube.com/watch?v=Ku8OQNyI2io
   Transcript: www.rt.com/news/438356-rt-petrov-boshirov-full-interview/

11 'Paul's Security Weekly,' Episode 548. Feb. 15, 2018. 21m; youtu.be/xb9BljytXds?t=1279

12 P. W. Singer and Emerson T. Brooking, *Like War: The Weaponization of Social Media*, Houghton Mifflin Harcourt, 2018, p. 80.

1 REVOLUTION ON A LAPTOP

1 Andy Carvin, *Distant Witness: Social Media, the Arab Spring and a Journalism Revolution*, CUNY Journalism Press, 2012, pp. 23–33.

2 Ibid., p. 39.

3 www.youtube.com/watch?v=EnmMZ2bSlnc

4 www.telegraph.co.uk/news/worldnews/africaandindianocean/libya/8754375/Gaddafis-ghost-town-after-the-loyalists-retreat.html

5 www.theguardian.com/world/middle-east-live/2011/aug/12/syria-libya-middle-east-unrest

6 af.reuters.com/article/libyaNews/idAFLDE77A0UN20110811?sp=true

7 en.wikipedia.org/wiki/Fourth_Battle_of_Brega

8 www.youtube.com/watch?v=4UGBP043dz8

9 www.google.com/maps/d/u/0/viewer?ie=UTF&msa=0&mid=1c5sA598QOpHNvFox08yrPsjHy4U&ll=30.486213501292106%2C19.72388699999999&z=19

10 www.bellingcat.com/resources/how-tos/2014/07/09/a-beginners-guide-to-geolocation/

11 www.theguardian.com/world/2012/oct/20/muammar-gaddafi-killing-witnesses
www.bbc.co.uk/news/world-africa-15390980www.youtube.com/watch?v=EnmMZ2bSlnc

12 web.archive.org/web/20130513032123/http://www.pressgazette.co.uk/node/33247
www.nytimes.com/2006/05/09/business/media/us-newspaper-circulation-fell-25-in-latest-period.html

13 www.theguardian.com/media/2011/nov/23/hugh-grant-leveson-inquiry-statement

14 www.theguardian.com/media/2011/jul/11/phone-hacking-news-international-gordon-brown

15 www.theguardian.com/uk/2011/jul/04/milly-dowler-voicemail-hacked-news-of-world

16 www.bbc.co.uk/news/uk-14040841

17 www.afr.com/business/media-and-marketing/tv/pay-tv-piracy-hits-news-20120328-iu4j1

18 brown-moses.blogspot.com/2012/03/ray-adams-and-his-friends-bulgarian.html

19 www.huffpost.com/entry/the-people-formerly-known_1_b_2411
    3?guccounter=1&guce_referrer=aHR0cHM6Ly93d3cuZ29vZ2xl
    LmNvbS8&guce_referrer_sig=AQAAANLEwO62uZJ71rUqJDA
    WsvuAa977q-qTZMO2nRR6xKSYZFyOdkQVeGOICRpbhO
    HzSNWO4K9mNsLpJdMtt4O1k4gDOpN5O3NEDwkFm1Q9
    pfoPrtBbaY1ft2GIQTpEOBm3bMZ798cD4dRNYasAh1xfXHnf
    4IaeNLHa2fKxabFd9eT9

20 mariecolvincenter.org/stories-by-marie-colvin/escape-from-chechnya/
    www.newyorker.com/books/page-turner/a-book-that-captures-the-singular-life-of-marie-colvin

21 edition.cnn.com/2012/02/22/world/marie-colvin-interview-transcript/index.html
    youtu.be/xfrVJSRMuhs?t=27www.newyorker.com/books/page-turner/a-book-that-captures-the-singular-life-of-marie-colvin

22 www.csmonitor.com/World/Middle-East/2012/0801/Syria-s-iPhone-insurgency-makes-for-smarter-rebellion

23 cpj.org/2014/02/attacks-on-the-press-syria-analysis.php

24 brown-moses.blogspot.com/2012/04/daily-selected-syria-videos-april-2nd.html

25 brown-moses.blogspot.com/2012/04/daily-selected-syria-videos-april-3rd.html

26 brown-moses.blogspot.com/2012/05/syria-houla-massacre.html

27 See EH tweets of 25 May 2012.

28 www.bbc.co.uk/news/world-middle-east-14482968

29 brown-moses.blogspot.com/2012/05/syria-houla-massacre.html

30 www.bbc.co.uk/news/world-middle-east-18233934

31 www.aljazeera.com/news/middleeast/2012/05/20125279530938874.html

32 https://www.nytimes.com/2012/05/30/world/middleeast/kofi-annan-meets-with-bashar-al-assad.html

33 www.ohchr.org/Documents/HRBodies/HRCouncil/
    PRCoISyria15082012_en.pdf

34 www.npr.org/sections/thetwo-way/2012/05/26/153792544/
    brutal-and-appalling-attack-on-syrian-city-of-houla-kills-32-
    children?sc=tw&cc=share

35 hassan699721, FreedomAlhoula, nontherful and samerd3

36 sabotagetimes.com/life/how-i-accidentally-became-an-expert-
    on-the-syrian-conflict

37 www.youtube.com/watch?time_continue=47&v=dRJnStU4izg

38 A prolific Twitter poster, @HamaEcho, pointed this out to me.
    On 5 December 2012, the account tweeted: '#offline forever.
    We are going to Ghouta soon. I have a bad feeling about this
    but the only thing that can happen is martyrdom or victory.'
    That was the last recorded tweet. (twitter.com/HamaEcho/
    status/276416201943576576)

39 en.wikipedia.org/wiki/9K32_Strela-2

40 brown-moses.blogspot.com/2012/06/even-more-increasingly-
    well-armed-free.html

41 web.archive.org/web/20130124155321/http://spectator.org/
    archives/2012/06/12/arming-the-free-syrian-army/

42 www.pri.org/stories/2012-06-07/inside-syria-you-will-
    never-guess-who-arms-rebels
    www.pri.org/stories/2012-06-14/syria-s-rebels-learn-
    value-prisoner

43 www.telegraph.co.uk/news/worldnews/middleeast/
    syria/9334707/US-holds-high-level-talks-with-Syrian-rebels-
    seeking-weapons-in-Washington.html

44 brown-moses.blogspot.com/2012/06/increasingly-well-armed-
    fsa-and-other.html
    brown-moses.blogspot.com/2012/06/even-more-increasingly-
    well-armed-free.htmlwww.youtube.com/watch?v=
    vJG698U2Mvo

45 Cq. twitter.com/EliotHiggins/status/222821174600663040

46 www.youtube.com/watch?v=GvCZNWxOZXg&feature=plcp

47 www.aljazeera.com/news/middleeast/2012/06/
    201261115143642086.html

48 www.hrw.org/news/2012/07/12/syria-evidence-cluster-
    munitions-use-syrian-forces

brown-moses.blogspot.com/2012/06/evidence-of-unguided-bombs-being.html

49 en.wikipedia.org/wiki/A-IX-2

50 www.un.org/disarmament/convarms/clustermunitions/

51 www.stopclustermunitions.org/en-gb/cluster-bombs/what-is-a-cluster-bomb.aspx
www.stopclustermunitions.org/en-gb/the-treaty/treaty-status.aspxwww.stopclustermunitions.org/en-gb/cluster-bombs/use-of-cluster-bombs/a-timeline-of-cluster-bomb-use.aspx

52 youtu.be/F92m9eqKP14

53 www.uxoinfo.com/blogcfc/client/index.cfm

54 brown-moses.blogspot.com/2012/07/evidence-of-cluster-bombs-being.html

55 cjchivers.com/post/27009844587/has-the-syrian-government-used-cluster-bombs

56 www.hrw.org/news/2012/07/12/syria-evidence-cluster-munitions-use-syrian-forces

57 cjchivers.com/post/27063587043/syria-and-the-use-of-cluster-munitions-why-it

58 www.globalsecurity.org/military/world/russia/ofab-250-270.htm
www.armaco.bg/en/product/aerial-ammunitions-c17/ofab-250-270-p566arconpartners.net/products/ammunition/aircraft-bombs/ofab-250-270-high-explosive-fragmentation-bomb-he-frag/brown-moses.blogspot.com/2012/06/evidence-of-unguided-bombs-being.html

59 foreignpolicy.com/2012/07/30/syrias-diy-revolt/

60 Robin Yassin-Kassab and Leila al-Shami, *Burning Country: Syrians in Revolution and War*, Pluto Press, 2016, p. 213.

61 www.youtube.com/watch?v=fn6HWOXlCzo

62 brown-moses.blogspot.com/2012/05/syrian-regime-propaganda-at-work.html

63 www.rt.com/news/syrian-rebels-desecrate-christian-churches-897/

64 brown-moses.blogspot.com/2012/06/russia-today-and-their-anti-fsa.html

65 translate.google.com/translate?sl=auto&tl=en&u=https%3A%2F%2Fwww.kommersant.ru%2Fdoc%2F1911336

66 www.InfoWars.com/shocking-videos-reveal-truth-behind-syrian-freedom-fighters/

67 www.infowars.com/al-qaeda-rebel-pictured-with-un-observers-in-syria/

68 www.infowars.com/al-qaeda-rebel-pictured-with-un-observers-in-syria/
    brown-moses.blogspot.co.uk/2012/05/more-syrian-propaganda-fake-al-qaeda.html

69 https://archives.infowars.com/al-qaeda-rebel-pictured-with-un-observers-in-syria/

70 www.nytimes.com/2017/11/02/world/americas/allahu-akbar-terrorism.html

71 brown-moses.blogspot.com/2012/07/alex-jones-InfoWars-and-their-anti-free.html
    brown-moses.blogspot.com/2012/07/alex-jones-InfoWars-and-their-anti-free.html?showComment=1342251080915#c8464224251801792476

72 youtu.be/s0YBroyNDIM

73 brown-moses.blogspot.com/2012/08/the-mystery-of-syrian-barrel-bombs.html

74 www.youtube.com/watch?v=M95ta3_mZBA

75 www.telegraph.co.uk/news/worldnews/middleeast/syria/9512719/Syrian-regime-deploys-deadly-new-weapons-on-rebels.html

76 web.archive.org/web/20130926070111/http:/rt.com/op-edge/barrel-bomb-syria-claim

77 brown-moses.blogspot.com/2012/10/clear-evidence-of-diy-barrel-bombs.html
    www.bellingcat.com/news/mena/2015/07/08/a-brief-open-source-history-of-the-syrian-barrel-bomb/

78 sn4hr.org/blog/2017/12/25/49915/

79 www.bbc.co.uk/news/world-middle-east-47572294

80 derstandard.at/1353207433435/Selbstgebastelte-Sprengsaetze-immer-wichtiger?ref=article

81 edition.cnn.com/2012/11/29/world/meast/syria-missiles/index.html

82 www.csmonitor.com/World/Middle-East/2012/1116/Where-Syria-s-opposition-groups-get-their-rockets

83 app.ft.com/cms/s/5dc1e0e6-3a23-11e2-a00d-00144feabdco.html

84 www.npr.org/2012/10/27/163760135/variety-of-weapons-increases-in-syrian-conflict

85 brown-moses.blogspot.com/2013/01/are-yugoslavian-anti-tank-weapons-being.html

86 brown-moses.blogspot.com/2013/01/evidence-of-multiple-foreign-weapon.html
    brown-moses.blogspot.com/2013/02/foreign-smuggled-weapons-spread.html

87 C. J. Chivers and Eric Schmitt, www.nytimes.com/images/2013/02/26/nytfrontpage/scan.jpg

88 www.nytimes.com/2013/02/26/world/middleeast/in-shift-saudis-are-said-to-arm-rebels-in-syria.html

89 www.publications.parliament.uk/pa/cm201213/cmhansrd/cm130304/debtext/130304-0001.htm#1303049000716

90 www.theguardian.com/world/2013/mar/21/frontroom-blogger-analyses-weapons-syria-frontline

91 www.indiegogo.com/projects/the-brown-moses-blog#/

92 www.vdc-sy.info/index.php/en/martyrs/1/c29ydGJ5PWEua2lsbGVkX2RhdGV8c29ydGRpcj1ERVNDfGFwcHJvdmVkPXZpc2libGV8ZXhocmFkaXNwbGF5PTB8Y29kTXVsdGk9MTV8dGhpcoRhdGU9MjAxMyowOCoyMXw=
    https://www.msf.org/syria-thousands-suffering-neurotoxic-symptoms-treated-hospitals-supported-msf

93 obamawhitehouse.archives.gov/the-press-office/2012/08/20/remarks-president-white-house-press-corps

94 www.armscontrol.org/factsheets/Timeline-of-Syrian-Chemical-Weapons-Activity

95 www.chathamhouse.org/sites/default/files/field/field_document/INTA91_5_11_Strong_0.pdf

96 obamawhitehouse.archives.gov/the-press-office/2013/08/30/government-assessment-syrian-government-s-use-chemical-weapons-august-21

97 firstdraftnews.org/piecing-together-open-source-evidence-from-the-sarin-attacks/

98 brown-moses.blogspot.com/2013/08/finding-exact-location-of-alleged.html

99 brown-moses.blogspot.com/2013/08/were-un-inspectors-examining-chemical.html

100 www.bellingcat.com/news/mena/2014/07/17/august-21st-the-rebels-did-it/

101 www.buzzfeednews.com/article/rosiegray/the-inside-story-of-one-websites-defense-of-assad#.xqRAzld18

102 brown-moses.blogspot.com/2013/09/chemical-weapons-specialists-on-claims.html

103 brown-moses.blogspot.com/2013/08/diy-weapon-linked-to-alleged-chemical.html

104 brown-moses.blogspot.com/2013/09/why-un-report-on-chemical-weapons-in.html

105 www.bbc.co.uk/news/world-middle-east-23876085

106 www.un.org/disarmament/content/slideshow/Secretary_General_Report_of_CW_Investigation.pdf

107 www.bellingcat.com/news/mena/2014/07/15/identifying-government-positions-during-the-august-21st-sarin-attacks/

108 Google Earth later updated its satellite imagery of the area, adding pictures of 24 August 2013, which showed tanks and checkpoints that matched my investigation of the videos, adding further confirmation of what I'd found.

109 www.nytimes.com/2013/09/17/world/europe/syria-united-nations.html

110 web.archive.org/web/20140122001133/http://www.presstv.ir/detail/2013/09/17/324436/5-lies-invented-to-spin-un-report-on-syria/

111 brown-moses.blogspot.com/2013/09/videos-claim-to-show-jabhat-al-nusra.html

112 brown-moses.blogspot.com/2013/09/statement-on-russia-todays-use-of-my.html

113 brown-moses.blogspot.com/2013/10/making-sense-of-russias-evolving.html
www.bellingcat.com/news/mena/2014/07/17/august-21st-the-rebels-did-it/

114 www.lrb.co.uk/the-paper/v35/n24/seymour-m.-hersh/whose-sarin

115 www.newyorker.com/magazine/2013/11/25/rocket-man-2

116 ict4peace.org/activities/google-ideas-conflict-in-a-connected-world-summit-strengthening-digital-security-of-activists/
www.youtube.com/watch?v=qbWhcWizSFY

117 camp2013.tacticaltech.org/content/track-summaries

118 www.icfj.org/our-work/knight/profiles/paul-radu
www.occrp.org/staff

119 www.pri.org/stories/2016-06-02/panama-papers-pirates-and-argument-how-some-data-leaks-can-make-world-better
en.wikipedia.org/wiki/Sm%C3%A1ri_McCarthy

120 exposingtheinvisible.org/films/sketch/lydia-medland-from-freedom-of/
www.bristol.ac.uk/spais/people/person/lydia-k-medland/

121 www.webcitation.org/6CViaUTn5?url=http://www.foreignpolicy.com/articles/2011/11/28/the_fp_top_100_global_thinkers?page=0,23

122 academic.oup.com/bjc/article/57/2/341/2623876

123 Wikileaks had their Twitter group chat logs leaked by a former member in 2018. In those chat logs, the Wikileaks account – perhaps even run by Julian Assange himself – speculated that Britain's Ministry of Defence funded Bellingcat, a totally false claim.
emma.best/2018/07/29/11000-messages-from-private-wikileaks-chat-released/

2 BECOMING BELLINGCAT

1 en.wikipedia.org/wiki/List_of_Ukrainian_aircraft_losses_during_the_Ukrainian_crisis

2 www.rferl.org/a/ukraine-separatist-leader-boasts-downing-plane/25460930.html

3 youtu.be/MiI9s-zWLs4

4 republic.ru/posts/l/1129893

5 rusvesna.su/news/1405676334

6 www.pressgazette.co.uk/russia-today-london-correspondent-resigns-protest-disrespect-facts-over-malaysian-plane-crash
www.buzzfeed.com/jimwaterson/russia-today-correspondent-resigns-over-coverage-of-ukranian?bftw=main

7 www.dailymail.co.uk/wires/ap/article-2706045/What-happened-The-day-Flight-17-downed.html

8 www.groene.nl/artikel/het-mh17-complot

9 www.bellingcat.com/resources/case-studies/2014/07/18/ identifying-the-location-of-the-mh17-linked-missile-launcher-from-one-photograph/

10 twitter.com/GirkinGirkin/status/489884062577094656/photo/1

11 www.koreandefense.com/how-to-find-the-missing-buk-system/

12 youtu.be/L4HJmev5xg0

13 www.bellingcat.com/news/uk-and-europe/2014/07/18/buk-transporter-filmed-heading-to-russia-sighted-in-an-earlier-photograph/

14 youtu.be/4bNPInuSqfs

15 www.bellingcat.com/news/uk-and-europe/2018/01/05/ kremlins-shifting-self-contradicting-narratives-mh17/

16 www.bellingcat.com/news/uk-and-europe/2014/07/22/evidence-that-russian-claims-about-the-mh17-buk-missile-launcher-are-false/

17 evilmilker.livejournal.com/4379.html?thread=66587#t66587

18 www.bellingcat.com/news/uk-and-europe/2014/07/24/caught-in-a-lie-compelling-evidence-russia-lied-about-the-buk-linked-to-mh17/

19 it4sec.org/system/files/15.1.01_abrams.pdf

20 www.rollingstone.com/music/music-news/the-passion-of-kanye-west-71551/#ixzz3Ak9jIIed

21 it4sec.org/system/files/15.1.01_abrams.pdf

22 www.stopfake.org/en/anatomy-of-an-info-war-how-russia-s-propaganda-machine-works-and-how-to-counter-it/

23 mashable.com/2014/07/23/citizen-journalists-mh17-spies/?europe=true

24 twitter.com/DisinfoPortal/status/1113190404105568257

25 euvsdisinfo.eu/figure-of-the-week-111486-0619/ www.groene.nl/artikel/het-mh17-complot

26 www.bellingcat.com/news/uk-and-europe/2014/07/24/caught-in-a-lie-compelling-evidence-russia-lied-about-the-buk-linked-to-mh17/

27 ukraineatwar.blogspot.com/2014/07/another-photo-of-mh17-buk-transport.html

28 www.bellingcat.com/news/uk-and-europe/2014/07/28/ two-more-key-sightings-of-the-mh17-buk-missile-launcher/

29 www.bellingcat.com/news/uk-and-europe/2014/07/28/
    the-buk-that-could-an-open-source-odyssey/

30 www.bellingcat.com/news/uk-and-europe/2014/07/22/the-latest-
    open-source-theories-speculation-and-debunks-on-flight-mh17/
    www.bellingcat.com/resources/articles/2014/08/06/investigating-
    the-mh17-crash-site-with-meedans-checkdesk/web.archive.org/
    web/20140825231735/http://bellingcat.checkdesk.org/en/story/24

31 www.bellingcat.com/news/mena/2014/08/28/
    russias-version-of-the-navy-seals-may-be-fighting-in-ukraine/

32 www.bellingcat.com/news/uk-and-europe/2014/09/08/
    images-show-the-buk-that-downed-flight-mh17-inside-russia-
    controlled-by-russian-troops/

33 www.themoscowtimes.com/archive/activist-plans-protest-amid-
    outrage-over-talk-show-hosts-homophobic-meteor-comments

34 www.bellingcat.com/news/uk-and-europe/2014/10/11/russian-tv-
    inadvertently-demonstrates-mh17-wasnt-shot-down-by-aircraft-
    cannon-fire/

35 www.bellingcat.com/news/2014/11/14/russian-state-television-
    shares-fake-images-of-mh17-being-attacked/

36 www.bellingcat.com/news/uk-and-europe/2014/11/08/
    origin-of-the-separatists-buk-a-bellingcat-investigation/

37 www.bellingcat.com/resources/case-studies/2015/01/27/
    examining-the-mh17-launch-smoke-photographs/

38 www.youtube.com/watch?v=SkCcCmYlMZc

39 www.bellingcat.com/news/uk-and-europe/2015/01/27/is-this-
    the-launch-site-of-the-missile-that-shot-down-flight-mh17/

40 www.bellingcat.com/news/uk-and-europe/2015/05/31/mh17-
    forensic-analysis-of-satellite-images-released-by-the-russian-
    ministry-of-defence/

41 www.gofundme.com/bellingcatsat

42 www.bellingcat.com/news/uk-and-europe/2015/06/12/
    july-17-imagery-mod-comparison/

43 www.bellingcat.com/wp-content/uploads/2016/02/53rd-report-
    public.pdf

44 www.bellingcat.com/news/americas/2014/12/17/mexicos-
    guerra-al-narco-a-disaster-rooted-in-misinterpretations/
    www.bellingcat.com/news/americas/2015/03/20/assessing-
    mexicos-guerra-al-narco/www.bellingcat.com/news/

americas/2016/02/25/geolocating-mexican-sicarios-in-chihuahua/www.bellingcat.com/news/2015/08/07/tracking-swiss-watches-in-sinaloa-top-6-luxury-brands-among-mexican-drug-lords/

45 www.bellingcat.com/resources/2015/10/05/gangs-of-detroit-osint-and-indictment-documents/

46 www.bellingcat.com/news/mena/2016/02/05/yemens-bombed-water-infrastructure/

47 www.bellingcat.com/resources/articles/2015/10/05/crowdsourced-geolocation-and-analysis-of-russian-mod-airstrike-videos-from-syria/

www.bellingcat.com/news/mena/2015/10/26/what-russias-own-videos-and-maps-reveal-about-who-they-are-bombing-in-syria/

48 www.bellingcat.com/resources/how-tos/2015/03/15/how-tall-is-that-gantry/

www.bellingcat.com/resources/how-tos/2015/04/10/theres-a-map-for-that/

49 medium.com/1st-draft/baltimore-looting-tweets-show-importance-of-quick-and-easy-image-checks-a713bbcc275e

50 www.bellingcat.com/resources/how-tos/2015/05/08/manual-reverse-image-search-with-google-and-tineye/

51 www.bellingcat.com/resources/case-studies/2014/08/23/the-hills-of-raqqa-geolocating-the-james-foley-video/

52 www.bellingcat.com/resources/case-studies/2015/11/23/how-we-found-one-of-the-paris-suicide-bombers-on-facebook/

53 www.atlanticcouncil.org/images/publications/Hiding_in_Plain_Sight/HPS_English.pdf

54 By March 2019, they had funded 662 projects totalling 140 million euros.
www.blog.google/around-the-globe/google-europe/digital-news-innovation-fund-three-years-and-662-total-projects-supported/

55 www.bellingcat.com/resources/articles/2016/05/13/dataset-of-russian-attacks-against-syrias-civilians/

3 FIREWALL OF FACTS

1 threatconnect.com/blog/faketivist-vs-hacktivist-how-they-differ/

2 www.apnews.com/69b28dd8fc034cb0a2528048638d7893

3 threatconnect.com/blog/tapping-into-democratic-national-committee/
threatconnect.com/blog/does-a-bear-leak-in-the-woods/

4 threatconnect.com/blog/russia-hacks-bellingcat-mh17-investigation/

5 www.bellingcat.com/resources/articles/2015/10/05/crowdsourced-geolocation-and-analysis-of-russian-mod-airstrike-videos-from-syria/

6 www.rt.com/news/317971-bellingcat-russia-syria-videos-geolocation/

7 www.linkedin.com/in/richard-galustian-a834136

8 russia-insider.com/en/understanding-history-zionism/ri26852

9 www.bellingcat.com/resources/articles/2016/04/14/response-from-the-russian-ministry-of-foreign-affairs-to-bellingcat-regarding-fakery-allegations/
www.bellingcat.com/news/uk-and-europe/2016/04/22/mfa-plagiarism/

10 www.whitehelmets.org/en/

11 www.infowars.com/report-soros-linked-group-behind-chemical-attack-in-syria/
www.nytimes.com/2017/04/10/us/politics/factcheck-syria-strike-conspiracy-theories.html

12 www.bellingcat.com/resources/articles/2017/07/04/khan-sheikhoun-false-flag-conspiracy-actually-mean/

13 www.thedailybeast.com/the-kardashian-look-alike-trolling-for-assad

14 www.youtube.com/watch?v=4TgwkhmHHfY

15 www.dailymotion.com/video/x1400c0

16 twitter.com/ryliberty/status/1065935056722518016?lang=en

17 twitter.com/Partisangirl/status/548282352258936832

18 www.youtube.com/watch?v=pSriotY_7uA

19 twitter.com/Partisangirl/status/372811564728217601

20 twitter.com/Partisangirl/status/372812134230806528

21 www.bellingcat.com/news/mena/2018/04/13/doumafakenews/

22 www.bellingcat.com/news/mena/2018/12/18/chemical-weapons-and-absurdity-the-disinformation-campaign-against-the-white-helmets/

23 faculty.washington.edu/kstarbi/Alt_Narratives_ICWSM17-CameraReady.pdf

24 www.nybooks.com/daily/2018/10/16/why-assad-and-russia-target-the-white-helmets/

25 thewallwillfall.org/about/

26 www.rt.com/op-ed/449431-syria-white-helmets-organ-traders/

27 21stcenturywire.com/2019/01/24/white-helmets-organ-traffickers-child-kidnappersthieves-terrorists-propagandists-or-saints/

28 www.globalresearch.ca/white-helmets-alleged-organ-traders-child-kidnappers-condemned-condoned/5666222

29 medium.com/@katestarbird/content-sharing-within-the-alternative-media-echo-system-the-case-of-the-white-helmets-f34434325e77

30 www.fastcompany.com/40540411/erasing-history-youtubes-deletion-of-syria-war-videos-concerns-human-rights-groups
www.theatlantic.com/ideas/archive/2019/05/facebook-algorithms-are-making-it-harder/588931/www.buzzfeednews.com/article/meghara/facebook-youtube-icc-war-crimes

31 www.niemanlab.org/2019/07/full-fact-has-been-fact-checking-facebook-posts-for-six-months-heres-what-they-think-needs-to-change/

32 www.niemanlab.org/2019/02/it-doesnt-seem-like-were-striving-to-make-third-party-fact-checking-more-practical-for-publishers-it-seems-like-were-striving-to-make-it-easier-for-facebook/

33 www.gppi.net/media/GPPi_Schneider_Luetkefend_2019_Nowhere_to_Hide_Web.pdf

34 www.scmp.com/news/world/middle-east/article/2160348/secret-app-known-sentry-gives-syrian-civilians-minutes-escape

35 www.thetimes.co.uk/article/pilot-of-sarin-gas-jet-flew-in-previous-chemical-attack-3pn62d3xw

36 www.bellingcat.com/news/mena/2017/07/04/opcw-just-trashed-seymour-hershs-khan-sheikhoun-conspiracy-theory/
www.bellingcat.com/news/mena/2017/07/04/summary-claims-surrounding-khan-sheikhoun-chemical-attack/

37 www.bellingcat.com/news/mena/2018/05/01/lethality-chlorine-gas-possible-explanation-high-casualties-deaths-following-april-7-2018-attacks-douma-syria/

38 syriapropagandamedia.org/wp-content/uploads/2019/05/Engineering-assessment-of-two-cylinders-observed-at-the-Douma-incident-27-February-2019-1.pdf

39 syriapropagandamedia.org/

40 hitchensblog.mailonsunday.co.uk/2019/05/strange-news-from-the-opcw-in-the-hague-.html

41 hitchensblog.mailonsunday.co.uk/2010/02/can-bears-turn-into-whales.html
hitchensblog.mailonsunday.co.uk/2013/02/can-bears-turn-into-whales-part-two-charles-darwin-revisited.html

42 www.independent.co.uk/voices/douma-syria-opcw-chemical-weapons-chlorine-gas-video-conspiracy-theory-russia-a8927116.html

43 wikileaks.org/opcw-douma/releases/
www.counterpunch.org/2019/11/15/the-opcw-and-douma-chemical-weapons-watchdog-accused-of-evidence-tampering-by-its-own-inspectors/

44 www.bellingcat.com/news/mena/2019/12/12/chlorines-unique-fingerprints-the-april-7-2018-douma-incident-through-a-chemistry-lens/

45 www.rt.com/news/476137-newsweek-bellingcat-opcw-leak-reuters/

46 www.opcw.org/media-centre/news/2020/02/opcw-independent-investigation-possible-breaches-confidentiality-report

47 twitter.com/zdroberts/status/896519908795854848

48 twitter.com/shaunking/status/896831149019992065

49 www.politico.com/gallery/2017/08/12/photos-charlottesville-white-nationalist-rally-002467?slide=29

50 twitter.com/AricToler/status/896860175046500352

51 eu.cincinnati.com/story/news/2019/01/06/commie-killer-ex-mason-student-daniel-borden-convicted-charlottesville-beating/2480871002/
www.nbcnews.com/news/us-news/ohio-man-gets-nearly-4-year-sentence-beating-black-man-n955961

52 www.topic.com/decoding-the-language-of-extremist-clothing

53 twitter.com/IGD_News/status/1157431843563683840

54 www.bellingcat.com/news/americas/2017/08/29/database-august-12-charlottesville-videos/

55 www.politico.com/magazine/story/2017/03/memes-4chan-trump-supporters-trolls-internet-214856

56 discordleaks.unicornriot.ninja/discord/view/3883?q=power+level#msg
www.bellingcat.com/news/americas/2018/08/17/fascist-activists-spent-last-year-trying-win-police/

57 discordleaks.unicornriot.ninja/discord/view/761140?q=redpilled#msg

58 discordleaks.unicornriot.ninja/discord/view/27908?q=redpilled#msg

59 ifstudies.org/blog/the-demography-of-the-alt-right

60 discordleaks.unicornriot.ninja/discord/view/554199?q=redpilled#msg

61 www.bellingcat.com/news/americas/2018/10/11/memes-infowars-75-fascist-activists-red-pilled/

62 timeline.com/louis-beam-white-supremacy-history-20d028315d?gi=c97ddd846f5f
timeline.com/white-supremacist-early-internet-5e91676eb847

63 simson.net/ref/leaderless/1984.inter-klan_newsletter.pdf

64 citeseerx.ist.psu.edu/viewdoc/download?doi=10.1.1.552.239&rep=rep1&type=pdf

65 www.aljazeera.com/news/2019/03/brother-muslim-worshipper-words-gunman-190315152715528.html

66 www.washingtonpost.com/world/2019/03/15/with-strobe-lights-guns-bearing-neo-nazi-slogans-new-zealand-gunman-plotted-massacre/

67 www.bellingcat.com/news/rest-of-world/2019/03/15/shitposting-inspirational-terrorism-and-the-christchurch-mosque-massacre/

68 www.cjr.org/analysis/christchurch-shooting-media-coverage.php

69 www.buzzfeed.com/markdistefano/the-daily-mail-let-readers-download-the-new-zealand-mosque

70 www.bellingcat.com/news/americas/2019/04/28/ignore-the-poway-synagogue-shooters-manifesto-pay-attention-to-8chans-pol-board/

71 www.bellingcat.com/news/americas/2019/08/04/the-el-paso-shooting-and-the-gamification-of-terror/

72 www.bellingcat.com/news/americas/2019/04/28/ignore-the-poway-synagogue-shooters-manifesto-pay-attention-to-8chans-pol-board/

73 encyclopediadramatica.rs/High_Score

74 www.nytimes.com/2019/08/04/technology/8chan-shooting-manifesto.html

75 www.nytimes.com/2019/08/04/technology/8chan-shooting-manifesto.html

76 www.theverge.com/2019/11/4/20947429/8chan-8kun-online-image-board-shooter-gunmen-manifesto

77 twitter.com/rcallimachi/status/734053117109624836

78 twitter.com/rcallimachi/status/734053117109624836

79 twitter.com/jenanmoussa/status/734054748031160320

80 twitter.com/jenanmoussa/status/734105719612407808

81 www.bellingcat.com/news/uk-and-europe/2017/06/01/crowdsourcing-europols-stop-child-abuse-trace-object-campaign/www.bellingcat.com/news/uk-and-europe/2017/06/15/update-crowdsourcing-europols-stop-child-abuse-trace-object-campaign/www.youtube.com/watch?v=XrOAy6PfYlYwww.europol.europa.eu/stopchildabuse

82 www.europol.europa.eu/newsroom/news/you-have-identified-70-objects-taken-child-sexual-abuse-images
www.europol.europa.eu/newsroom/news/your-help-we-are-21-000-steps-closer-to-saving-child-sexual-abusewww.bellingcat.com/news/uk-and-europe/2017/08/28/stop-child-abuse-2nd-update/

83 www.bellingcat.com/news/uk-and-europe/2020/04/22/creating-impact-a-year-on-stop-child-abuse-trace-an-object/

84 www.europol.europa.eu/newsroom/news/241-victims-of-child-sexual-abuse-safeguarded-thanks-to-global-law-enforcement-efforts

85 en.wikipedia.org/wiki/Russians_in_the_Baltic_states

86 www.thedailybeast.com/the-baltic-elves-taking-on-pro-russian-trolls

87 www.bbc.co.uk/news/av/world-europe-48401922/how-finland-fights-the-fake-news-trolls

88 disinfoportal.org/governments-countering-disinformation-the-case-of-sweden/

89 stacks.stanford.edu/file/druid:fv751yt5934/SHEG%20
Evaluating%20Information%20Online.pdf
amp.usatoday.com/amp/2769781002?__twitter_impression=true

90 www.npr.org/2019/03/22/705809811/students-in-ukraine-learn-how-to-spot-fake-stories-propaganda-and-hate-speech?t=1553365503768

91 euvsdisinfo.eu/trolls-in-your-feed/

92 www.cjr.org/special_report/students-of-truth.php

93 reporterslab.org/category/fact-checking/

94 www.bbc.co.uk/news/av/world-africa-46828293/debunking-fake-news-in-nigeria

95 fullfact.org/blog/2019/jun/how-fact-checking-works/

96 www.bellingcat.com/news/2020/04/10/covid-19-monitoring-the-global-slowdown/

4 MICE CATCH CAT

1 Urban, op. cit., pp. 199–202.

2 www.bbc.co.uk/news/uk-43315636

3 www.wired.com/story/roman-dobrokhotov-insider-russia-gru-bellingcat/?mbid=social_twitter_onsiteshare

4 theins.ru/uncategorized/76960?lang=en.

5 www.telegraph.co.uk/news/2018/07/13/twelve-russian-intelligence-officers-charged-us-election-hacking/
www.telegraph.co.uk/news/2018/10/04/unit26165-russias-elite-military-hacking-centre/

6 cgrozev.wordpress.com/page/7/

7 www.bellingcat.com/news/uk-and-europe/2017/12/08/russian-colonel-general-delfin/

8 https://tass.com/world/979971

9 www.bellingcat.com/news/uk-and-europe/2018/05/25/mh17-russian-gru-commander-orion-identified-oleg-ivannikov/

10 www.kcl.ac.uk/policy-institute/assets/weaponising-news.pdf

11 www.ft.com/content/c655aa4a-3b82-11e9-b856-5404d3811663

12 www.nytimes.com/2018/09/12/world/europe/putin-russia-skripal.html

13 www.bellingcat.com/news/uk-and-europe/2018/09/14/skripal-poisoning-suspects-passport-data-shows-link-security-services/

14 www.bellingcat.com/news/uk-and-europe/2018/09/20/skripal-suspects-confirmed-gru-operatives-prior-european-operations-disclosed/

15 www.bellingcat.com/news/uk-and-europe/2018/09/26/skripal-suspect-boshirov-identified-gru-colonel-anatoliy-chepiga/

16 www.bellingcat.com/news/uk-and-europe/2018/10/02/anatoliy-chepiga-hero-russia-writing-wall/

17 www.bellingcat.com/news/uk-and-europe/2018/10/09/full-report-skripal-poisoning-suspect-dr-alexander-mishkin-hero-russia/

18 www.telegraph.co.uk/news/2018/09/27/gru-agent-carried-skripal-reconnaissance-mission-identified/

19 www.fontanka.ru/2018/10/10/124/

20 www.bellingcat.com/news/uk-and-europe/2019/02/07/third-skripal-suspect-linked-to-2015-bulgaria-poisoning/

21 www.bellingcat.com/news/uk-and-europe/2019/02/14/third-suspect-in-skripal-poisoning-identified-as-denis-sergeev-high-ranking-gru-officer/
www.bellingcat.com/news/uk-and-europe/2019/02/21/the-search-for-denis-sergeev-photographing-a-ghost/

22 www.bellingcat.com/news/uk-and-europe/2019/06/28/the-gru-globetrotters-mission-london/

23 Michael Schwirtz, www.nytimes.com/2019/10/08/world/europe/unit-29155-russia-gru.html?smid=nytcore-ios-share

24 forum.faleristika.info/viewtopic.php?t=101954&start=30

25 www.bellingcat.com/news/uk-and-europe/2019/10/14/averyanov-chepiga/

26 www.bellingcat.com/news/uk-and-europe/2019/10/14/averyanov-chepiga/

27 www.ncbi.nlm.nih.gov/pmc/articles/PMC6039123/

28 www.theguardian.com/world/2018/mar/14/nerve-agent-novichok-produced-russia-site-expert

29 webcache.googleusercontent.com/search?q=cache:9zJUlh4VkbwJ:old.redstar.ru/2008/07/09_07/2_01.html+&cd=6&hl=en&ct=clnk&gl=uk&client=safari

30 www.polygraph.info/a/lavrov-alleges-ties-between-bellingcat-and-intelligence-services-fact-check/29551448.html

31 www.buzzfeed.com/heidiblake/from-russia-with-blood-14-suspected-hits-on-british-soil

32 www.bellingcat.com/news/uk-and-europe/2019/08/14/the-russians-and-ukrainians-translating-the-christchurch-shooters-manifesto/

33 www.bellingcat.com/news/uk-and-europe/2019/08/10/guccifer-rising-months-long-phishing-campaign-on-protonmail-targets-dozens-of-russia-focused-journalists-and-ngos/

34 medium.com/dfrlab/dont-watch-the-new-zealand-mosque-attack-video-just-don-t-e7d30c7ca96a

35 dartcenter.org/media/advice-dealing-vicarious-trauma

36 dartcenter.org/content/working-with-traumatic-imagery

37 www.bellingcat.com/resources/how-tos/2018/10/18/prevent-identify-address-vicarious-trauma-conducting-open-source-investigations-middle-east/
dartcenter.org/media/advice-dealing-vicarious-trauma

5 NEXT STEPS

1 www.icc-cpi.int/CaseInformationSheets/al-werfalliEng.pdf

2 saltonline.org/en/1092/images-ethics-action-online-video-human-rights-and-civic-activism-in-syria

3 (time-stamped, part 1 of his question) youtu.be/2u2DylH9 VCU?t=4434

4 www.bellingcat.com/news/mena/2017/09/04/geolocating-libyas-social-media-executioner/#_ftn1

5 www.bellingcat.com/news/mena/2017/10/03/how-an-execution-site-was-geolocated/

6 www.hrw.org/news/2015/12/16/syria-stories-behind-photos-killed-detainees

7 www.spiegel.de/international/world/spiegel-reporting-supports-accounts-of-torture-and-execution-in-syria-a-945760.html
www.bellingcat.com/resources/case-studies/2015/03/18/3062/

8 www.buzzfeednews.com/amphtml/craigsilverman/facebook-graph-search-war-crimes?__twitter_impression=true

www.janes.com/images/assets/793/89793/Social_media_changes_force_OSINT_practitioners_to_adapt.pdf

9 www.bellingcat.com/news/uk-and-europe/2019/02/20/russias-anti-selfie-soldier-law-greatest-hits-and-implications/

10 keyfindings.blog/2019/01/04/the-golden-age-of-osint-is-over/

11 Lindsay Freeman, 'Digital Evidence and War Crimes Prosecutions: The Impact of Digital Technologies on International Criminal Investigations and Trials', *Fordham International Law Journal*, Volume 41, Issue 2, 2018.
ir.lawnet.fordham.edu/cgi/viewcontent.cgi?article=2696&context=ilj

12 Freeman, op. cit.
ir.lawnet.fordham.edu/cgi/viewcontent.cgi?article=2696&context=ilj

13 youtu.be/o3dOCsqxiUM?t=26141

14 youtu.be/iil6p-zd6qo?t=1292

15 mobile.abc.net.au/news/2018-12-03/syrian-war-crimes-evidence-strongest-since-nuremberg-trials/10577206?pfmredir=sm

16 www.aljumhuriya.net/en/content/narrative-war-coming

17 news.un.org/en/story/2019/02/1032811

18 www.transparency.org/news/feature/regional-analysis-MENA
www.gfmag.com/global-data/economic-data/richest-countries-in-the-world

19 www.theatlantic.com/international/archive/2013/02/gun-control-yemen-style/273058/

20 www.acleddata.com/2019/06/18/press-release-yemen-war-death-toll-exceeds-90000-according-to-new-acled-data-for-2015/

21 www.ncbi.nlm.nih.gov/pmc/articles/PMC6278080/

22 news.un.org/en/story/2019/03/1035501

23 mwatana.org/en/day-of-judgment/

24 yemen.bellingcat.com/work

25 www.bellingcat.com/news/mena/2019/04/22/the-yemen-project-announcement/

26 yemeniarchive.org/en

27 www.youtube.com/watch?v=cQ54GDmieLo

28 www.youtube.com/watch?v=sDOo5nDJwgA

29 www.whichfaceisreal.com/

30 www.wsj.com/articles/fraudsters-use-ai-to-mimic-ceos-voice-in-unusual-cybercrime-case-11567157402

31 amp.theguardian.com/technology/2019/feb/14/elon-musk-backed-ai-writes-convincing-news-fiction?__twitter_impression=true
https://openai.com/blog/better-language-models/

32 www.vice.com/en_us/article/594qx5/there-is-no-tech-solution-to-deepfakes

33 lab.witness.org/projects/synthetic-media-and-deep-fakes/

34 www.youtube.com/watch?time_continue=1&v=Qh_6cHw5olo

35 amp.axios.com/deepfake-authentication-privacy-5fa05902-41eb-40a7-8850-5450bcad0475.html?__twitter_impression=true

36 open.nytimes.com/introducing-the-news-provenance-project-723dbaf07c44?gi=5f9c26d709a7
www.newsprovenanceproject.com/FAQs

37 ai.facebook.com/blog/deepfake-detection-challenge/

38 syrianarchive.org/en/tech-advocacy

39 syrianarchive.org/en

40 amp.theguardian.com/world/2019/aug/18/new-video-evidence-of-russian-tanks-in-ukraine-european-court-human-rights?CMP=share_btn_tw&__twitter_impression=true

41 forensic-architecture.org/investigation/the-beating-of-faisal-al-natsheh

42 www.bbc.co.uk/news/av/world-africa-45599973/cameroon-atrocity-finding-the-soldiers-who-killed-this-woman

43 digiday.com/media/the-wall-street-journal-has-21-people-detecting-deepfakes/amp/?__twitter_impression=true

44 digiday.com/media/reuters-created-a-deepfake-video-to-train-its-journalists-against-fake-news/

45 www.bellingcat.com/resources/articles/2015/12/08/women-in-osint-diversifying-the-field/

AFTERWORD

1 www.spiegel.de/international/world/alexei-navalny-on-his-poisoning-i-assert-that-putin-was-behind-the-crime-a-ae5923d5-20f3-4117-80bd-39a99b5b86f4

2 www.polygraph.info/a/fact-check-russia-navalny-poisoning-disinfo/30802987.html

3 *Ibid.*

4 www.bellingcat.com/news/uk-and-europe/2020/10/23/russias-clandestine-chemical-weapons-programme-and-the-gru-unit-21955/

5 www.bellingcat.com/news/uk-and-europe/2020/12/14/fsb-team-of-chemical-weapon-experts-implicated-in-alexey-navalny-novichok-poisoning/

6 www.youtube.com/watch?v=AeQXc182r1A

7 www.bellingcat.com/news/uk-and-europe/2020/12/21/if-it-hadnt-been-for-the-prompt-work-of-the-medics-fsb-officer-inadvertently-confesses-murder-plot-to-navalny/

8 *Ibid.*

9 twitter.com/aceurasia/status/1338602531291848714?lang=en

10 www.nytimes.com/2020/12/17/world/europe/russia-putin-navalny-press-conference.html

11 www.bellingcat.com/news/uk-and-europe/2021/01/27/navalny-poison-squad-implicated-in-murders-of-three-russian-activists/

12 www.bellingcat.com/news/uk-and-europe/2021/02/11/vladimir-kara-murza-tailed-by-members-of-fsb-squad-prior-to-suspected-poisonings/

13 www.bellingcat.com/news/2021/06/09/russian-poet-dmitry-bykov-targeted-by-navalny-poisoners/

14 www.dw.com/en/alexei-navalny-says-he-is-being-tortured-in-prison/a-56995363

15 www.reuters.com/world/europe/russian-editor-decries-destruction-media-before-election-2021-09-02/

16 twitter.com/clarissaward/status/1443045137211437061

17 www.bellingcat.com/app/uploads/2021/05/Bellingcat-Annual-Report-2020-1.pdf

18 www.bellingcat.com/app/uploads/2020/09/Editorial-Standards-Practices.pdf

19 www.bellingcat.com/news/americas/2021/01/05/how-the-insurgent-and-maga-right-are-being-welded-together-on-the-streets-of-washington-d-c/

20 www.bellingcat.com/news/mena/2021/02/08/how-instagram-celebrities-promote-dubais-underground-animal-trade/

21 www.bellingcat.com/news/2019/12/03/the-dilan-cruz-shooting-tracking-officer-003478/

22 www.bellingcat.com/news/uk-and-europe/2020/06/23/masked-men-on-a-hellenic-coast-guard-boat-involved-in-pushback-incident/

23 www.gq-magazine.co.uk/politics/article/eliot-higgins-bellingcat-interview

24 www.bbc.co.uk/news/world-africa-54238170

25 www.bbc.co.uk/news/uk-58635137

26 www.bellingcat.com/news/uk-and-europe/2019/02/14/third-suspect-in-skripal-poisoning-identified-as-denis-sergeev-high-ranking-gru-officer/

27 www.bellingcat.com/news/uk-and-europe/2019/08/30/suspected-assassin-in-the-berlin-killing-used-fake-identity-documents/

28 www.bellingcat.com/news/uk-and-europe/2019/12/03/identifying-the-berlin-bicycle-assassin-part-1-from-moscow-to-berlin/

29 www.bellingcat.com/news/uk-and-europe/2019/12/06/identifying-the-berlin-bicycle-assassin-russias-murder-franchise-part-2/

Acknowledgements

I want to start by thanking Tom Rachman, without whose skills as a journalist and talent as a writer this book could not have been written; I feel lucky to have found such a brilliant collaborator. Thanks are due too to my editors Alexis Kirschbaum, Jasmine Horsey, Ben Hyman and all the team at Bloomsbury, as well as my agents, Natasha Fairweather, who believed in the power of the Bellingcat story from the start, and Elyse Cheney in New York.

As you will have read, everything that I have achieved has been a group effort and I am hugely grateful to the many people – too numerous to name – in the open-source community and the Bellingcat Investigation Team who transformed a hobby into a truly global endeavour.

And finally to my wife, Nuray: thank you for being the catalyst and companion on this journey.

Index

ABC News 123
al-Abdallah, Hadi 40
'active measures' 75
Adams, Ray 19
Addounia TV 37
Adra 53
Afghanistan 214
Agnes, Mother 55, 120
Al Aan 147
Al Dabaa 43
Al-Arabiya 41
Al-Hamza Brigade 29
Al-Jazeera 22, 40
Al-Jinah mosque 121
Al-Qaeda 42, 46, 115
Al-Saiqa Brigade 194
Aleppo 36, 41, 107, 125
Aleppo University 23
Alexeyevka 87–8
Allen, Timmi 90, 92, 94, 213
alt-right and alt-left 116, 119
Amanpour, Christiane 56
Amnesty International 33, 58, 91,
        215–16, 220
ANNA news agency 54
Anti-Communist Action 138
anti-Semitism 120, 133, 136,
        139, 143–5
Antonova, Natalia 166–7, 219

Apushka 175
ARD 48
Ardern, Jacinda 144
Arias, Fernando 131
Armed Conflict & Event Data
        Project 202
artificial intelligence (AI) 207–11, 220
Aryan Liberty Net 140
al-Assad, Bashar 6, 13, 22, 24, 26, 28,
        31, 36–8, 40, 42–3, 47, 104, 107,
        121, 137, 194, 197, 201
    and chemical attacks 50, 53–6, 108,
        115–18, 123, 125–6
    and disinformation 115–18, 120
Assange, Julian 58
Associated Press 68–9, 71–2, 119, 123
Atlantic Council Digital Forensic
        Research Lab 107, 188
Australian Financial Review 19
Averyanov, Andrey 180–5

Balkan conflict 199
Baltic states 150
Baltimore riots 105
Bambuser 25, 28, 197
Ban Ki-moon 54
Bank of America 68
Bataclan concert hall 105
Batbo 41

Battle of the Camel 10
Bazzell, Michael 7
BBC 43, 89, 177, 187, 203, 215–16, 219
Beam, Louis 140
Beeley, Vanessa 120
Bellingcat
  crowdfunding 49, 60, 121
  ethics 106
  funding 107–8, 121
  motto 60, 116
  name and mission 61
  payments for closed sources 163–5
  personality types 60
  risks 186–91
  spirit of collaboration 14
  staffing 166, 219–20
  supervisory board 121
  training programme 216–17
  transparency principle 13, 122
Bellingcat Anti-Equality Monitoring Group 187
Bellingcat Online Investigation Toolkit 217
BellingChat 153
Benetech 211
Benghazi 193–5
Benjamin, Carl ('Sargon of Akkad') 139
Bhatti, Tariq 130
Biggers, Chris 104
Bikov, V. N. 183
Blair, Tony 128
Bogdanov, General Vladimir 229
Boogaloo movement 153
Borden, Dan 135–6
Boshirov, Ruslan, *see* Chepiga, Anatoliy
Boston bombings 58, 188
Brace, Chris 67
Braha, Sébastien 130
Breaking the Silence 213
Brega 13–16

Brennan, Fredrick 146
Browne, Malachy 59, 215
Buk missile system 64–6, 68–9, 71–4, 77–83, 86–8, 90, 92–5, 97–103, 132, 159, 212
Bulgarian assassination attempt 179
BuzzFeed News 186

Cameron, David 50
Cameroon 215–16
Carvin, Andy 10, 12, 33, 58, 188–9
Catalonian independence movement 180
Channel 4 News 48, 67, 219
'channers' (4chan and 8chan) 137–46, 187
Charlottesville, Virginia 6, 132–6, 138
Chechnya 169–70, 177
Check 149, 194
Checkdesk 83, 104, 149
Chepiga, Anatoliy ('Ruslan Boshirov') 4–5, 162–3, 165, 167–72, 174–6, 178–80, 182
Chepur, Sergey 183–5
child sexual abuse 149–50
China 104, 124
Chivers, C. J. 32–4, 47
chlorine gas 125–30
Christchurch shootings 141–2, 144–6, 187–8, 190
Christian Science Monitor 44
citizen journalism, rise of 21–2, 89, 109
climate-change denial 120
Clinton, Hillary 58, 112
CNN 39, 44, 48, 56
Columbine massacre 188
Colvin, Marie 22, 89
confirmation bias 122
Congo 205
Counterfactual Community 115–22, 125, 127–8, 130–1, 137, 150, 153, 156, 162, 170, 186, 219

Covid-19 pandemic 7, 114, 152–3,
    232, 235–7
Cracked 137
Crimea, Russian annexation of 84,
    151, 174, 179
criminal justice 105–6
CrowdStrike 112
cyberspace, US domination of 76–7
Czuperski, Maks 107

Dagestan 177
Daily Mail 144
Damascus 34, 38, 65, 115, 125
    chemical attacks 49–56, 115–16,
        118, 120, 125–30
Daraa 46
Dawes, Kevin 24
Dawson, Ryan 115
de Kock, Peter 212
De Wereld Draait Door 153
'death flights' 140
Deep State 115
Deepfake Detection Challenge 209
'deepfakes' 206–9, 216
Democratic National Convention 112
Denmark 151
Detroit street gangs 104
'digilantism' 58
DigitalGlobe 99, 105
Discord 138
disinformation 75–7, 93–4,
    114–32, 215
    resistance to 150–3
    and Skripal poisoning 162
    and social media 123–4
    and Syrian conflict 114–20,
        125–30, 207
    see also Counterfactual
    Community
diversity, and online
    community 218–19
Dix, Jacob 134–5

DNA profiling 199
Dobrokhtov, Roman 156–8, 163,
    174, 186–8
Donetsk 63, 78–80, 86, 94
Douma, *see* Damascus, chemical
    attacks
Dowler, Milly 19
doxxing 134, 140–1
drones 104
drugs cartels 103–4
Duke, David 115
Dutch Safety Board 89, 91

Edwards, Maxim 236
El Paso shooting 145
Ellis, Hannah 190
'elves' 150
emergency-dispatch calls 212
Encyclopedia Dramatica 146
environmental damage 214
Escher, Federico 67
ethnic cleansing 12
European Center for Constitutional
    and Human Rights
    (ECCHR) 214
Europol 149–50
Evans, Robert 136–8, 140–1,
    143–6, 187
Extreme Toxicology 183

fact-checking projects 151–2
Faktenfinder 152
Fall of Kabul, 2021 239
'false triangulation' 119
Falun Gong 124
Fancy Bear 112, 187
Far Eastern Military Command
    Academy 169–70, 172
Fedotov, Sergey, *see* Sergeev, Denis
53rd Anti-Aircraft Missile Brigade
    88, 90, 94, 100–2, 106, 111, 135,
    200, 211

Financial Times 44
Finland 151
Fiorella, Giancarlo 238
First Draft News 152
Firth, Sara 68
Fisk, Robert 128
Fitzpatrick, Catherine A. 77
Floyd, George 153
Flynn, General Michael 7
Foley, James 24, 105
Fontanka 175
Foreign Policy 36, 40, 203
Forensic Architecture 210, 213–14
Forensic Science Centre of
    Lithuania 159
Fox News 131, 140
Free Syrian Army 28–9, 36, 38, 41, 47
Freeman, Lindsay 200
FSB 63, 75, 158–9, 185
Full Fact 152

Gab 140
Gaddafi, Muammar 11–12, 14, 16–18,
    26, 32, 193
Galustian, Richard 113
Gamergate 141, 219
geolocation 16, 59, 65, 70, 77,
    108, 195
GetContact 178
Ghouta, *see* Damascus, chemical
    attacks
Global Legal Action Network
    (GLAN) 203–4
GlobalResearch 119–20
GNII VM 225
Google Digital News Initiative 108
Gorelyh, Ilya 84–5
Grant, Hugh 19
Graph Search 198
Gray, Freddie 105
'Great Replacement, The' 142
Gregory, Sam 207–8

Grozev, Christo 157–8, 163, 165–6,
    176, 180, 182, 186–7
GRU 5, 127, 134, 155–8, 160, 168–9,
    171–4, 176–85
Guardian 11, 13–14, 16–18, 25, 33, 39,
    48, 85, 115, 187
gun control 145

Hadi, Abdrabbuh Mansur 202
Haftar, General Khalifa 193
Haggard, Andrew 71–2, 74, 94, 100
Hague, William 33
Hama 22, 29, 32, 194
al-Hamwi, Sami 31
Hanham, Melissa 104
Hayden, General Michael 76
Hebron 213
Helsingin Sanomat 175
Henderson, Ian 127, 129–30
Hersh, Seymour 55–6
Heyer, Heather 136
Hitchens, Peter 127–8
Hitler, Adolf 145
Holocaust 113, 115
Homs 22–3, 25, 29–30, 37–8,
    40–1, 125–6
Houla massacre 25–7, 37, 55
Houthis 202
Human Rights Center 199–200
Human Rights Watch 33–4, 43, 58, 91
Hunchly 204
Hussein, Saddam 8

Identity Evropa 136
Ilovaysk, Battle of 210
IMINT (imagery intelligence) 104
India 104
Information Wars 39, 109, 114, 132
InfoWars 39–40, 115, 120, 139
Insider, The 156–7, 159, 161, 163, 168,
    174–5, 183
International Criminal Court 194, 199

international criminal law, and
     technological advances 199
Internet Research Agency 77
Interpreter, The 77
Iran 104, 123, 215
Iraq 37, 76, 117, 128, 137
ISIS 6, 24, 104–5, 119, 147–9, 189
Israel 34, 213
Issacharoff, Dean 213
ITAR-TASS 75
Ivannikov, Oleg Vladimirovich 160–1

Jabal Shashabo 31, 34
Jabhat al-Nusra 46
Jespersen, Bjørn 33
Joint Investigation Team 91, 103, 106,
     157, 159
Jones, Alex 38–9, 139
Jukes, Peter 61, 67

Kahn Sheikhoun sarin attack 115, 125–6
Kaszeta, Dan 67
KGB 1–2, 63, 75
Khashoggi, Jamal 186, 215
Al Khatib, Hadi 57, 108, 201
Khrushchev, Colonel Evgeny 42
King, Shaun 133
Kivimäki, Veli-Pekka (VP) 81–3,
     92–4, 112
Koenig, Alexa 200
Koettl, Christoph 58, 215
Kommersant 39
Kovalchuk, Alexander 184
Krasikov, Vadim 241
Krasnodon 158
Ku Klux Klan 115, 132, 140
Kudryavtsev, Konstantin 230, 232–3
Kuhotkin, Sergey 184–5
Kursk 88, 94

Al-Laham, Mimi 115
Lane, David 142

Lange-Damianova, Dessi 236
Las Vegas shootings 215
Lavrov, Sergey 1, 171, 185
Lebanon 34
Leicestershire Police 91
Lens Young Homsi 38
Leroy, Aliaume 103, 215
Les Décodeurs 152
Libya 11–17, 23, 26, 29, 32, 34, 57, 59,
     103, 188
     Al-Saiq Brigade atrocities 193–6
Libyan National Army 193, 195
Litvinenko, Alexander 1
LiveJournal 74
London Review of Books 56
Loyga 174
Luhansk 74, 95, 160
Lyons, Josh 42, 58

McClatchy DC Bureau 158–9
Macguire, Eoghan 236
Macron, Emmanuel 157
Magnitsky, Sergei 85–6
Makarenko, Vladimir 159
Makshakov, Colonel Stanislav 228–230
Malaysia Airlines Flight MH17 6,
     63–103, 106, 113, 123, 131, 156,
     158–61, 163–4, 167, 181, 189–90,
     200, 210–12
Malaysia Airlines Flight 370, 214
Mamontov, Arkady 93
Martin, Ryan 134–5
mass shootings, conspiracy
     theories 119
Matrix, The 138
May, Theresa 2
Medvedev, Dmitri 157
Mein Kampf 145
Middle East Live 11
Military Medical Academy 172–3
Millerovo 94, 101
MintPress News 53, 119

'miserabilism' 8, 124, 147
Mishkin, Alexander ('Alexander
    Petrov') 4–5, 162–3, 165–9,
    171–80, 184–5
Misrata 12, 32
Mnemonic 204
Moldova 179
Montenegro coup plot 157, 172,
    179
Morgan, Daniel 67
Moussa, Jenan 147
Mubarak, Hosni 9
Münster 147–8
Murdoch, Rupert 19
Musk, Elon 207
al-Musulmani, Ahmad 196
Myanmar 205
Mystery Munitions 34–5, 51

National Center for Media
    Forensics 159
NATO 12, 42, 115
Navalny, Alexey 185
Nayda, Vitaly 79
Nazi affiliations 132–3, 135–6,
    139, 144–5
New York Times 47, 181–2, 203, 215
    News Provenance Project 208–9
New Yorker 56
News of the World 19
Newsweek 130–1
Newtral 152
Nimmo, Ben 75
North Korea 58, 83
NPR 26–7, 43–4
Nuremberg trials 199

Obama, Barack 50, 52–3, 56,
    206, 209
Odnoklassniki 101, 171
Oliphant, Roland 97
OpenAI 207

Organisation for the Prohibition of
    Chemical Weapons (OPCW) 3,
    125–31, 171
OSINT (open-source intelligence) 7
Ostanin, Iggy 85–9, 92, 94, 99
Owens, Candace 143

paedophiles 141
Pagella Politica 152
Pakistan 105
Pandora Intelligence 212
Panoramio 96
Paris Match 78–9, 86–7, 90, 92, 103
Paris terrorist attacks 105
Patriot Prayer 138
Peele, Jordan 206
Pelosi, Nancy 206, 209
Pepe the Frog 137, 145
Periscope 132
Peskov, Dmitry 170
Petrov, Alexander, see Mishkin,
    Alexander
phone-hacking scandal 18–21, 23, 33,
    48, 103, 134
Pinochet, General Augusto 140
Pittsburgh synagogue attack 140
Postal, Chris 79
Postma, Foeke 238
post-traumatic stress disorder
    (PTSD) 189
Poway synagogue attack 144–6
Press TV 54
Prigozhin, Yevgeny 224
Prison Planet 38
Professional Pilots Rumour
    Network 82
Protocol on Open Source
    Investigations 200
ProtonMail 187
Proud Boys 138
Putin, Vladimir 1–2, 64, 75, 102, 107,
    121, 138, 166, 170–1, 174, 185

Radio Free Europe/Radio Liberty 182
Radio Svoboda 170
Rapp, Stephen 201
Reddit 58, 138–9
'red-pilling' 138–9, 144–5
Rees, Gavin 189
Regular Contributor, The 20–1
Reporters' Lab 152
Respekt 175
Reuters 216, 219
reverse image searches 105
Revolution Man 118
rhino poaching 154
Roberts, Zach D. 133
Romein, Daniel 95, 97, 100, 163, 182
Rosen, Jay 21
Roshka, Georgy Petrovich 157
RosPassport database 176
Rostov Oblast 101
RTL Nieuws 96
Russia-1 93
Russia Today (RT) 26, 38–40, 42, 68,
    73, 89, 112, 117, 119–20, 131, 162
    Petrov/Boshirov interview 4,
    165–8, 171, 173–5, 186
Russian databases, leaked 163, 211
Russian Defence Ministry 68, 77, 98,
    102, 113, 158–9, 168, 184
Russian Foreign ministry 113–14
Rwanda 199

St Petersburg 172–3
Saleh, Ali Abdullah 13, 202
Saoud, Sari 40
sarin gas 52–4, 56, 115, 124–6
satellite imagery 104–5, 164,
    195–6, 199
Saudi Arabia 41, 47, 52, 121, 124,
    186, 201–3
SC Signal 225, 228–9
Schiphol Airport 148
Schmitt, Eric 47

Second Life 90
Second World War 197, 199
Senezh 182
Sergeev, Denis ('Sergey
    Fedotov') 175–80
shabiha 25–6
Shaif, Rawan 203–4
Shikhany institute 184–5
'shitposting' 143–4, 187
Simon, Scott 43–4
Simonyan, Margarita 39
Skripal poisoning 1–6, 39, 125, 127,
    131, 134, 155–6, 162–85, 191
Sky News 89
Slack 92, 165
Snizhne 64–6, 68–9, 71–2, 78–81,
    94, 96–7
Snopes 123–4, 152
social media
    algorithms 123–4
    archiving 196–9
    ISIS and 147–9
    searching 101–2
Sofronov, G. A. 183
Something Awful 12, 18–20, 137,
    141, 143
Soros, George 115
Spain 180
spear-phishing attacks 111–12
Speiz laboratory 168
Spencer, Richard 136
Spetsnaz soldiers 85, 99, 158, 169, 172
SputnikNews 26, 112, 119–20, 162
Spyro the Dragon 143
Stalin, Josef 75, 206
Stamboliyska, Rayna 219
Starbird, Kate 119
Stary Oskol 87–8, 92
Stasi 90
State Experimental Institute for
    Scientific Research in Military
    Medicine 183

Storyful 59, 81, 189–90, 215, 219
Stover, Eric 200
Strelkov, Igor 63–4, 68
SunCalc 71, 78–9, 195
Susli, Maram 115–16
Sweden 151
Syria 6, 10, 13, 18, 22–58, 65, 86, 89,
    91, 103–4, 106, 112, 121, 123, 137,
    159, 170, 188, 215
  arms-smuggling 29, 46–7, 57, 215
  barrel bombs 41–3, 189
  'Caesar' pictures 196–7
  chemical attacks 49–56, 108, 115–
    18, 123, 125–30, 168, 215
  cluster munitions 32–4
  disinformation 114–20,
    125–30, 207
  documentation 57–8, 108, 194–8,
    201, 205–6, 210, 213–14
  pipe bombs 44
Syria Civil Defence (White Helmets)
    114–15, 118–20, 127
Syrian Air Force 31, 35–6, 41
Syrian Archive 108, 201, 204,
    210, 214
Syrian Network for Human Rights
    43, 126
Syrian Sentry 126

Tactical Technology Collective
    57–9, 108
Tahrir Square 9–11
Technical University of Delft 96
ThreatConnect 112
Tice, Austin 24
Tiji 16–17
Tkachev, Nikolai Fedorovish 158–9
Toler, Aric 68–70, 72, 92, 94, 107,
    112, 132–3, 135–6, 163, 165, 182
Torez 64, 69–72, 79–80, 96, 103
Tottenham 148
Trace an Object 149–50

Traditionalist Worker Party 136
Triebert, Christiaan 108, 153–4, 215
TrueCaller 160
Trump, Donald 7, 21, 112, 131, 137,
    139, 206
Turkish military coup 104, 153
21stCenturyWire 119–20

Ugail, Hassan 173, 177
Ukraine 63–103, 107, 113, 134,
    137, 150–1, 156, 158–61,
    169–70, 210–12
Ukraine International Airlines Flight
    PS572 123, 215
Ukraine@War blog 79–81, 96
Ukrainian Air Force 64, 74,
    86, 93
Ukrainian neo-Nazis 187
Unicorn Riot 138
Unite the Right 132–3, 136
US Capitol riot, 2021 238
US Defense Intelligence Agency 7
US National Geospatial-Intelligence
    Agency 104
US presidential elections 112, 157
Utrecht terrorist attack 217
Uxoinfo 33

van Ess, Henk 101–2
van Huis, Pieter 182
Vanguard America 136
Vasilyev, General Kirill 229
Venezuela 205
Vietnam War 140
virtual reality 213
VKontakte 63, 87–8, 100–2, 182

Wagner Group 224
Wall Street Journal 216
Ward, Clarissa 233
Waters, Nick 128, 203–4
Watson, Tom 48

al-Werfalli, Mahmoud 193–6
Which Face Is Real 207
White Helmets, *see* Syria Civil
    Defence
white supremacy 140–1
WikiLeaks 58, 93, 112, 128
Working Group on Syria,
    Propaganda and Media 127
World Anti-Doping Agency 179
World Health Organization 152
World Wildlife Fund 154

Yanukovych, Viktor 63, 174
Yekaterinburg cadet school 158
Yemen 13, 104, 121, 124, 201–5
Yemeni Archive 204
Yugoslavia, former 45–8

Zakharova, Maria 113
Zappa, Frank 18
Zaroschinskoe 99
Zello app 97
Zuhres 78–80

A Note on the Type

The text of this book is set in Adobe Garamond. It is one of several versions of Garamond based on the designs of Claude Garamond. It is thought that Garamond based his font on Bembo, cut in 1495 by Francesco Griffo in collaboration with the Italian printer Aldus Manutius. Garamond types were first used in books printed in Paris around 1532. Many of the present-day versions of this type are based on the *Typi Academiae* of Jean Jannon cut in Sedan in 1615.

Claude Garamond was born in Paris in 1480. He learned how to cut type from his father and by the age of fifteen he was able to fashion steel punches the size of a pica with great precision. At the age of sixty he was commissioned by King Francis I to design a Greek alphabet, and for this he was given the honourable title of royal type founder. He died in 1561.